D1713853

SPYING

SPYING

ASSESSING US DOMESTIC INTELLIGENCE SINCE 9/11

Darren E. Tromblay

LYNNE
RIENNER
PUBLISHERS

BOULDER
LONDON

*The views expressed in this book are solely those of the author,
Darren E. Tromblay, and do not reflect the views of any
US government agency or other entity.*

Published in the United States of America in 2019 by
Lynne Rienner Publishers, Inc.
1800 30th Street, Boulder, Colorado 80301
www.rienner.com

and in the United Kingdom by
Lynne Rienner Publishers, Inc.
Gray's Inn House, 127 Clerkenwell Road, London EC1 5DB

Library of Congress Cataloging-in-Publication Data
Names: Tromblay, Darren E., author.
Title: Spying : assessing US domestic intelligence since 9/11 /
  Darren E. Tromblay.
Description: Boulder, Colorado : Lynne Rienner Publishers, Inc., [2019] |
  Includes bibliographical references and index.
Identifiers: LCCN 2018048489 (print) | LCCN 2018059687 (ebook) |
  ISBN 9781626378018 (e-book) | ISBN 9781626377806 (hardcover : alk. paper)
Subjects: LCSH: Domestic intelligence—United States. | United States.
  Department of Homeland Security. | United States. Federal Bureau of
  Investigation. | National security—United States.
Classification: LCC HV6432.4 (ebook) | LCC HV6432.4 .T76 2019 (print) | DDC
  363.250973—dc23
LC record available at https://lccn.loc.gov/2018048489

British Cataloguing in Publication Data
A Cataloguing in Publication record for this book
is available from the British Library.

Printed and bound in the United States of America

The paper used in this publication meets the requirements
∞ of the American National Standard for Permanence of
Paper for Printed Library Materials Z39.48-1992.

5 4 3 2 1

To my cabinet of choristers—especially Joe, Jim, KT and Pat, Connie, Sylvia, and the inimitable Dame Judith—for whose friendship, intelligence, wit, and wisdom I am most grateful

Contents

Acknowledgments

If this book is a success, there are many people to thank. If it is a failure, well, mea culpa. First, there are many people whom I have met in the course of my career who inspired me to make a second career out of assessing how to get intelligence right within the domestic setting. Chief among these people is my good friend John F. Fox Jr., who has dubbed me the "loyal opposition." I also owe much to Fred, Molly, Rob, Deborah, Joe, Dan, Brian, Jenny, Chris, Jeff, and J. D. Many thanks as well to Kathy Pherson, Rob Atkinson, Devin Stewart, Loch Johnson, Richard Valcourt, Stephen Slick, Bo Miller, Gerry Sherrill, Thomas Van Wagner, and Kate Brannen, all of whom have given me platforms to try out my ideas.

It's a bad idea to dive into the icy and lonely waters of writing (and editing—more on that in a minute) without good friends who can help you return to reality once you come up for air. I am fortunate to have a coterie from my undergraduate and graduate school days whom I know I can call on—John, Brent, Kamran, Heather, Aaron, Daina, Meagan, Carla, and Megan, thank you for being there.

As I mention in the dedication, I am blessed to have a cabinet of choristers at Holy Trinity Catholic Church in Washington, DC, for whose friendship I am eternally grateful. In addition to those whom I have already named, I would be remiss if I didn't tip my hat to a broader circle of 11:30 denizens (as well as a few honorary members). Here's looking at you Kathy DeJ, Kathleen, Nick and Elena (and your well-stocked bar), Pam and Dennis Lucey ("you're the best"), BZ and George, Dick and

Charlotte, Richard and Karen, Kerry and David, Matthew, Emily, Bryan, D. Pennington, Kay Frances, Bob and Denise, and Suzanne, with a special remembrance of the late Bill Noonan, who always had a smile and an encouraging word. Apologies to anyone I missed. Meet me at the bar of 1789 and I'll buy you a round or two of rye Manhattans in apology.

Many thanks also to my editor, Marie-Claire Antoine, who has enthusiastically shepherded several of my projects to publication. Poor Marie-Claire had to answer my email in the spring of 2018 announcing that I'd somehow overshot the 75,000-word limit . . . and ended up with a book of 140,000 words! Remember what I said about editing? Even after that she gamely got me my next contract!

Last, the views expressed in this book are solely mine and do not reflect the views of any US government agency or other entity.

1

The US Intelligence Enterprise

Intelligence in the US domestic setting—beyond the topic of counterterrorism—has received insufficient assessment and theorization. American political discourse turns to the topic only in the wake of an intelligence failure (Pearl Harbor, the September 11 attacks, etc.) or a scandal (such as the activities unearthed by the congressional Church and Pike Committees). However, these questions of security and civil liberties are inextricably linked to ensuring that the domestically oriented intelligence enterprise is functioning effectively. This enterprise does not consist solely of—or even primarily of—the formal sixteen-member US intelligence community (plus the nonoperational Office of the Director of National Intelligence). Instead, it is an intricately interlinked network of federal and subfederal agencies.

There are a number of interdisciplinary analogies—from the fields of mechanics, biology, and even art—that can help in thinking about the organization of the domestically oriented intelligence enterprise. However, architecture is the most appropriate for this book, as it highlights what is absent from the enterprise as well as the qualities of which the enterprise is desperately in need. An architect designs with purpose—unlike for an ecosystem, which evolves with no specific objective other than the survival of its constituent elements—and architecture, once it becomes physical reality, not only houses an organization but also contributes to second-order effects such as an agency's self-perception and corporate culture.

The design of the domestically oriented intelligence enterprise should reflect the same degree of thought as the blueprints for an edifice built for the public. However, this has not been the case. Instead, the design process—to the extent that it has existed at all—for the

1

bureaucratic interplay of the intelligence elements within the domestic setting has been ad hoc. Agencies did not emerge from US—or in some cases state and local—government strategic planning, but instead originated as responses to identified threats or crises that had already transpired. This process has produced an intelligence enterprise that resembles an increasingly unstable pile of sediment that is unable to support US policymakers. Individual agencies are not immune from this accretion of responsibilities—the Federal Bureau of Investigation (FBI), for instance, was the only entity capable of handling most internal, national-level threats for the better part of a century and, as a result, accumulated an overly diversified portfolio of responsibilities.

Architecture as Analogy

The physical architecture, including the current state of it, that houses the two most significant domestically focused intelligence services in the United States—the FBI and the Department of Homeland Security (DHS)—is a metaphor for those agencies' respective conditions. Both agencies' headquarters are physically ill-suited to their current missions and impose constraints on the agencies' operations. More important, the facilities are inconsistent with the corporate cultures that would complement the missions of the FBI and the DHS and send unintentionally counterproductive messages to the American public, whom these agencies are supposed to serve and from whom these agencies require assistance.

FBI Headquarters

As of this writing, the FBI's headquarters building, an example of unmitigated brutalism, remains on Pennsylvania Avenue NW, between Ninth and Tenth Streets, in Washington, DC, an unfortunate choice for the headquarters of a law enforcement agency. The timing of the building's erection and opening was even worse. When the National Capital Planning Commission approved the design—developed by C.F. Murphy & Associates of Chicago—for the FBI's headquarters in 1964, there was no way to know that the Bureau was in the midst of operations such as the controversial COINTELPRO.[1] Construction started in 1967—a bad year for intelligence, thanks to the disclosures published by *Ramparts*—about domestic activities of the Central Intelligence Agency (CIA).[2] By 1974, when FBI personnel first began moving into the building, and 1975, when the building was formally dedicated, the United States was in the thick of a recriminations, notably those of the Church and Pike Committees, about alleged abuses by multiple intelligence services, including the FBI.[3] It was bad timing to unveil a building that consciously conjured the Big Brotherish image of a "central core of files."[4] Bare-knuckled brutalism (seven stories in front, rising to eleven stories on the opposite side)—not to mention the way the building rose ominously over Pennsylvania Avenue, the thoroughfare that tied together the elements of US government—created an ominous public image for an agency about which the American public already had a reason to be concerned.

The building—named after J. Edgar Hoover—was also inefficient. Although it comprises 2.4 million square feet, only 53 percent of it is usable, since the building's footprint includes an extensive, open, interior courtyard.[5] Despite this deficiency, the FBI's headquarters was nevertheless the most expensive—at $126 million—federal building erected up to that point.[6] The original design concept had been a "solid block type structure" of eight stories.[7] This had been modified to the current configuration in order to conform with the requirements of the National Capital Planning Commission, the Commission of Fine Arts, and the Pennsylvania Avenue Advisory Council.[8] Even the process of designing the building provides an interesting analogy for intelligence within the domestic setting. Whereas external sensibilities imposed design constraints on the Bureau, external factors including political whims and public opinion have distorted how intelligence agencies function (or fail to do so) domestically.

With the Bureau's evolution, its headquarters became ever less suited to its purpose. Building renovations occurred reactively as the FBI's mission grew.[9] The tenth floor, which originally housed 35 million fingerprint cards, has been converted into staff space, as has the area previously occupied by the crime laboratory—which relocated to Quantico.[10] Approximately 200,000 square feet of basement and cafeteria spaces were converted into offices. However, these modifications encountered impediments imposed by the building's original design. For instance, the Bureau was unable to convert some areas into open-plan spaces. Furthermore, according to the General Services Administration (GSA), new offices created from old space might not be adequately ventilated and cooled.[11] The GSA deemed the FBI's headquarters building to be functionally obsolete, and Bureau officials have admitted that the structure is so inefficient that it has hindered the agency's mission.[12] As the FBI's role grew, via aggregation of missions rather than by design, its organizational and conceptual frameworks—just like its physical presence—ceased to accommodate what the Bureau had become.

Furthermore, as the Bureau grew and its bureaucracy became increasingly unwieldy, physical limitations led to breakdowns in communication. In 2011, the Government Accountability Office (GAO) assessed that the building's design was "a significant barrier to staff collaboration and information sharing across teams."[13] Space constraints are so severe that the FBI has been unable to physically co-locate various analysts and specialists. The building, even its most jury-rigged configuration, cannot actually contain the totality of its staff. In 2001, when the headquarters staff numbered 9,700, the Bureau had to distribute that staff across seven locations. As of 2011, the headquarters staff of 17,300 was housed in more than forty annexes.[14] The fragmentation of the headquarters presence is a metaphor for the agency's atomization of information across field offices—a problem identified but not rectified after the September 11 attacks.

The increasingly spit-and-baling-wire nature of the FBI's headquarters has only worsened with physical decay. Its interiors are characterized by peeling paint, ragged carpet, and stained light fixtures.[15] One of the Bureau's architectural features is a dry moat. There is, however, water elsewhere—notably in the basement, which is prone to flooding from the courtyard during periods of rain.[16] Employees must have been unnerved when, according to the *Washington Post,* half of the building's alarms failed to sound during a July 2015 drill.[17] Even worse, the disrepair has started to imperil the very people whom the FBI is supposed to protect. Areas of the upper-level exterior façade had deteriorated to the point that concrete could fall onto unsuspecting pedestrians. The GSA and FBI had to install netting to catch falling debris. Director James Comey actually kept in his office a large piece of concrete that had fallen from the building's Ninth Street façade.[18] A Bureau hobbled by a muddled mission and an incoherent corporate culture is—like its headquarters—endangering the people it has promised to serve.

Department of Homeland Security

The Department of Homeland Security is a relatively young agency, having come into existence only with 2002 legislation. Nevertheless, its experience with architecture draws some unwanted comparisons. Its first headquarters complex—on Nebraska Avenue, in northwest Washington, DC—is a secondhand facility that had originally housed the

Naval Communications Annex. It is unintentionally appropriate that a department cobbled together from elements of twenty-two different agencies should have a headquarters that reflects the lack of a unique identity. (The bureaucratic justification for this location was that the campus could accommodate a headquarters operation.)[19]

If the Naval Communications Annex location sent an unflattering message, the DHS's new headquarters complex—a former mental hospital—sent a worse one. In 2013, the DHS officially opened its consolidated headquarters campus at the former site of St. Elizabeth's Hospital in southeast Washington, DC.[20] The DHS undertook this consolidation project to bring together entities—scattered across more than forty sites—into one location.[21] However, when that location is an insane asylum, it does give pause, especially when the department in question does suffer from bureaucratic multiple personality disorder. The primary occupants of the St. Elizabeth's complex will be the US Coast Guard, DHS headquarters elements, the Federal Emergency Management Agency (FEMA), the National Operations Center, the Transportation Security Administration, Customs and Border Protection, and Immigration and Customs Enforcement, as well as liaison presences from other DHS elements.[22]

Architecture of the US Intelligence Enterprise in the Domestic Setting

The domestically oriented intelligence enterprise did not develop with the benefit of a blueprint. Instead, it is an aggregation of agencies—both federal and subfederal—that developed in response to specific challenges. In addition to this organizational fragmentation, the foundation of the domestically oriented intelligence enterprise is further fractured by two competing taxonomies for organizing intelligence functions. Some entities, such as the FBI—in its Counterterrorism, Counterintelligence, and Criminal Investigative Divisions—have historically focused on threat actors, while others, including the Bureau of Alcohol, Tobacco, Firearms, and Explosives (ATF) and the Drug Enforcement Administration (DEA), are organized around implements, rather than who uses or benefits from them. Even a single agency can be inconsistent about the concepts around which it organizes. For instance, the FBI created a Weapons of Mass Destruction Directorate (WMDD) and a Cyber Division (CyD)—both of which are ostensibly organized around implements rather than actors. Not surprisingly, unleashing agencies working from intersecting points of view leads to collisions as intelligence collectors and analysts pull on different threads that lead to the same threats.

As agencies—and US strategic interests—have evolved, new capabilities have emerged and new gaps have become apparent. For instance, the FBI, when its history is parsed, has a lengthy history in the field of weapons of mass destruction (WMD) but did not consolidate this work into its WMD Directorate until the middle of the first decade of the twenty-first century (and may never have done so without intervention by the findings of the WMD Commission, which itself was a onetime initiative, in response to an intelligence failure). Of course, whether this expertise should have remained in the Bureau or been consolidated into the DHS is an argument for debate. Similarly, the Bureau's counterintelligence, counterterrorism, and criminal investigative missions all identified opportunities for the collection of positive foreign intelligence (the kind of information that would give US policymakers a decision-advantage, rather than just a warning). However, the FBI has yet to find a way to systematically exploit these opportunities for collection.

Evolution by aggregation, throughout the twentieth century, created an increasingly confused distribution of missions. The FBI accumulated an increasingly broad set of responsibilities. While the DHS, created after 9/11, has been roundly criticized as a hodgepodge of dissimilar organizations, the Bureau, through its growth, encountered a similar crisis of identity. Was it an intelligence service, a cop-shop, a linchpin for information sharing with law enforcement agencies, or a first responder (through entities such as the Hostage Rescue Team)? Confusion became even more acute when newer agencies such as the DEA and ATF emerged and took on issues that ran up against the Bureau's mandate. Finally, the picture became even more muddled when the CIA, which is prohibited by statute from domestic security functions, took on responsibility for the domestic collection of foreign intelligence information, through what is now known as the National Resources Division, within the Bureau's area—both geographically and conceptually—of responsibility.

Finally, the increasing incorporation of subfederal entities into developing the national-level intelligence picture has introduced additional complexities to assessing the domestically oriented intelligence enterprise. There is no argument that these entities need to be involved (and they, to varying extents, have been, and certainly well before "fusion" became the buzzword after 9/11), since they have a frontline perspective on trends that may develop into national-level problems.

However, judicious tradeoffs are necessary. The federal government, which has increasingly engaged these entities through fusion centers (DHS) and joint terrorism task forces (FBI), must ensure that it is not leveling demands that drain resources from local issues. On the other hand, the federal government should be making a serious assessment of how it might bolster subfederal agencies' capabilities to address issues that would free up federal-level resources to address problems of a national scope that federal agencies are uniquely suited to address.

After the September 11, 2001, attacks on the United States, the US government implemented sweeping reforms—which were not nearly as sweeping as they should have been. Rather than assessing the totality of the domestically focused intelligence infrastructure that had accumulated throughout the twentieth century, reformers focused on a single issue—terrorism—and proceeded to build a bureaucracy around this problem set. This approach—of attempting to solve new problems without first fixing the underlying ones—did not ameliorate the entrenched fragmentation and incongruity that had increasingly characterized the intelligence infrastructure within the domestic environment. Instead, intelligence reforms gave the American public a false sense of confidence that the government had addressed points of failure while creating a single-issue infrastructure (the National Counterterrorism Center [NCTC], the DHS, and the reorientation of nearly every agency toward a counterterrorism mission) that is ill-equipped to address nonterrorism threats or exploit opportunities for positive intelligence collection that might provide decisionmakers with a decision-advantage.

This book is organized around the evolution—intentional or otherwise—of the domestically oriented intelligence enterprise in the years following the attacks of September 11, 2001. However, policymakers were not working with a clean slate as they attempted to rectify the failures in bureaucratic structures that the al-Qaeda hijackers exploited. Instead, they had to contend with a century's worth of history. Chapter 2 provides a summary of the key themes that emerged from this history and sets the stage for discussion of whether reforms addressed underlying deficiencies that resulted from the evolution-by-aggregation approach to intelligence in the domestic setting.

In addition to entrenched bureaucratic inertia, policymakers seeking to sort out the deficiencies in domestically oriented intelligence had to navigate political realities. Chapter 3 addresses how competition between the executive and legislative branches of government, as well as between executive branch agencies seeking to protect their own turf—arguably at a cost to national security—stymied reform efforts. Additionally, the chapter highlights the issue-oriented nature of reform. Rather than addressing the structural deficiencies of the domestically oriented intelligence enterprise, the immediacy of terrorism meant that many of the reforms to intelligence focused extensively on that topic—and left the United States vulnerable to other threats.

Chapters 4, 5, and 6 examine the implications of post-9/11 reform for the Federal Bureau of Investigation. Prior to 9/11 the Bureau was an organizationally schizophrenic entity. It had been present at the creation of the modern US intelligence community but remained culturally divided between reactive investigative and proactive intelligence mindsets. Without a strong organizational identity, the reforms in which the post-9/11 FBI engaged tended to be superficial and confusing. It was clear that the Bureau needed to show progress, but it was less clear what the end-goal of that progress should be; consequently, for nearly two decades, the Bureau pursued what often looked like change for change's sake.

Following 9/11, the US government responded—following a political standoff between the president and Congress—by creating the Department of Homeland Security. The presence of politics and bureaucratic jockeying that informed the creation of DHS meant, perhaps inevitably, that the result would be less than the sum of its parts. Chapters 7 and 8 parse the DHS's role in the domestically oriented intelligence enterprise—reaching the conclusion that the DHS is primarily a passive collector with some outliers (e.g., the Homeland Security Investigations component of Immigration and Customs Enforcement) that engage in active collection, in furtherance of solving specific cases.

The domestic intelligence enterprise also includes other federal agencies, both within and outside the formal sixteen-member intelligence community (plus the Office of the Director of National Intelligence). As mentioned earlier, among these are the Central Intelligence Agency and the Drug Enforcement Administration—both of which are members of the intelligence community—as well as others, such as the Bureau of Alcohol, Tobacco, Firearms, and Explosives, that are not part of the community but nonetheless have mission sets that overlap with those of community entities. Chapter 9 discusses these additional participants and the potential for redundancies, additional points of failure (due to fragmentation), and competition for turf (e.g., the rivalry between the FBI and ATF over terrorism investigations) that their involvement creates.

Chapters 10 and 11 cover efforts to create synergies between agencies through interagency collaboration. These chapters assess the complications created by a domestically oriented enterprise that exists only partially under the auspices of the Office of the Director of National Intelligence. They also shed light on the counterterrorism-centric nature of collaboration, which threatens to prevent the identification of other threats and opportunities. Finally, these chapters discuss the role that state and local agencies play in shaping—rather than simply participating in—the evolution of the domestically oriented intelligence enterprise.

The book reaches the conclusion that there is not the political will to create a new, dedicated, domestically oriented intelligence service. Therefore, policymakers should focus on conducting a net assessment of the resources available within existing agencies and moving mission sets and capabilities among existing agencies in furtherance of creating comparative advantages and eliminating redundancies. Additionally, policymakers will need to reassess the changing nature of federal-subfederal relationships as well as the role of the private sector, an increasingly significant factor, in continuing to refine the domestically oriented intelligence architecture.

The purpose of this book is to break crockery. No agency goes unscathed in this account of how the domestically oriented US intelligence enterprise has arrived at where it is. This approach owes a bit to Joseph Schumpeter. The purpose of this tome is to drive the design of a domestically oriented intelligence architecture, as opposed to reforming individual agencies within a vacuum. A primary premise is that, for multiple reasons, there is not a political willingness to create a new agency; thus, reform should focus on unpacking the missions of the domestic oriented US intelligence entities and realigning them, as necessary, to create comparative advantages across agencies. The objective of this realignment would be not only the introduction of greater efficiency and effectiveness but also the establishment of a concept for assessing future growth or retrenchment.

Notes

1. General Accounting Office, Federal Bureau of Investigation: Actions Needed to Document Security Decisions and Address Issues with Condition of Headquarters Buildings (Washington, DC, 2011); Roger K. Lewis, "A Daunting but Worthy Mission for the FBI: Soften Headquarters' Hard Edges," *Washington Post*, June 3, 2009.

2. General Accounting Office, Federal Bureau of Investigation.

3. Ibid.

4. Lewis, "A Daunting but Worthy Mission for the FBI."

5. General Accounting Office, Federal Bureau of Investigation; Jonathan O'Connell, "The FBI's Headquarters Is Falling Apart: Why Is It So Hard for America to Build a New One?" *Washington Post*, October 16, 2015.

6. O'Connell, "The FBI's Headquarters Is Falling Apart."

7. Departments of State, Justice, and Commerce, the Judiciary, and Related Agencies Appropriations for 1976, Before a Subcommittee of the Committee on Appropriations, House of Representatives, 94th Cong., pt. 2 (1975).

8. Ibid.

9. General Accounting Office, Federal Bureau of Investigation.

10. O'Connell, "The FBI's Headquarters Is Falling Apart."

11. General Accounting Office, Federal Bureau of Investigation.

12. Ibid.; O'Connell, "The FBI's Headquarters Is Falling Apart."

13. General Accounting Office, Federal Bureau of Investigation.

14. Ibid.

15. O'Connell, "The FBI's Headquarters Is Falling Apart."

16. General Accounting Office, Federal Bureau of Investigation.

17. Ibid.; O'Connell, "The FBI's Headquarters Is Falling Apart."

18. O'Connell, "The FBI's Headquarters Is Falling Apart."

19. "History of the Nebraska Avenue Complex," https://www.dhs.gov/history-nac.

20. "DHS Opens New Headquarters on St. Elizabeth's Campus," DHS Press Office.

21. General Services Administration, Prospectus—Construction; Department of Homeland Security, Consolidation, Infrastructure, Site Acquisition, and Development of St. Elizabeth's Campus (Washington, DC, 2010).

22. Ibid.

2

Emergence of a Domestically Oriented Intelligence Enterprise

The September 11, 2001, attacks on the United States triggered a reassessment of US intelligence, especially as it pertained to the domestic setting. This was just one more episode in the crisis-driven development of the US national security community—both the formal intelligence community and the broader network of federal and subfederal entities that collect and use intelligence. Since 1908, the year of the FBI's creation, the domestically oriented national security community has developed in an ad hoc manner, and by the end of the twentieth century it was an assemblage without architecture, the majority of it having its origins in responding to an already identified threat—whether spies or narcotics traffickers—rather than built toward providing policymakers with an informational advantage.

At the center of the domestically oriented intelligence architecture is the Federal Bureau of Investigation. The Bureau has evolved by aggregation. Its original purpose—as simply the Bureau of Investigation—was to serve as a detective force for the Department of Justice (DoJ).[1] This orientation toward ferreting out criminal threats, closing cases, and moving on to the next investigation would inform the FBI's approach to an increasingly disparate set of missions. In 1939, the Bureau became indisputably responsible for counterintelligence when President Franklin D. Roosevelt tasked that "all espionage, counterespionage, and sabotage matters" would be handled by the Federal Bureau of Investigation, the Military Intelligence Division of the War Department, and the Office of Naval Intelligence of the Navy Department. The directors of these three agencies were to function as a committee to coordinate their activities.[2] In the same year, FDR put the FBI into what would now be called counterterrorism when he made the Bureau responsible for matters relating to sabotage.[3] The FBI's entrance into these fields had less to do with the organization's expertise and much more to the fact that it was the nation's default civilian intelligence service.

The FBI has accrued such a wide array of responsibilities due to its vaguely defined mission. Its only statutory sanction is the 1871 legislation authorizing the Department of Justice to use investigators for the prosecution of crimes against the United States.[4] Many of its responsibilities are those assigned by piecemeal legislation and by executive orders, notably Executive Order 12333, which invests the Bureau with national security responsibilities. When Congress did consider a charter, starting in 1979, a fundamental problem became apparent: the Bureau was really two distinct organizations under one roof. The charter would have defined the FBI's duties and responsibilities "except those relating to foreign intelligence collection and foreign counterintelligence investigations" as well as foreign-based terrorist groups.[5] A separate charter would govern these activities.[6] This is a division that the Bureau has yet to resolve and one that stumped Robert Mueller III, who served as the FBI's director between 2001 and 2013, during a time of reform that produced more smoke and noise than results.

With no charter, the FBI is especially susceptible to the outlooks of successive administrations. The Attorney General Guidelines provide the Bureau with much of its mission. Attorneys general, from Harlan Fiske Stone, who demanded that newly appointed J. Edgar Hoover focus only on reactive investigations, to Nicholas deBelleville Katzenbach, who in 1965 stipulated more stringent oversight for the Bureau's use of wiretaps and microphones, have asserted authority over the FBI's operations.[7] However, it was not until 1976 that Attorney General Edward Levi issued the first formal set of Attorney General Guidelines.[8] Levi and subsequent attorneys general issued discrete sets of guidelines for various topics, including domestic security investigations, informants, civil disturbances, counterintelligence, and international terrorism.[9] In 2008, a significant change occurred when a new, unified set of Attorney General Guidelines did away with the artificial trisection between criminal investigations, national security investigations, and foreign intelligence collection.[10]

Arguably, the lack of a charter and of strong organizational identity has produced an overabundance of caution about how to proceed with intelligence activities in the domestic setting. FBI and Department of Justice overinterpretation of restrictions reached their nadir in the form of the "Wall," which stemmed from a 1995 Department of Justice memo that Bureau personnel eventually interpreted as a preclusion to sharing of all classified information between the intelligence and criminal investigative aspects of the FBI.[11] According to the 9/11 Commission, the 1995 decision, which provided a basis for the Wall, applied only to sharing of information between agents and criminal prosecutors, not between two kinds of FBI agents. Even Jamie Gorelick (a member of the 9/11 Commission), who authored the memo, at the direction of then–attorney general Janet Reno, admitted that what she had written went beyond what was legally required.[12] Reno and Gorelick were not entirely responsible for the creation of the Wall, as a concept, since the 1995 memo was only a capstone to an ongoing process of interpretation that had, over the course of decades, created a growing sense of prohibition against information sharing across the Bureau's various components and between the Bureau and criminal prosecutors.[13]

The FBI's accumulation of responsibilities throughout the twentieth century made it difficult for the Bureau's work force to become specialists in specific topics. Instead, the FBI tended to surge its special agents to whatever the crisis du jour was, sometimes at the expense of the Bureau's counterterrorism and counterintelligence programs.[14] For instance, following the end of the Cold War, the FBI reprogrammed agents from counterintelligence to health care fraud investigations.[15] Similarly, in 1992, the FBI moved approximately 300 counterintelligence agents to the violent crimes and major offenders program.[16]

Furthermore, the FBI's efforts to establish a professional analytic cadre were largely unsuccessful. When it did hire experts, such as those it brought in to staff the Terrorist Research and Analytical Center (TRAC), which the FBI established in 1980, strategic products often fell victim to demands for tactical pieces.[17] The FBI also had a tendency to equate analysis with data manipulation, which meant that glorified clerks—such as those responsible for entering information in the Organized Crime Information System—earned the title "analyst."[18]

By the 1990s, the Bureau's analytic positions fell into two categories—intelligence operations specialists, including individuals who lacked any formal training in analytical work, and intelligence research specialists, all of whom possessed at least college degrees.[19] In 1999, Congress took the FBI to the woodshed—in the wake of the loss of sensitive US technology to China—for failing to analyze foreign intelligence and counterintelligence information, and stated that the Bureau needed to develop a capability for all-source analysis.[20] In answer to this demand, the FBI created an Investigative Services Division (ISD), which consolidated the FBI's intelligence research specialists (the

FBI's all-source analysts), as well as other analytic resources.[21] It was first time that the FBI had made strategic analysis independent of the operational divisions.[22]

The differentiation in aptitude between the intelligence research specialists and the intelligence operations specialists produced internecine warfare. Intelligence operations specialists—with their tactical orientation, which was more in line with the FBI's ethos—directed the work of the more qualified intelligence research specialists and used them to perform the work that they "did not like to do."[23] A CIA manager detailed to the FBI told the Department of Justice's Office of the Inspector General (OIG) that intelligence research specialists were considered "second class citizens" at the FBI.[24] As the twentieth century closed out, intelligence operations specialists had become chokepoints with any work by an intelligence research specialist having to be coordinated through an intelligence operations specialist.[25] Chokepoints, in turn, became points of failure. Intelligence operations specialists, according to a joint congressional inquiry, refused to share information with their strategic analytic counterparts.[26] These developments created conditions that would undermine the FBI's efforts to transform its analytical cadre after 9/11.

Two Taxonomies

As the domestically oriented intelligence enterprise developed, two distinct taxonomies for organizing agencies emerged. The first of these was the FBI's approach, which focused on threat actors. The Drug Enforcement Administration and the Bureau of Alcohol, Tobacco, and Firearms took a second approach, which focused on the implements—rather than the perpetrators—of crime. The DEA entered into existence—under the auspices of the Department of Justice—in mid-1973, as the successor to several federal antinarcotics initiatives.[27] The previous year, 1972, had seen the creation of the ATF as part of the Department of the Treasury.[28] It was inevitable that the actor-focused and implement-focused models would result in bureaucratic collisions, as agencies closed in on the same threats from different angles.

Although the FBI, throughout much of the twentieth century, was an actor-centric organization, its work in several fields would lead the Bureau to establish implement-centric components shortly before 9/11 and even more substantively in the decade after the attacks. The foundations for what would become the FBI's post-9/11 Cyber Division and

Weapons of Mass Destruction Directorate evolved along with the rest of the FBI's mission. As early as World War II, the Bureau was already working in the WMD field, with its CINRAD (Communist Infiltration of Radiation Laboratory) at the University of California–Berkeley.[29] The FBI similarly had decades of experience with cyber issues. In 1975, then-director Clarence Kelley explained that it was necessary for Bureau personnel to become more familiar with computer fraud.[30] At the time, Kelley's primary concern was individuals' use of computers to perpetrate fraud, since Kelley believed that there was sufficient security built into computer systems to ward off intrusions.[31] Unlike WMD, however, the Bureau began to separate out cyber as a unique discipline—detached from the threat actors who used it—in the mid-1990s with the creation of the Computer Investigations and Infrastructure Assessment Center in 1996 and the National Infrastructure Protection Center in 1998.[32]

Foreign Intelligence in the Domestic Setting

The FBI's work on counterintelligence, counterterrorism, and criminal investigative matters has consistently put the Bureau into opportunities for the collection of foreign intelligence. At least one of these instances—codenamed SOLO—provided early information about the Sino-Soviet split after originating in a counterintelligence investigation.[33] Bureau officials have long recognized the value that foreign intelligence could bring to policymakers. For instance, in 1965, J. Edgar Hoover explained that "a great deal of positive intelligence information is produced from [the FBI's] investigations and sources" and this was "made available to the White House, the Department of State, [US] military services, [and] the Central Intelligence Agency."[34] Hoover's successors endorsed this perspective. In 1984, William H. Webster acknowledged that "in the course of [the FBI's] sensitive investigative techniques in place to develop counterintelligence, [the Bureau] pick[ed] up positive intelligence and that, in turn, is referred to CIA."[35] In 1989, then-director William Sessions echoed Hoover and Webster when he suggested that "the FBI serves the policy making levels of the United States Government by providing an overview of foreign intelligence activities within the United States" that assisted US government officials with "making informed decisions concerning national security policy requirements."[36] Despite these acknowledgments, the FBI never established a component dedicated to thoroughly identifying and exploiting opportunities, within its area of responsibility, for the collection of foreign intelligence information.

Certain aspects of foreign intelligence collection within the domestic setting are the responsibility of the Central Intelligence Agency. The Agency consolidated its overt and covert collection of foreign intelligence on US soil in 1991 within the National Resources Division.[37] With its creation, this division inherited two CIA functions—debriefing Americans, on a voluntary basis, who had traveled abroad, as well as recruitment of foreigners in the United States who planned to return abroad—that began during the Cold War.[38] However, neither the gleaning of information from American travelers, nor the development of contacts with foreigners returning abroad, fully exploits opportunities, domestically, for the collection of foreign intelligence. The Bureau's need for involvement in this area is indicated by the 1942 statement of a Bureau official who groused that "the field is inclined to overlook the necessity for establishing confidential informants in embassies, legations and consulates" even though "the best possible informant coverage is within the embassies, legations, and consulates."[39]

Federally Driven Fusion

After 9/11, "fusion" became a buzzword in the domestically oriented intelligence enterprise. However, the structures to facilitate fusion grew steadily throughout the twentieth century. The FBI and DEA were two of the most notable agencies in the field of information sharing and interagency coordination.

The FBI was an early leader in the area of information sharing, through its establishment of an increasingly expansive apparatus that culminated with the founding of the Criminal Justice Information Services Division (CJIS). The FBI's Identification Division, formed in 1924, served as a national clearinghouse for fingerprint records.[40] In 1967, the Bureau enhanced its role as an information-sharing enterprise when it established the National Crime Information Center—a joint federal/nonfederal law enforcement system. This system contained files on wanted persons and stolen vehicles, guns, and license plates.[41] In subsequent years, the FBI incorporated additional categories into this system, including, in 1971, criminal histories.[42] The FBI merged these functions, as well as several other components, in 1992 to create the Criminal Justice Information Services Division. Then–FBI director

William Sessions claimed that the CJIS would "greatly improve the quality of [the FBI's] customer-driven law enforcement information services to agencies across the country."[43] The CJIS subsequently grew to become the largest division in the FBI. The mission of the CJIS is "to equip [the FBI's] law enforcement, national security, and intelligence community partners with the criminal justice information they need to protect the United States while preserving civil liberties."[44]

The Drug Enforcement Administration established the El Paso Intelligence Center (EPIC) in 1974. EPIC is the primary, tactical antinarcotics intelligence center in the United States and draws resources from member agencies. When established, EPIC was envisioned as a prototype for a national narcotics intelligence system that would serve federal and subfederal law enforcement agencies.[45] EPIC was responsible for providing "a complete and accurate picture of drug trafficking, immigration violations and smuggling."[46] Although administered by the DEA's Intelligence Division, it has grown to include representatives from multiple federal entities including the CIA, Defense Intelligence Agency (DIA), National Security Agency (NSA), FBI, Federal Aviation Administration (FAA), ATF, US Coast Guard, Internal Revenue Service (IRS), Marshals DHS, and the US Digital Service (USDS).[47]

Interagency Influences

Beyond formalized structures for information sharing, there was significant cross-pollination between federal agencies throughout the twentieth century. The FBI, as the nation's primary domestically focused intelligence service, has, as expected, had the most significant impact on how other federal and subfederal agencies in the domestic setting do business.

The Bureau has had a long-standing opportunity to work with and shape the practices of subfederal agencies. As early as 1922, the Bureau of Investigation noted the "close cooperation established with local authorities."[48] Hoover used the FBI's National Academy program for training subfederal agencies as a venue for cementing cooperation. Testifying to Congress in 1937, Hoover said that "within the course of the next 3 or 4 years we will have in every community in the country one man who will have had the benefit of this expert training that we try to give all of our own agents."[49] In 1942, Hoover noted that nearly every US law enforcement agency had a squad—ranging anywhere from two to twenty men—responsible for cooperating with the FBI and to which the FBI referred complaints that came from those squads' home communities.[50] Directors after Hoover continued to acknowledge the value of these relationships. When queried about state and local officials' willingness to bring the FBI in on a terrorist situation, then-director Webster assessed that this "depend[ed], in large measure, upon the success and effectiveness of [the Bureau's] liaison and interrelationships which have been developed and fine-tuned in most major cities and in other parts of the country"; according to Webster, the FBI could "count on almost immediate notification."[51]

The Bureau's other significant contribution to the development of the domestically oriented intelligence infrastructure was its role in shaping the Drug Enforcement Administration. Although Hoover had objected to the Bureau's entry into counternarcotics work, the FBI became increasingly involved with the field following Hoover's death. By the late 1970s, there was serious consideration—reflecting concerns about the DEA's dysfunctionality—about merging the two agencies.[52] In 1982, the DoJ gave the DEA and the FBI concurrent jurisdiction over narcotics matters and directed the DEA to function under the supervision of the FBI's director.[53] Although this arrangement ended in 1987, with the two agencies remaining separate entities, their work was increasingly intertwined. In 1986, for instance, the Bureau introduced its first National Drug Strategy.[54] The FBI would remain in this line of work, as indicated by the need to reallocate resources from counternarcotics to counterterrorism following the September 11, 2001, attacks.

The DEA also developed new competencies as a result of its experience with the Bureau. Of particular note, the FBI brought competencies in the area of electronic surveillance to DEA intelligence-gathering operations. According to then-director Webster, the Bureau assisted the DEA with Title III–authorized wiretaps, since the DEA lacked the personnel, resources, and equipment to implement these activities on its own.[55] With the FBI's expertise, the number of court-authorized drug-related wiretaps tripled.[56]

The Bureau's influence in the form of technical collection was apparent in the DEA's establishment of the Special Operations Division (SOD). In 1992, the DEA's Office of Major Investigations implemented the Kingpin Strategy—an investigative approach that relied primarily on wiretaps and other types of electronic surveillance—to identify and target drug kingpins.[57] It is difficult to imagine that, without the influx of wiretap expertise that the DEA received from the FBI between 1982 and 1987, this approach would have been feasible. The Kingpin Strategy evolved into the SOD, which placed greater emphasis on intercepting the communications between top-level drug traffickers and their subordinates, in furtherance of dismantling entire illicit networks.[58] The SOD became operational, as a DEA-only entity, in 1994.[59] The FBI began assigning representation to it starting in 1995.[60] By 1997, congressional documents characterized the SOD as being run jointly by the FBI and DEA to support major drug investigations through the provision of operational intelligence.[61] The SOD assists intelligence collectors with building multijurisdictional cases that are based primarily on wiretaps.[62]

Sub–Federally Driven Fusion

Although subfederal fusion centers are often talked about as post-9/11 institutions, their roots are actually in this earlier era of nonfederal intelligence institutions (albeit assisted through federal guidance and programs). In 1973, the National Advisory Committee on Criminal Justice Standards and Goals concluded that each state should establish a central institution for intelligence analysis and dissemination and that every police agency in the state should be an active participant in this initiative.[63] This system was to be further institutionalized through the designation of at least one individual in each police department as a liaison to the state intelligence apparatus.[64]

In addition to the fusion of substate authorities, multiple states banded together in regional arrangements. In 1956, twenty-six police departments from seven states established the Law Enforcement Intelligence Unit.[65] Additional examples include the Regional Organized Crime Information Center, which operated in fourteen southeastern states and assisted member agencies with tracking and apprehending narcotics traffickers and other mobile criminals. The Western States Information Network—which linked California, Oregon, Washington, Alaska, and Hawaii—existed to increase the effectiveness of law enforcement in identifying and reducing narcotics-related crime through collection, analysis, and dissemination of information. Several of these regional initiatives incorporated federal input through liaison with agencies including the FBI, DEA, and ATF.[66] Part of the discussion of fusion centers, after 9/11, has been an attempt to identify their purpose. Some have returned to an all-hazards approach, which brings them back around to their origins, by bringing intelligence regarding criminal threats back into the picture.

The development of these agencies invited further federal involvement beyond liaison with individual agencies. In 1978, the DoJ's Law Enforcement Assistance Administration (LEAA) established an Intelligence Systems and Policy Review Board to oversee a program of grants to interjurisdictional intelligence projects.[67] As a General Accounting Office report from 1980 stated, the DoJ was put in a position of having to define the role of these interstate projects in the context of intergovernmental law enforcement, in order to work in conjunction with federal agencies that were focusing on similar areas of crime.[68]

Blueprint for Domestic Intelligence in the Twenty-First Century

The domestically oriented intelligence architecture of the United States evolved throughout the twentieth in a largely ad hoc manner, as federal and subfederal entities attempted to address specific problems ranging from local and regional crime to international state and nonstate actor-driven threats. This approach resulted in gaps on issues—notably foreign intelligence—that did not immediately endanger the nation's security. Furthermore, the ways in which the federal government defined issues produced two different taxonomies for organizing US efforts against identified threats. The first of these taxonomies stressed actors (the FBI's approach), whereas the second focused on implements of criminality (the DEA's approach). This was bound to result in collisions, as different agencies, following different investigative threads, converged on the same threat actors.

Turning the corner into the twenty-first century, the domestically oriented intelligence enterprise was in need of significant reform. Agencies such as the FBI had accumulated an increasingly diverse set of missions that arguably spread their resources too thin. Meanwhile, new agencies had emerged with little effort, on the part of policymakers, to reassess which entity was doing what (and what functions might warrant transfer from existing agencies to new ones—as well as which functions subfederal entities might be able to capably address with minimal federal support). However, consistent with the evolution of US intelligence, substantive reform would occur only in response to a crisis. September 11 represented such a crisis and precipitated more than a decade of massive change that focused on a specific type of threat, rather than taking stock of, and reforming, what had evolved into a complex domestically oriented intelligence enterprise.

Notes

1. *United States Secret Service: An Agency in Crisis,* Committee on Oversight and Government Reform, House of Representatives, 114th Cong. (2015).

2. *Federal Bureau of Investigation,* Hearings on S. Res. 21, Before the Select Committee to Study Governmental Operations with Respect to Intelligence Activities, 94th Cong. (1975).

3. *Domestic Intelligence Operations for Internal Security Purposes,* Before the Committee on Internal Security, House of Representatives, 93rd Cong., pt. 1 (1974).

4. *Intelligence Activities,* Hearings on S. Res. 21, Before the Select Committee to Study Governmental Operations with Respect to Intelligence Activities, Senate, 94th Cong., vol. 6 (1975).

5. *FBI Charter Act of 1979,* Hearings on S. Res. 1612, Before the Committee on the Judiciary, Senate, 96th Cong., pts. 1– 2 (1980).

6. Ibid.

7. *FBI Oversight,* Before the Subcommittee on Civil and Constitutional Rights of the Committee on the Judiciary, House of Representatives, 95th Cong., pt. 1 (1977); *Final Report of the Select Committee to Study Governmental Operations with Respect to Intelligence Activities,* book 2, *Intelligence Activities and the Rights of Americans,* S. Doc. 94-755 (1976).

8. *Domestic Security (Levi) Guidelines,* Before the Subcommittee on Security and Terrorism of the Committee on the Judiciary, Senate, 97th Cong. (1982).

9. Jim McGee, "The Rise of the FBI: Congress Is Handing the Bureau New Powers and Funds, Creating a National Police System That Draws on Military and Intelligence Resources," *Washington Post,* July 20, 1997.

10. "Attorney General's Guidelines for Domestic FBI Operations," https://www.justice .gov/archive/opa/docs/guidelines.pdf.

11. *FBI Oversight: Terrorism and Other Topics,* Before the Committee on the Judiciary, Senate, 108th Cong. (2004).

12. Amy Zegart, *Spying Blind* (Princeton: Princeton University Press, 2007), p. 153.

13. *FBI Oversight; Report of the Joint Inquiry into the Terrorist Attacks of September 11, 2001,* House Permanent Select Committee on Intelligence and the Senate Select Committee on Intelligence, 107th Cong., S. Doc. 107-351, H. Rep. 107-792 (2002).

14. *The Federal Bureau of Investigation's Strategic Plan and Progress on Reform,* Before the Select Committee on Intelligence, Senate, 110th Cong., S. Doc. 110-793 (2007); 9/11 Commission, "Law Enforcement, Counterterrorism, and Intelligence Collection in the United States Prior to 9/11," Staff Statement no. 9, undated, https://govinfo.library.unt.edu /911/staff_statements/staff_statement_9.pdf, http://govinfo.library.unt.edu/911/staff_statements /staff_statement_9.pdf; *Oversight of the FBI,* Before the Committee on the Judiciary, Senate, 107th Cong., S. Doc. 107-447 (2001).

15. *FBI Oversight and Authorization, Fiscal Year 1993,* Before the Subcommittee on Civil and Constitutional Rights of the Committee on the Judiciary, House of Representatives, 102nd Cong. (1992) (testimony of William Sessions).

16. *FBI Oversight and Authorization, Fiscal Year 1993.*

17. Stanley A. Pimentel, Society of Former Special Agents, "Interview of Former Special Agent Richard A. Marquise," unpublished interview, April 11, 2008.

18. *Departments of State, Justice, and Commerce, the Judiciary, and Related Agencies Appropriations for Fiscal Year 1980,* Before a Subcommittee of the Committee on Appropriations, Senate, 96th Cong. (1979).

19. "Law Enforcement, Counterterrorism, and Intelligence Collection in the United States Prior to 9/11"; Department of Justice, Office of the Inspector General, *The Federal Bureau of Investigation's Efforts to Hire, Train, and Retain Intelligence Analysts* (Washington, DC, 2005).

20. *Departments of Commerce, Justice, and State, the Judiciary, and Related Agencies Appropriations for 2001,* Before a Subcommittee of the Committee on Appropriations, House of Representatives, 106th Cong., pt. 2. (2000).

21. *Departments of Commerce, Justice, and State, the Judiciary, and Related Agencies Appropriations for 2005,* Before a Subcommittee of the Committee on Appropriations, House of Representatives, 108th Cong., pt. 10 (2004); *Departments of Commerce, Justice, and State, the Judiciary, and Related Agencies Appropriations for 2001,* pt. 2.

22. "Law Enforcement, Counterterrorism, and Intelligence Collection in the United States Prior to 9/11."

23. Department of Justice, *A Review of the FBI's Handling of Intelligence Information Related to the September 11 Attacks* (Washington, DC, 2004) (publicly released in 2006).

24. Ibid.

25. Ibid.

26. *Joint Inquiry into Intelligence Community Activities Before and After the Terrorist Attacks of September 11, 2001,* Before the Select Committee on Intelligence, Senate, and the Permanent Select Committee on Intelligence, House of Representatives, S. Doc. 107-1086, vol. 1 (2002).

27. *Federal Drug Enforcement,* Before the Permanent Subcommittee on Investigations of the Committee on Government Operations, Senate, 94th Cong., pt. 4 (1976).

28. *Enforcement Efforts of the Bureau of Alcohol, Tobacco, and Firearms,* Before the Subcommittee on Crime of the Committee on the Judiciary, House of Representatives, 97th Cong. (1982).

29. "Communist Infiltration of Radiation Laboratory," University of California–Berkeley, January 31, 1947.

30. *Departments of State, Justice, and Commerce, the Judiciary, and Related Agencies Appropriations for 1976,* Before a Subcommittee of the Committee on Appropriations, House of Representatives, 94th Cong., pt. 2 (1975).

31. Ibid.

32. *Departments of Commerce, Justice, and State, the Judiciary, and Related Agencies Appropriations for 1999,* Before a Subcommittee of the Committee on Appropriations, House of Representatives, 105th Cong., pt. 6 (1998); *Improving Our Ability to Fight Cybercrime: Oversight of the National Infrastructure Protection Center,* Before the Subcommittee on Technology, Terrorism, and Government Information of the Committee on the Judiciary, Senate, 107th Cong., S. Doc. 107-366 (2001).

33. See John Barron, *Operation SOLO* (Washington, DC: Regnery, 1992).

34. *Departments of State, Justice, and Commerce, the Judiciary, and Related Agencies Appropriations for 1966,* Before a Subcommittee of the Committee on Appropriations, House of Representatives, 89th Cong. (1965).

35. *Departments of Commerce, Justice, and State, the Judiciary, and Related Agencies Appropriations for 1985,* Before a Subcommittee of the Committee on Appropriations, House of Representatives, 98th Cong., pt. 8 (1984).

36. *Departments of Commerce, Justice, and State, the Judiciary, and Related Agencies Appropriations for 1990,* Before a Subcommittee of the Committee on Appropriations, House of Representatives, 101st Cong., pt. 2 (1989).

37. Matt Apuzzo and Adam Goldman, *Enemies Within: Inside the NYPD's Secret Spying Unit and Bin Laden's Final Plot against America* (New York: Simon and Schuster, 2013), p. 30.

38. Henry A. Crumpton, *The Art of Intelligence: Lessons from a Life in the CIA's Clandestine Service* (New York: Penguin, 2012), p. 289; Jeffrey Richelson, *The U.S. Intelligence Community,* 6th ed. (Boulder: Westview, 2011), p. 21; Henry A. Crumpton, "U.S. Department of State" (last updated August 3, 2005), http://2001-2009.state.gov /outofdate/bios/c/50493.htm; Richard Helms, *A Look over My Shoulder: A Life in the Central Intelligence Agency* (New York: Random, 2003), p. 288; *National Intelligence*

Reorganization and Reform Act of 1978, Before the Select Committee on Intelligence, Senate, 95th Cong. (1978); *Notification to Victims of Improper Intelligence Agency Activities,* Before a Subcommittee of the Committee on Government Operations, House of Representatives, 94th Cong. (1976).

39. Harry M. Kimball to D. M. Ladd, November 9, 1942.

40. *Department of Justice Appropriations Bill 1930,* Before the Subcommittee of House Committee on Appropriations, 70th Cong. (1928); *Departments of Commerce, Justice, and State, the Judiciary, and Related Agencies Appropriations for 1988,* Before a Subcommittee of the Committee on Appropriations, House of Representatives, 100th Cong., pt. 4. (1987).

41. *FBI Oversight,* Before the Subcommittee on Civil and Constitutional Rights of the Committee on the Judiciary, House of Representatives, 96th Cong. (1980).

42. Ibid.

43. *FBI Oversight and Authorization, Fiscal Year 1993,* Before the Subcommittee on Civil and Constitutional Rights of the Committee on the Judiciary, House of Representatives, 102nd Cong. (1992).

44. Federal Bureau of Investigation, "Criminal Justice Information Services," http://www.fbi.gov/about-us/cjis.

45. *Federal Drug Enforcement,* Before the Permanent Subcommittee on Investigations of the Committee on Government Operations, Senate, 94th Cong., pt. 4 (1976).

46. Ibid.

47. Michael C. Kenney, "Intelligence Games: Comparing the Intelligence Capabilities of Law Enforcement Agencies and Drug Trafficking Enterprises," *International Journal of Intelligence and Counterintelligence* 16, no. 2 (2003): 212–243; Department of Justice, *Review of the Drug Enforcement Administration's El Paso Intelligence Center* (Washington, DC, 2010).

48. *Appropriations, Department of Justice, 1924,* Before the Subcommittee of House Committee on Appropriations, 77th Cong., pt. 2 (1922).

49. *Department of Justice Appropriation Bill for 1938,* Before the Subcommittee of the Committee on Appropriations, House of Representatives, 75th Cong. (1937).

50. *Department of Justice Appropriation Bill for 1943,* Before the Subcommittee of the Committee on Appropriations, House of Representatives, 76th Cong. (1942).

51. *FBI Budget and Oversight for Fiscal Year 1987,* Before the Subcommittee on Security and Terrorism of the Committee on the Judiciary, Senate, 99th Cong., S. Doc. 99-1013 (1986).

52. Frederick Kaiser, *Law Enforcement Reorganization at the Federal Level* (Washington, DC: Congressional Research Service, 1979).

53. *Departments of Commerce, Justice, and State, the Judiciary, and Related Agencies Appropriations for 1985,* pt. 8.

54. *Departments of Commerce, Justice, and State, the Judiciary, and Related Agencies Appropriations for 1990,* pt. 2.

55. *Departments of Commerce, Justice, and State, the Judiciary, and Related Agencies Appropriations for 1985,* pt. 8 (1984).

56. *DEA Oversight and Authorization,* Before the Subcommittee on Security and Terrorism of the Committee on the Judiciary, Senate, 98th Cong., S. Doc. 98-91 (1983).

57. General Accounting Office, *Drug Control: DEA's Strategies and Operations in the 1990s* (Washington, DC, 1999).

58. Ibid.

59. "Drug Enforcement Administration: 1994–1998," https://www.dea.gov/about/history/1994-1998%20p%2076-91.pdf.

60. *Departments of Commerce, Justice, and State, the Judiciary, and Related Agencies Appropriations for 1998,* Before a Subcommittee of the Committee on Appropriations, House of Representatives, 105th Cong. (1997); "Drug Enforcement Administration: 1994–1998"; General Accounting Office, *Drug Control.*

61. *Departments of Commerce, Justice, and State, the Judiciary, and Related Agencies Appropriations for 1998; Departments of Commerce, Justice, and State, the Judiciary, and Related Agencies Appropriations for 1999*, pt. 6.

62. General Accounting Office, *Drug Control.*

63. *Focus on Fusion Centers: A Progress Report,* Before the Ad Hoc Subcommittee on State, Local, and Private Sector Preparedness and Integration of the Committee on Homeland Security and Governmental Affairs, Senate, 110th Cong. (2008).

64. Ibid.

65. Ibid.

66. General Accounting Office, *The Multi-State Regional Intelligence Projects—Who Will Oversee These Federally Funded Networks?* (Washington, DC, 1980).

67. Ibid.

68. Ibid.

3

Crisis and Competition

In the aftermath of 9/11, there was a scramble to understand what had gone wrong and how to fix it. Unfortunately, this devolved into a bureaucratic melee as Congress fought the White House over the best approach to homeland security—which resulted in the establishment of an incoherent department—and the FBI fought back proposals to divide it into two agencies.

Origins of the Department of Homeland Security

Shortly after the attacks, then-president George W. Bush formally introduced the concept of homeland security into the US executive branch. On October 8, 2001, via Executive Order 13228, Bush established the Office of Homeland Security (OHS).[1] This office had the role of adviser to the White House and—according to the executive order—was supposed to "develop and coordinate the implementation of a comprehensive strategy to secure the United States from terrorist threats or attacks."[2] Although the OHS had a broad mandate to work with US government executive departments and agencies, state and local governments, and private entities in furtherance of this mission, it had no authority to compel action by the more than one hundred US government entities that had a homeland security role.[3]

Even before the White House had established the OHS, Congress, notably through Senator Joseph Lieberman, was criticizing the White House's proposal. The legislators' concern was that the OHS would lack the tools—especially budgetary authority—that it would need to implement its mission. Lieberman leaped to introduce legislation that would establish a permanent agency for homeland security functions.[4] On October 11, 2001, Lieberman introduced his bill to create a new department, led by an official who would have cabinet rank and serve as a member of the National Security Council.[5] Lieberman's idea was not new. The concept for a Department of Homeland Security predated the attacks of September 11, 2001. In January 2001, the US Commission on National Security in the 21st Century (commonly known as the Hart-Rudman Commission) had recommended the creation of a national homeland security agency.[6]

The political, rather than policy, impetus for Lieberman's action was nakedly apparent in the failure to define terms for the purpose of this new cabinet department. The Congressional Research Service in May 2002 issued a report stating that no definition of homeland security, beyond Bush's initial executive order, had been established.[7] Opponents of the OHS, therefore, had no defined end-goal, beyond scoring political points against the White House, in mind. (It is worth bearing in mind that less than a year prior to Lieberman's objection, he had been the vice presidential candidate on a ticket that had lost an ugly race to Bush and was considering a presidential bid in 2004.[8])

The White House, which had initially attempted to argue that the creation of a homeland security agency would be a bureaucratic nightmare, decided to compete with the congressional challenge by offering its own vision of a new department. As early as November 2001, the OHS indicated that the administration was giving consideration to merging agencies responsible for border security.[9] Several months later, in April 2002, the White House hinted that it might be amenable to implementing what the Lieberman bill requested.[10]

Then, in June 2002, the Bush administration made a high-profile announcement that introduced a competitor to Lieberman's legislation. Bush directed a small group of advisers to begin developing the White House proposal from a clean slate.[11] The group—which began working in late April—referred to previous studies, including those of the Hart-Rudman Commission, and used the premise of seeking reactions to the Lieberman bill, which was a topic of discussion, to inform the closely held process of developing an alternative proposal.[12] However, the secrecy of the White House's deliberations also meant that it was unable to seek direct input from the heads of departments that would be impacted by the legislation.[13] Using a televised speech, Bush announced his plan to create a Department of Homeland Security that would merge components from eight cabinet departments.[14] On June

18, 2002, the White House transmitted its proposed legislation to the House of Representatives.[15]

The administration's high-profile entry into the legislative fray introduced additional points of friction. In July 2002, the White House threatened to veto a version of the legislation after assessing that the Democrats had stripped the proposed department of management flexibility by making it more difficult to reward good employees and fire poor performers.[16] Furthermore, Bush's version of the bill was the target of elements within Congress who did not believe that the legislation sufficiently addressed intelligence-sharing deficiencies between the FBI and CIA, even as the legislation defined the DHS as a passive recipient of information, reliant on these two agencies.[17]

When the Homeland Security Act became law in late November 2002, it created a bloated and imprecisely organized department. The reorganization was the largest in the federal government since the creation of the Department of Defense in 1947 and combined twenty-two agencies, along with 170,000 employees, under the new DHS.[18] During debate on the creation of the department, Tom Ridge, who at the time was the head of the OHS and who would become DHS secretary, acknowledged that the new agency would include a number of programs not directly related to counterterrorism.[19] However, the problem was more pronounced than the DHS's components spilling over from the counterterrorism arena into other areas of concern. Rather, prior to the creation of the DHS the majority of the agencies that combined to form the organization were focused on neither homeland security nor counterterrorism functions.[20]

As originally envisioned by Lieberman and others, the DHS would have carved out territory claimed by the FBI and CIA. Lieberman had wanted to give the DHS undersecretary for intelligence the authority to direct the CIA and FBI to carry out counterterrorism-related intelligence collection within the United States as well as abroad.[21] Furthermore, Lieberman was toying with the idea of folding the FBI or at least parts of it into the DHS.[22] Congressman Richard K. Armey went even further by suggesting that both the CIA and the FBI might have to be placed "more formally" within the DHS.[23] There was also support, in certain corners of Congress, for the DHS to subsume the CIA's counterterrorism center.[24] However, the FBI ultimately did not lose much to the DHS. The president's proposal led to the movement of the National Infrastructure Protection Center (NIPC)—which the Bureau had never effectively led—to the DHS, while leaving responsibility for cyber-related investigations with the FBI. The DHS also acquired the FBI's National Domestic Preparedness Office, which as a nonoperational coordinator of first-responder preparedness never fit comfortably within the Bureau.

Shortly after creation of the DHS, the administration made a decision that profoundly undercut the department's analytic element. Intelligence analysts within the DHS were supposed to fuse information that they received from the FBI and the CIA.[25] However, in his 2003 State of the Union speech, delivered just as the DHS was forming, Bush announced that he had instructed the heads of the FBI, CIA, DHS, and Department of Defense (DoD) to create a Terrorist Threat Integration Center (TTIC), which would merge and analyze all threat information in a single location.[26] The TTIC would include DHS analysts and would receive information from DHS entities such as the US Coast Guard and the Transportation Security Administration (TSA), as well as from state and local authorities.[27] Ridge, in response to the creation of the TTIC, drew a distinction between threat assessments, which the TTIC would handle, and vulnerability assessments, for which the DHS's Information Analysis and Infrastructure Protection Directorate (IAIP) took responsibility. According to Ridge, the IAIP would receive information from the intelligence community about the possibilities of attacks and potential targets. In response, the DHS would work with the industry sector in which the potential target was located, to take protective measures. In furtherance of assessing and hardening vulnerabilities, Ridge believed that the DHS could task analysts at the TTIC with intelligence requirements for additional information from analysts' respective agencies and even to make inquiries of detained individuals.[28] Despite Ridge's sanguine assessment, the creation of the TTIC (and its successor, the National Counterterrorism Center) contributed to the stunting of the DHS's intelligence function.[29]

In the years since the department's creation, DHS secretaries have initiated multiple efforts to reorganize it. These reorganizations have been directed at fixing a haphazardly designed organization. The shoddy, politically driven circumstances that surrounded the establishment of the DHS are perhaps nowhere so evident as in the fact that the legislation reported to the US House of Representatives did not even define the term "homeland security."[30] Imprecise terms of reference laid a foundation onto which entire agencies—rather than homeland-specific programs—were transferred. As the General Accounting Office noted, sorting out the programs would be a task for future Congresses.[31] Originally, the DHS was divided into five primary directorates: management; science and technology; information analysis and infrastructure protection; border and transportation security; and emergency preparedness and response. However, approximately a dozen other units existed outside of any directorate and instead reported directly to the DHS secretary.[32] This indigestion suggested that the DHS had indeed absorbed functions that did not fit within its mission.

Secretary Michael Chertoff implemented the first significant DHS reorganization. In mid-2005, Chertoff announced the results of the Second Stage Review, a process that he had initiated upon being confirmed as secretary. The review entailed a systematic evaluation of DHS operations, policies, and structures, and included an assessment of whether the DHS was organized to best support its mission.[33] The result of review was the identification of six imperatives: increase preparedness, with particular focus on catastrophic events; strengthen border security and interior enforcement and reform immigration processes; harden transportation security without sacrificing mobility; enhance information sharing with partners, especially those at the state, local, and tribal government levels, as well as with the private sector; improve DHS stewardship in areas including human resources and information technology; and realign the DHS organization to maximize mission performance.[34] Organizationally, the review resulted in the creation of a chief intelligence officer (CINT). According to Chertoff, the role of the CINT was not simply one of chasing terrorists but instead involved understanding border operations, Coast Guard operations, and how to work with subfederal partners.[35] The review also resulted in the dismantlement of the Information Analysis and Infrastructure Protection Directorate; the breakup's outcome was the establishment of a new Office of Intelligence and Analysis (OI&A) and the transfer of the Office of Infrastructure Protection into the Preparedness Directorate.[36] The review also drove the creation of the Directorate of Policy, which would coordinate department-wide policies, regulations, and other initiatives.[37]

DHS secretaries during the presidency of Barack Obama continued to struggle with developing the department into a coherent organization. In 2009, Secretary Janet Napolitano announced her "One DHS" initiative, which was directed at establishing a unified departmental identity across its various components.[38] According to a DHS progress report, one near-term outcome of the One DHS initiative was a moratorium on external contracts for branding and logos for components, which would instead use the existing, common DHS logos and seals.[39] This inconsequential step was worthy of Jack Welch, in comparison to

Napolitano's flat-out gaffe, later in 2009, when she claimed that "the system worked" after the "underwear bomber" nearly detonated an explosive device on a flight inbound to Detroit and was foiled only by the alertness of passengers, rather than by anything that the DHS had done.[40] Despite this misstep, which rivaled Alexander Haig's "I am in control here," Napolitano remained in office. Under Napolitano, the DHS completed its first Quadrennial Homeland Security Review—which established a unified strategic framework for homeland security mission goals—and the first Bottom-Up Review—which aligned DHS's programmatic activities and organizational structure to the first review's findings.[41] These activities identified six DHS missions: preventing terrorism and enhancing security; securing and managing borders; enforcing and administering immigration laws; safeguarding and securing cyberspace; ensuring resilience in disasters; and providing essential support to national and economic security.[42]

Napolitano's successor, Jeh Johnson, launched a more ambitious effort to reform the DHS. In 2014, Johnson introduced his "Strengthening Departmental Unity of Effort" initiative.[43] Under the initiative, the DHS would take a new approach to developing joint operational plans that incorporated the DHS secretary's priorities. The initiative would strengthen and enhance DHS programming and budgeting processes by incorporating the results of strategic analysis and joint-requirements planning into portfolios for review by cross-component, issue-focused teams. Organizationally, Unity of Effort spurred the redesign, consolidation, and reorganization of DHS headquarters elements.[44]

The FBI's Response to US Government Reorganization

Another bureaucratic brouhaha—regarding the FBI—was ginning up while the debate over the DHS played out, and this controversy—like the continued dissatisfaction with the DHS—would persist throughout the first decade of the twenty-first century. The 9/11 attacks prompted significant questions about whether the FBI was effective in the field of national security, or whether the United States should establish a separate, MI-5-like intelligence service to operate within the domestic setting.

Skepticism of the FBI's ability to handle an intelligence mission ran rampant—or at least resounded loudly—throughout Washington. Members of Congress repeatedly aired their concerns about the Bureau's role.[45] This questioning did not stop even after Mueller began implementing structural changes such as establishing the National Security Branch (NSB) and the Weapons of Mass Destruction Directorate. For instance, according to Senator Patrick Leahy, speaking in 2007, Congress was still aware of calls to take away the Bureau's role in domestic intelligence.[46] In that same year, Senator Arlen Specter suggested that creation of an MI-5 model continued to "warrant very serious deliberation."[47] In 2009, Congressman Steve Cohen brought up an issue that had been developing for a century when he asked whether "the FBI [had] grown so much that maybe it [needed] to have two different bureaus, one for homeland security and counterterrorism and counterintelligence . . . and another for the criminal section."[48] This comment was consistent with a reality that had been emerging for much of the twentieth century and had become apparent during the discussion of creating an FBI charter several decades prior. Mueller himself was not above reproach. At least one senator, in 2007, questioned whether the then–FBI director was capable of doing his job.[49]

Mueller fought tenaciously to keep the FBI unified, refusing to acknowledge the agency's inability to surmount the inherent tension between proactive intelligence collection and reactive investigations. According to at least one author, Mueller was able to make this argument with credibility because he had not been responsible for the Bureau's missteps prior to 9/11 and thus was not burdened with having to prove that the agency had functioned effectively under his watch.[50] This, however, tamped down scrutiny of the Bureau's structure when there was a moment of political opportunity to make significant changes that would improve intelligence within the domestic setting.

Although he was an apotheosis of personal integrity and patriotism, Mueller's track record did not include substantial experience with intelligence. Despite this, he was the head of an agency and was not going to have it dismantled out from under him. In 2003, he explained to Congress that the FBI had "the benefit of having the capability of looking at a set of facts or circumstances from the intelligence point of view and then understanding that, particularly when it comes to terrorists, at some point in time, you have to neutralize or address the possibility that the terrorist will take action."[51] The FBI was unique in that it had "under one roof the decision makers who [could] look at [an issue] from the intelligence point of view in gathering . . . intelligence and yet on the other hand, invoking the criminal processes to address the threat to the nation."[52] In 2007, Mueller continued to stick with this premise, telling Congress that "the FBI [believed] the United States [was] better served by enhancing the FBI's dual capacity for law enforcement and intelligence gathering."[53] Mueller's argument reflected his military and prosecutorial approach to intelligence—the identification, reaction, and resolution of a specific problem, rather than the forward-looking navigation of perpetual ambiguity.

In addition to his mission-oriented arguments, Mueller resorted to justifications based on logistical concerns. Speaking in 2003, he stated that creating a separate intelligence service would necessitate replicating much of what the FBI had "in terms of resources, manpower, and technical capabilities. . . . [Y]ou would have to replicate the technological capabilities of doing electronic surveillances, the physical surveillance, and aerial surveillance."[54] By keeping the FBI unified, Mueller argued that resources could be "shift[ed] back and forth between [the FBI's] programs."[55] However, this argument failed to acknowledge that competing proactive and reactive approaches to intelligence would create competition for resources. The FBI—by this logic—would find itself "robbing Peter to pay Paul" rather than exploiting its resources efficiently.

Notes

1. Rensselaer Lee, *Homeland Security Office: Issues and Options* (Washington, DC: Congressional Research Service, 2002).
2. "Executive Order 13228," http://www.presidency.ucsb.edu/ws/index.php?pid=61509.
3. David Von Drehle and Mike Allen, "Bush Plan's Underground Architects: In Silence and Stealth Group Drafted Huge Security Overhaul," *Washington Post,* June 9, 2002.
4. Eric Pianin, "Unresolved Issues for Ridge's Job: Some Say Security Post Lacks Needed Powers," *Washington Post,* September 29, 2001.
5. Harold C. Relyea, *Homeland Security: Department Organization and Management* (Washington, DC: Congressional Research Service, 2002).
6. Lee Hamilton and Thomas Kean, *Without Precedent: The Inside Story of the 9/11 Commission* (New York: Vintage, 2007), p. 11.
7. Lee, *Homeland Security Office.*
8. Richard L. Berke, "Lieberman Has One Eye on '04 Run, the Other, Quite Expectantly, on Gore," *New York Times,* May 2, 2002.
9. David S. Broder and Eric Pianin, "Border Agencies May Be Merged, Ridge Says; Consolidation Plans Could Be in Budget," *Washington Post,* November 4, 2001; Alison Mitchell, "Disputes Erupt on Ridge's Needs for His Job," *New York Times,* November 4, 2001.
10. Elizabeth Becker, "Bush Is Said to Consider a New Security Department," *New York Times,* April 12, 2002.
11. Von Drehle and Allen, "Bush Plan's Underground Architects."
12. Ibid.; Dana Milbank, "Plan Was Formed in Utmost Secrecy; Final Proposal Came from 4 Top Bush Aides; Most Others Out of Loop," *Washington Post,* June 7, 2002.
13. Von Drehle and Allen, "Bush Plan's Underground Architects."

14. James Gerstenzang, "Response to Terror: Bush Proposes a Cabinet-Level Homeland Security Department," *Los Angeles Times,* June 7, 2002.

15. Relyea, *Homeland Security.*

16. David Firestone, "Bill on Security Backed in Senate; Veto Threatened," *New York Times,* July 26, 2002.

17. William Neikirk and Jeff Zeleny, "Legislators Challenge Bush Plan," *Chicago Tribune,* June 2, 2002; Aaron Zitner, "Senators Urge Flexibility in Bush's Plan to Expand Cabinet," *Los Angeles Times,* June 10, 2002.

18. Helen Dwar, "Senate Passes Homeland Security Bill," *Washington Post,* November 20, 2002.

19. Relyea, *Homeland Security.*

20. *Department of Homeland Security Status Report: Assessing Challenges and Measuring Progress,* Before the Committee on Homeland Security and Governmental Affairs, Senate, 110th Cong., S. Doc. 110-588 (2007).

21. Bill Miller and Walter Pincus, "Senate Panel Shapes Homeland Dept Bill," *Washington Post,* July 25, 2002.

22. Alison Mitchell and Carl Hulse, "Congress Seeking to Put Own Stamp on Security Plan," *New York Times,* June 12, 2002.

23. Jim VandeHei and Dan Eggen, "Hill Eyes Shifting Parts of FBI, CIA; Homeland Security Department Would Get Own Operatives," *Washington Post,* June 13, 2002.

24. Walter Pincus, "Homeland Security Issues Abound," *Washington Post,* August 7, 2002.

25. Ibid.

26. Harold C. Relyea and Henry B. Hogue, *Department of Homeland Security Reorganization: The 2SR Initiative* (Washington, DC: Congressional Research Service, 2005).

27. *How Is America Safer? A Progress Report on the Department of Homeland Security,* Before the Select Committee on Homeland Security, House of Representatives, 108th Cong. (2003).

28. Ibid.

29. Testimony of the Honorable Jane Harman, Senate Homeland Security and Governmental Affairs Committee, July 12, 2012.

30. Relyea, *Homeland Security.*

31. Ibid.

32. Relyea and Hogue, *Department of Homeland Security Reorganization.*

33. Ibid.

34. *Department of Homeland Security: Second Stage Review,* Before the Committee on Homeland Security and Governmental Affairs, Senate, 109th Cong., S. Doc. 109-359 (2005).

35. Ibid.

36. *Department of Homeland Security Status Report: Assessing Challenges and Measuring Progress,* Before the Committee on Homeland Security and Governmental Affairs, Senate, 110th Cong., S. Doc. 110-588 (2007).

37. Ibid.

38. "Testimony of Secretary Janet Napolitano Before the House Committee on Homeland Security on DHS: The Path Forward," February 15, 2009, https://www.dhs.gov/news/2009/02/25/secretary-napalitanos-testimony-dhs-path-forward.

39. "Progress Report: Department of Homeland Security (DHS)," April 29, 2009, https://www.hsdl.org/?view&did=37202.

40. Benjamin Carlson, "Janet Napolitano: 'The System Worked,'" *The Atlantic,* December 27, 2009, https://www.theatlantic.com/politics/archive/2009/12/janet-napolitano-the-system-worked/341568.

41. *Homeland Security Department's Budget Submission for Fiscal Year 2012,* Before the Committee on Homeland Security and Governmental Affairs, Senate, 112th Cong., S. Doc. 112-196 (2011).

42. Ibid.

43. *Department of Homeland Security Appropriations for 2016,* Before a Subcommittee of the Committee on Appropriations, House of Representatives, 114th Cong., pt. 1A (2015).

44. Ibid.

45. Michael Allen, *Blinking Red: Crisis and Compromise in American Intelligence After 9/11* (Washington, DC: Potomac, 2016).

46. *Federal Bureau of Investigation,* Before the Committee on the Judiciary, Senate (2007).

47. Ibid.

48. *Federal Bureau of Investigation,* Before the Committee on the Judiciary, House of Representatives (2009).

49. *Federal Bureau of Investigation,* Before the Committee on the Judiciary, Senate (2007).

50. Allen, *Blinking Red.*

51. *Departments of Commerce, Justice, and State, the Judiciary, and Related Agencies appropriations for 2004,* Before a Subcommittee of the Committee on Appropriations, House of Representatives, 108th Cong., pt. 10 (2003).

52. Ibid.

53. *Oversight of the Federal Bureau of Investigation,* Before the Committee on the Judiciary, Senate, 110th Cong., S. Doc. 110-881 (2007).

54. *Departments of Commerce, Justice, and State, the Judiciary, and Related Agencies appropriations for 2004,* pt. 10.

55. Ibid.

4

The Vision of the FBI
After 9/11

The FBI—because it lacks a formal charter—has been at the mercy of its directors for a vision. Mueller was the wrong man at the wrong time and the wrong place. Although Mueller fought to keep the Bureau united, he could never find a way to bring it together conceptually. The lack of unity was not a new problem by any means, but it was one for which Mueller became responsible when he decided to fight against splitting the FBI into separate organizations. Furthermore, Mueller squandered an opportunity to cohere the Bureau around National Intelligence Priorities Framework (NIPF)–informed collection requirements. The use of intelligence requirements as a shared point of orientation would have helped to solidify a culture of intelligence within the FBI, as well as align the Bureau with the intelligence community, by introducing a shared point of reference. Instead, by the end of his (extended) term, Mueller had failed to transform the FBI from a reactive law enforcement organization to one that accepted its responsibility to serve as the country's primary intelligence service within the domestic setting. Even worse, he set the Bureau back to a pre-9/11 footing by implementing the Threat Review and Prioritization (TRP) process, which institutionalized a pathology of parochialism that 9/11 had demonstrated was untenable.

Too Many Missions and a Lack of Vision

Because the FBI lacks a formal charter, the vision that its leadership establishes is uniquely important. The directorship of the FBI, since 9/11, has set out a confused vision of the organization's purpose (a reflection, perhaps, of the Bureau's organic, rather than designed, evolution, which has brought too many disparate elements under its purview). One theme, which multiple directors emphasized, was that the Bureau was an agency bifurcated between law enforcement and intelligence (a theme that stretched back to Hoover and showed up in the aborted FBI charter). Both Mueller and James Comey also made sporadic efforts to integrate the two missions, but the way in which they did so continued to emphasize the FBI's traditional, reactive approach to its responsibilities. The possibility that intelligence collection might identify opportunities that would afford US decisionmakers an informational advantage vis-à-vis adversaries of both foreign and domestic nature remained largely unaddressed.

To be fair, when Robert Mueller III became the director of the FBI days before the September 11 attacks, the former prosecutor had no idea that he would be thrust into a national debate about intelligence failures and the FBI's role as an intelligence service. He acknowledged the Bureau's cultural shortcomings, explaining that it had been a reactive organization and had perceived itself as such.[1]

However, what Mueller did not do was recognize the extent to which the Bureau's perception needed to change. In 2002, he correctly stated that the FBI could not wait until it had evidence of a crime being committed, but rather needed to "take what evidence [the FBI had] and make predictive observations to avoid the next attack."[2] This was not fundamentally different from what the FBI had been doing. The Bureau continued to focus on identifying evidence that malefaction was afoot—it simply attempted to identify threat activity in its earlier stages, before it had culminated in an attack or other damage to US security. Mueller seemed to confirm this approach when, in 2004, he explained that the FBI would "focus on the threat" although "not necessarily the instrumentality of the crime."[3] Again, Mueller's underlying premise was that there was a criminal/threat that had already formed and that the FBI needed to find.

Although Mueller attempted to enhance the FBI's intelligence capabilities, his efforts simply put a veneer of new terminology on the existing, reactive agency. This was apparent in many of his descriptions of the FBI that perpetuated the Bureau's split personality. In 2004 he told Congress that the Bureau was taking full advantage of its "dual role as both a law enforcement, as well as an intelligence agency."[4] The bifurcated description of the FBI that Mueller presented was adopted by his successor. In 2014, then-director Comey referred to the FBI as a "national security and law enforcement organization" and then, the following year, similarly described it as "the lead domestic intelligence and law enforcement agency."[5] As of 2013, the FBI was making this bifurcated description part of its training for new employees. The Directorate of Intelligence and the Training Division developed a "Dual Mission from Day One" initiative that was supposed to provide "clear expectations that responsibilities of the intelligence mission assume the same stature of a law enforcement mission."[6]

In his description of the FBI's resources, Mueller tended to erroneously conflate intelligence collection and investigation. While the two are related, they are not synonymous: investigations are a subset of intelligence collection. Mueller, in 2004, claimed that intelligence functions were "woven throughout the fabric of the Bureau."[7] He further conflated reactive investigations with intelligence when, in 2008, he claimed that the "FBI has always excelled at gathering intelligence . . . and using it to build cases that led to courtroom convictions."[8] Subsequently, in 2011, he stated that "the talents and capabilities that enabled [FBI personnel] to be good criminal investigators . . . are the same talents and capabilities that enable [the Bureau] to address the other priorities."[9] However, investigations are deductive—they are premised on identifying the perpetrator of an act (or the perpetrator of activities leading to a larger act such as a terrorist attack)—whereas intelligence also encompasses the navigation of uncertainty, forecasting based on indicators and trends.

Intelligence information, as Mueller described it, was something ancillary to reactive investigations of existing threats. For instance, in 2004, he stated that the FBI's Directorate of Intelligence would be responsible for a strategic intelligence campaign to support major cases.[10] Furthermore, Mueller suggested that intelligence collection was merely a by-product of the FBI's work, rather than an objective in its own right. In 2006, he explained that the FBI had traditionally derived intelligence from cases.[11] By Mueller's logic, the Bureau looked for intelligence among only a subset of actors—those that were already suspected of being threats—and gathered it only as an afterthought to the primary objective of disrupting a nefarious entity.

Mueller was never able to extricate himself—or the Bureau—from this reactive approach. Even after the FBI launched a program of dedicated human intelligence (HUMINT) collectors who were oriented toward intelligence requirements, rather than disruption of specific malignant activities, Mueller remained mired in terms of investigations, stating that these agents' mission was to recruit and use human sources to fill in "the spaces between the cases."[12] Therefore, according to Mueller, the Bureau's understanding of its domain was still reliant on reactive investigations to define the topography, rather than assessing the topography to identify the anomalies on which cases might be predicated. Mueller's failure to move the Bureau beyond a reactive, investigative approach—and instead allowing investigations to stand in for intelligence collection—was an acquiescence to the unsatisfactory, pre-9/11 status quo.

This could all become quite circular. In 2012, Mueller described a model of intelligence collection that produced information, which in turn informed a threat picture, which in turn drove how the FBI understood the threats and how it investigated threats.[13] "Intelligence," according to Mueller's previous statement, was derived from cases (i.e., investigations of threats), which meant that investigation of threats was producing the information that the FBI was using to develop a threat picture, on which the Bureau would premise future collection (i.e., investigations). Consequently, the FBI would seemingly continue to collect against the threats about which it was already cognizant. There would be no mechanism to identify emerging issues (whether threat or opportunity). This, as the section on the Threat Review and Prioritization process—which the Bureau instituted in 2012—describes, is exactly what happened.

Building on his early statements of bifurcation and conflation, Mueller and his successors began—to their credit—attempting to develop a unified definition of the FBI. In 2009, Mueller gave a clunky explanation, stating that "today's FBI is not an intelligence service that collects but does not act, [nor is the FBI] a law enforcement services that acts without knowledge. [The FBI] is a security service fusing the capability to understand the breadth and the scope of threats with the capability to dismantle those same threats, whether they're terrorist or criminal."[14] Then in 2013, Mueller more concisely described the FBI as "threat-focused, intelligence-driven" (a variation on his 2011 statement that the Bureau was "threat-focused, intelligence-led").[15] Mueller's successor, Comey, adopted similar language. Even Comey's unexpected successor, Christopher Wray, continued to use the "threat-focused, intelligence-driven" language.[16] However, this is not radically different from where the FBI was prior to 9/11, since—unpacking these statements—the FBI is an agency that continues to use its resources only to ferret out individuals who are guilty either of committing a crime, or of planning one.

What FBI directors since 9/11 have expected to achieve through collection and analysis is only one part of the picture that the FBI is entrusted with developing. Mueller in 2002 admitted that the FBI had not focused on its analytical capability, which he defined as having to "take every piece that may be provided to [the FBI] and put it in a larger framework, in a larger puzzle."[17] (This, of course—like "connecting the dots"—is a misleading analogy, since not all of the pieces may fit the same puzzle, or any puzzle.) Ten years later, Mueller was still focusing on developing a "comprehensive threat picture" that would enable the FBI to "effect strategic disruptions of terrorist networks before they act."[18] What Mueller did not take account of in his picture is that threats are not the only things available in the domestic setting—there are also opportunities for collection of foreign intelligence information that can provide US decisionmakers not simply a warning but also a decision-advantage.

Intelligence Requirements as an Organizing Concept (or Not)

One area of the FBI's work, where Mueller had the opportunity to set the Bureau on the right path but failed to do so, was the agency's relationship to intelligence requirements. These requirements are how policymakers articulate informational needs and are supposed to provide the intelligence community with direction. Although the FBI has linked its intelligence collection to requirements, it has done so—even before Mueller's tenure—as an afterthought, focusing instead on its own, parochially identified priorities. Mueller—as in other aspects of intelligence—used the right terminology to dress up a fundamentally broken process for a few years. However, he then knocked the Bureau back onto a pre-9/11 footing—which treated the intelligence community and its policymaking customers as an afterthought—when he introduced the Threat Review and Prioritization process as the Bureau's organizing rubric.

The FBI Relationship to Intelligence Requirements

The FBI has, for much of its history, been an intelligence collector capable of addressing other agencies' needs. During World War II, the FBI explicitly acknowledged that it would disseminate material to the Department of State, Department of the Navy, War Department, Office of the Coordinator of Inter-American Affairs, Office of the Coordinator of Information, Department of the Treasury, Maritime Commission, and Board of Economic Warfare "in accordance [with those departments'] particular interest."[19] Similarly, during the Cold War, the Bureau provided information to the CIA from the SOLO operation, which Allen Dulles, the director of central intelligence, praised highly.[20] As of the late 1970s, the FBI maintained a component, consistent with Executive

Order 11905, to collect and disseminate foreign intelligence acquired in support of other intelligence agencies.[21] These activities were effectively answering intelligence requirements. However, the Bureau did not orient its collection activity around external requirements and instead provided information that was developed as a byproduct to its own work. As then–FBI director Webster told Congress in the mid-1980s, the FBI shared intelligence "to the extent that in the course of [its] sensitive investigative techniques in place to develop counterintelligence, [the FBI] pick[ed] up positive intelligence and that in turn [was] referred to the CIA."[22]

Following the conclusion of the Cold War, the Bureau did begin orienting itself toward collection in response to intelligence requirements rather than specific cases. For instance, as of 1992 the FBI had developed enhanced analytical capabilities for counterterrorism requirements that responded to the Gulf War.[23] This emphasis ebbed as the decade progressed. However, by the late 1990s, then-director Freeh, reflecting on the development of the FBI's 1998–2003 strategic plan, stated that a principal deficiency in the FBI's operation was the "absence of systematic intelligence collection requirements from Headquarters program managers to field offices."[24]

The FBI requested analytic enhancements specifically to help the Bureau "transition from a system in which collection requirements are derived to fill the needs of individual investigations to one that allows for the monitoring and evaluating of collection requirements on a programmatic and national level."[25] Part of this analytic enhancement would take the form of hiring fifty-six intelligence operations specialists (i.e., intelligence analysts) to serve as collection management officers, who would implement systematic collection requirements, with each field office acquiring an analyst who would concentrate on establishing a reporting and requirements system applicable to all FBI programs.[26] Furthermore, these collection management officers would "identify information of national intelligence interest to be disseminated . . . for national policy makers."[27] This new initiative, if implemented with commitment, would have helped transform the FBI from a case-based, reactive organization into one tied to the intelligence community.

This new requirements-oriented process would have treated sources as organizational, rather than case-specific, assets. A standard debriefing guide would help to determine all areas about which the source might have information. Furthermore, a source "inventory" would facilitate the direction of new requirements to existing sources across programs.

Importantly, the collection management initiative would include "routine reporting to United States policy makers of foreign intelligence information collected by FBI sources."[28]

However, this new effort included an inherent flaw. Information was still derived from cases. Although sources might be leveraged corporately, there would still be a "specific activity for which [the source] was developed."[29] Consequently, although the FBI might overlay requirements on its existing base of sources, it was still not poised to develop sources expressly to address requirements. This meant that the Bureau would ultimately not exploit the full range of information within the domestic setting. Instead, its ability to collect intelligence was limited to the space that reactive investigations had opened up. Confirming this was the Bureau's statement that it needed analysts who understood national intelligence requirements as well as foreign and domestic priorities, capable of "extract[ing] national foreign intelligence information collected as a byproduct of FBI investigation and process it for dissemination to policy makers."[30] Although the Bureau was learning to speak the language of intelligence, it remained unable to fully implement the concepts that this language expressed.

As part of its effort to institutionalize intelligence, following 9/11 the FBI began to place more emphasis on requirements and collection management functions. The new Directorate of Intelligence included an Intelligence Requirements and Collection Management Unit (IRCMU).[31] This unit focused full-time on identifying gaps and developing strategies for filling them.[32] It also provided a single point of entry to the Bureau for all information requests, and represented the FBI on the DCI's National Intelligence Collection Board and ensured that intelligence community taskings were passed to FBI field offices.[33] Contemporaneously, the FBI developed a "collection baseline" database, which defined the sum total of resources that the FBI could deploy against a specific threat.[34] This was a step in the right direction, as it meant that the Bureau was thinking about its resources as corporate, rather than case-specific, assets. However, the continued discussion of collection in terms of "threat" did not create conceptual room for the collection of positive intelligence that could provide decisionmakers with an informational advantage. Instead, the discussion continued to frame intelligence in reactive terms, which restricted the use of intelligence to identification and disruption of malign entities.

The FBI acknowledged that it shared a common point of reference with the intelligence community in the form of the National Intelligence

Priorities Framework. In 2004, according to the Bureau, the NIPF served as a "single prioritization scheme" for the Bureau's requirements process.[35] During that same year, the Bureau advised Congress that it applied its capacity to collect information on threats (i.e., investigations) against the NIPF requirements and used this disparity to identify intelligence gaps. The IRCMU, in conjunction with analysts embedded with headquarters and field entities, was supposed to develop targeting and collection strategies to address these gaps. However, the FBI's relationship with the NIPF was one of putting the cart before the horse. Rather than using the NIPF as a starting point for developing collection resources, the Bureau instead overlaid its own investigative priorities on the NIPF.[36] This approach was consistent with Mueller's benighted conception that intelligence was the by-product of investigations rather than the baseline from which to identify anomalies that might serve as the predication for specific investigations.

Unfortunately, the FBI never achieved a transformation into an NIPF-oriented agency. This would have entailed developing a baseline awareness of the domestic environment—through the collection and analysis of both positive and threat-oriented intelligence—which would identify anomalies warranting tactical collection and disruption (i.e., investigations) as well as provide decision-advantage to policymakers. Instead, the Bureau was increasingly captured by the gravitational pull of its tactical legacy. For instance, in 2004, John Pistole, the FBI's assistant director for counterterrorism, attempted to square the circle of intelligence and law enforcement by telling Congress that intelligence requirements allowed the FBI to focus "investigations on specific collection that may lead to a criminal prosecution."[37] Pistole's error was in making an imperfect analogy. Although case predications are a type of requirement, the two are not synonymous. Policymakers need not just intelligence that results from the investigation of threats; they also benefit from the insights that can be derived through the exploitation of opportunities where nothing has gone wrong for the United States but where, instead, circumstances are especially right for gaining an informational advantage.

Threat Review and Prioritization Process

After 2004, the Bureau was unable to recover from its descent into the tyranny of tactical thinking. This hit a new low when the FBI introduced its Threat Review and Prioritization process, which represented a drastic retreat from the NIPF. The FBI began developing the process in fiscal year 2010 and implemented it in fiscal year 2012.[38] TRP is disconnected from the intelligence community in both organization and ethos.

The TRP process—which the Directorate of Intelligence manages—is conducted on an annual basis, with the participation of FBI headquarters and field offices.[39] Based on a "Master Threat Issue List"—maintained by the Directorate of Intelligence—operational divisions, in advance of the TRP meetings, gather documentation, including case summaries and reviews, raw intelligence reporting, finished intelligence products, and threat mitigation strategies.[40] TRP, at headquarters, identifies the FBI's national threat priorities.[41] Field offices use the outcomes of the headquarters prioritization process to conduct their own iteration of the TRP process to prioritize the national threat priorities as well as other threat issues.[42] TRP's end result is the Consolidated Strategy Guide, which documents the annual prioritization of threats identified by headquarters and field offices.[43] As described by Comey in 2015, TRP is "a very disciplined and very, very complicated process."[44]

The FBI has tried to sell TRP as a standardized and objective process. According to the 9/11 Review Commission's report, TRP allows FBI headquarters to compare one field office's priorities—and resource allocation—with those of another field office.[45] However, the reality is far from objective. According to the office of the DoJ's inspector general, TRP is subjective and open to interpretation, and in certain contexts this has been a "substantial weakness."[46] FBI officials' descriptions have been consistent with the inspector general's assessment. For instance, one official referred to TRP as essentially a "gut check," while an FBI assistant director believed that outcomes could be determined by the "loudest person in the room."[47] Presenting TRP, as the FBI has, gives the Bureau's overseers a false sense of confidence in the efficacy of the process in place.

Organizationally, TRP disengages the FBI from the intelligence community. The process focuses the FBI's collection not on NIPF-informed requirements but instead on an internally oriented mechanism that emphasizes FBI-specific concerns.[48] TRP uses two criteria—impact level of the threat, and mitigation resources necessary to address the threat—as the basis for its judgments.[49] Missing from this rubric is any discussion of whether the Bureau has unique opportunities within the domestic setting to develop positive intelligence that addresses requirements and supports the strategic interests of the United States. In fact, the TRP process resulted in penalization of offices that addressed intelligence community priorities and produced information that was included in Presidential Daily Briefs, because collection did not address parochial TRP-mandated topics.[50] There is a clearly a problem when intelligence of interest to the highest level of the US government is not the same as the intelligence that the TRP process elicits.

TRP is, instead, institutionalized insularity. As the office of the DoJ inspector general has described, it is a "standardized . . . process for the FBI's operational divisions to align their resources against the most severe and substantial threats."[51] This fundamental premise turns the FBI into a self-licking ice cream cone, institutionalizing the FBI's reactive mission. The 9/11 Review Commission corroborated this when it determined that TRP incentivized field offices to align their resources against already identified threats.[52]

Not only does TRP place the Bureau in a reactive straitjacket, but it further impedes the FBI by creating an institutional myopia. The process does not look beyond a one-year horizon and, according to the 9/11 Review Commission, does not sufficiently encourage or reward the identification of new or emerging threats.[53] Additionally, TRP cannot effectively drive the prioritization of emerging threats identified by the interagency coordination process.[54] Allowing a threat to develop, as opposed to disrupting it at a nascent stage, puts the FBI (and the United States) at a disadvantage by narrowing the window within which the Bureau can act before a threat degrades US interests, whether kinetically or otherwise.

Notes

1. *Reforming the FBI in the 21st Century,* Before the Committee on the Judiciary, Senate, 107th Cong., S. Doc. 107-971 (2002).

2. Ibid.

3. *Departments of Commerce, Justice, and State, the Judiciary, and Related Agencies Appropriations for 2005,* Before a Subcommittee of the Committee on Appropriations, House of Representatives, 108th Cong., pt. 6 (2004).

4. *FBI Oversight: Terrorism and Other Topics,* Before the Committee on the Judiciary, Senate, 108th Cong., S. Doc. 108-804 (2004).

5. *Commerce, Justice, Science, and Related Agencies Appropriations for Fiscal Year 2015,* Before a Subcommittee of the Committee on Appropriations, Senate, 113th Cong. (2015); *Federal Bureau of Investigation,* Before the Committee on the Judiciary, House of Representatives, H.R. 113-77 (2014).

6. *Commerce, Justice, Science, and Related Agencies Appropriations for 2014,* Before a Subcommittee of the Committee on Appropriations, House of Representatives, 113th Cong., pt. 2B (2013).

7. *Departments of Commerce, Justice, and State, the Judiciary, and Related Agencies Appropriations for 2005,* pt. 10 (2004).

8. *Oversight of the Federal Bureau of Investigation,* Before the Committee on the Judiciary, Senate, 110th Cong., S. Doc. 110-910 (2008).

9. *Commerce, Justice, Science, and Related Agencies Appropriations for 2012,* Before a Subcommittee of the Committee on Appropriations, House of Representatives, 112th Cong., pt. 7 (2011).

10. *Departments of Commerce, Justice, and State, the Judiciary, and Related Agencies Appropriations for 2005,* pt. 10 (2004).

11. Testimony of the Honorable Robert S. Mueller III, 6 December 2006.

12. Statement of Robert S. Mueller III, Director, Federal Bureau of Investigation, Department of Justice, Before the United States Senate, Committee on the Judiciary, Concerning "Oversight of the Federal Bureau of Investigation," 17 September 2008.

13. *Ten Years After 9/11: 2011,* Before the Committee on Homeland Security and Governmental Affairs, Senate, 112th Cong. (2012).

14 *Oversight of the Federal Bureau of Investigation,* Before the Committee on the Judisicary, United States Senate, 111th Cong. (2009).

15. *Oversight of the Federal Bureau of Investigation,* Before the Committee on the Judiciary, House of Representatives, 113th Cong. (2013); *Oversight of the Federal Bureau of Investigation,* Before the Committee on the Judiciary, Senate, 112th Cong., S. Doc. 112-173 (2011); *Ten Years After 9/11: 2011.*

16. Statement of Christopher A. Wray, Director, Federal Bureau of Investigation, Before the Committee on the Judiciary, House of Representatives, December 7, 2017.

17. *Reforming the FBI in the 21st Century,* 2nd sess.

18. *Ten Years After 9/11: 2011.*

19. Federal Bureau of Investigation. *F.B.I. History of the S.I.S.,* vol. 1 (Washington, DC: undated).

20. Federal Bureau of Investigation, F. A. Frohbose to A. H. Belmont (Washington, DC, December 10, 1959); Federal Bureau of Investigation, R. O. L'Allier to A. H. Belmont (Washington, DC, January 13, 1961).

21. *Departments of State, Justice, and Commerce, the Judiciary, and Related Agencies Appropriations for 1979,* Before a Subcommittee of the Committee on Appropriations, House of Representatives, 95th Cong., pt. 6 (1978).

22. *Departments of Commerce, Justice, and State, the Judiciary, and Related Agencies Appropriations for 1985,* Before a Subcommittee of the Committee on Appropriations, House of Representatives, 98th Cong., pt. 8 (1984).

23. *Departments of Commerce, Justice, and State, the Judiciary, and Related Agencies Appropriations for 1993,* Before a Subcommittee of the Committee on Appropriations, House of Representatives, 102nd Cong., pt. 2B (1992).

24. *Departments of Commerce, Justice, and State, the Judiciary, and Related Agencies Appropriations for 2000,* Before a Subcommittee of the Committee on Appropriations, House of Representatives, 106th Cong., pt. 6 (1999).

25. *Departments of Commerce, Justice, and State, the Judiciary, and Related Agencies Appropriations for 2001,* Before a Subcommittee of the Committee on Appropriations, House of Representatives, 106th Cong., pt. 2 (2000).

26. *Departments of Commerce, Justice, and States, the Judiciary, and Related Agencies Appropriations for 2000,* pt. 2.

27. Ibid.

28. Ibid.

29. Ibid.

30. Ibid.

31. Alfred Cumming and Todd Masse, *Intelligence Reform Implementation at the Federal Bureau of Investigation: Issues and Options for Congress* (Washington, DC: Congressional Research Service, 2005).

32. *FBI Oversight: Terrorism and Other Topics.*

33. *Departments of Commerce, Justice, and State, the Judiciary, and Related Agencies Appropriations for 2005*, pt. 10.

34. *FBI Oversight: Terrorism and Other Topics.*

35. *Departments of Commerce, Justice, and State, the Judiciary, and Related Agencies Appropriations for 2005*, pt. 10.

36. Ibid.

37. Ibid.

38. Department of Justice, *Audit of the Federal Bureau of Investigation's Cyber Threat Prioritization* (Washington, DC, 2016).

39. Ibid.

40. Ibid.

41. *Commerce, Justice, Science, and Related Agencies Appropriations for 2017, Before a Subcommittee of the Committee on Appropriations, House of Representatives*, 114th Cong., pt. 2B (2016).

42. Ibid.

43. Department of Justice, *Audit of the Federal Bureau of Investigation's Cyber Threat Prioritization.*

44. *Commerce, Justice, Science, and Related Agencies Appropriations for 2016, Before a Subcommittee of the Committee on Appropriations, House of Representatives*, 114th Cong., pt. 6 (2015).

45. *Commerce, Justice, Science, and Related Agencies Appropriations for Fiscal Year 2015, Before a Subcommittee of the Committee on Appropriations, Senate*, 113th Cong. (2015); 9/11 Review Commission, *The FBI: Protecting the Homeland in the 21st Century* (Washington, DC, 2015).

46. Department of Justice, *Audit of the Federal Bureau of Investigation's Cyber Threat Prioritization.*

47. Ibid.

48. Darren E. Tromblay, "Information Technology (IT) Woes and Intelligence Agency Failures: The Federal Bureau of Investigation's Troubled IT Evolution as a Microcosm of a Dysfunctional Corporate Culture," *Intelligence and National Security* (2017). Pages 817–832 published online March 2, 2017; https://doi.org/10.1080/02684527.2017.1296947.

49. Department of Justice, *Audit of the Federal Bureau of Investigation's Cyber Threat Prioritization.*

50. Ibid.

51. Ibid.

52. 9/11 Review Commission, *The FBI.*

53. Ibid.

54. Ibid.

5

Reorganizing the Bureau

Since its earliest days, the FBI has tried to strike a balance between the role of headquarters and the field. After 9/11, the Bureau pursued massive reorganizations at both the field and headquarters levels. However, these changes did not fix but rather exacerbated the Bureau's existing shortcomings. Rather than facilitating information sharing, Mueller created a top-heavy organization—dominated by an expanded headquarters, even though headquarters personnel were the primary points of failure prior to 9/11. Furthermore, Mueller did little to unlock the Bureau's human capital, instead allowing field offices to control their human capital, rather than using the FBI's personnel, regardless of where they might be geographically located, as corporate resources. This was a needlessly inefficient approach in the twenty-first century.

Headquarters Reorganization

Director Mueller, informed by his conception of intelligence, reorganized the FBI by consolidating functions at headquarters that his predecessors, William Sessions and Louis Freeh, had delegated out to the field. Early on, Mueller established four executive assistant director positions; these directors would report directly to him and were responsible—respectively—for counterterrorism and counterintelligence; criminal investigations; criminal investigations and law enforcement services; and administration.[1] (There was also a deputy executive assistant director—which reduced into the unfortunate acronym DEAD—for counterintelligence and counterterrorism.[2]) Mueller's desire

47

was to reduce the deputy director's span of control—in response to congressional concern as well as concerns raised by internal and external reviews of the FBI.[3]

However, headquarters-happy Mueller—falling into the either/or fallacy of headquarters/field relations, quickly consolidated headquarters control over field-based activities. Mueller believed that the FBI should have "centralized management with distributed execution."[4] In 2001, Congress approved Mueller's proposal to reorganize the FBI, which, among other measures, consolidated management of counterterrorism cases and operations under the assistant director for the relatively new Counterterrorism Division.[5] Under Mueller, the Bureau also consolidated direction of its counterintelligence program at headquarters. In 2002, David Szady, then the assistant director for counterintelligence, stated that "a new more centralized and nationally directed" program was a more effective approach.[6] As of 2006, the FBI was establishing a national counterintelligence strategy that provided a centrally driven foreign counterintelligence program that would provide "strategic direction, priorities, guidance, and support flowing from FBI HQ to the field offices."[7] This top-down ethos seemed to provide no effective mechanism for field offices to help FBI headquarters refine its approach. In addition to counterterrorism and counterintelligence, Mueller emphasized national management of cyber crime activities.[8]

Mueller believed that this approach addressed the fact that counterterrorism had national and international dimensions that transcended field offices' arbitrary, geographically defined areas of responsibility. According to Mueller, he was fixing a problem of "stovepiping" of counterterrorism-related information by fifty-six field offices.[9] While the existence of these field offices did present problems for the FBI as a corporate entity, they were not the FBI's primary contributors to the Bureau's role in the 9/11 intelligence failure. Rather, headquarter mis-

Headquarters Expansion

The expansion of FBI headquarters is indicated by the growth in its counterterrorism bureaucracy. As of 1997, the Counterterrorism Center did not even constitute an entire section. By 2004, the FBI's Counterterrorism Division (which the Bureau had established in 1999) contained nearly ten sections (see Figure 5.1).

Figure 5.1 FBI Counterterrorism Structure Prior to 9/11

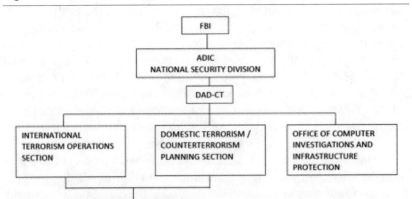

Source: Combating Terrorism: Federal Agencies' Efforts to Implement National Policy and Strategy (Washington, DC: General Accounting Office, 1997).

steps were far more damaging to the FBI's counterterrorism efforts. Mueller's consolidation of responsibility at headquarters, rather than facilitating the aggressive work that field offices had done, was a perverse decision that fixed nothing.

Headquarter actions, prior to 9/11, included errors of interpretation and incompetence on the part of analysts. It was headquarters that denied the Minneapolis special agent who was investigating Zacarias Moussaoui—who could have alerted the US government to the scope and nature of the September 11 attacks—the authority to conduct a Foreign Intelligence Surveillance Act (FISA)–authorized search directed at Moussaoui.[10] Confirming the weak pre-9/11 analytic culture, the country can lay multiple missteps at the feet of headquarters-based analysts. For instance, an FBI headquarters analyst was the point of failure who did not afford appropriate attention to a memo from an FBI agent in the Phoenix, Arizona, field office who advised FBI headquarters that there might be a "coordinated effort by Osama bin Ladin" to send students to civil aviation schools in the United States.[11] Furthermore, it was a headquarters analyst who gave the New York field office guidance regarding the Wall's prohibitions on information sharing—guidance that the 9/11 Commission later identified as having been based on the analyst's misunderstanding of the policy.[12] When in June 2001, after an FBI headquarters analyst met with agents in the New York field office and showed them photographs of soon-to-be 9/11 hijackers Khalid al-Mihdhar and Nawaf al-Hazmi, the analyst promised to provide additional information but did not follow through with furnishing the details that might have helped to disrupt the September 11 plot.[13] The office of the DoJ inspector general found that the analyst's inability to provide this data was not due to an inability to share information but rather because the analyst had failed to "plan the meeting adequately, or to ask sufficient questions from the CIA in advance of the meeting."[14] In other words, field offices were asking the right questions and getting the wrong answers from headquarter bodies.

FBI executives seemed to engage in magical thinking when they not only decided to consolidate management of operations at headquarters but also put even greater faith in the analytic enterprise at headquarters—the same analytical enterprise that had fumbled repeatedly and disastrously prior to 9/11. According to Mueller, he intended to create a centralized body of subject-matter experts who were knowledgeable about historical cases.[15] The Bureau not only believed that location somehow imparted expertise but also actually strove to separate field-based analysts from playing a role in developing the national picture by establishing "an independent analytic process that [was] a collaborative effort between FBI HQ analytical components and the [Office of Intelligence]."[16]

Given its history of analytic work, it was incongruous that Mueller thought that headquarters was not only capable of doing the work it was assigned but also in a position to drop in as a subject-matter expert on field offices. However, this is exactly what happened. As of 2002, headquarters established "flying squads" that were expected to augment field investigative capabilities by providing specialized personnel.[17] According to the FBI, these teams included expertise regarding FISA requirements, intelligence analysis, and familiarity with the intelligence community.[18] These were all areas in which headquarters had only recently demonstrated deadly ineptitude. In addition to counterterrorism, the FBI also assumed that expertise on cyber issues was resident at, and deployable from, headquarters. The Cyber Action Teams were surge capabilities to assist field offices that were working on complex computer intrusion incidents that represented an immediate threat to the US information technology infrastructure.[19]

The growth of headquarters was a slap in the face to field offices. Many of the FBI's agents in the field believed that Counterterrorism Division supervisors lacked sufficient expertise to guide the field's work.[20] This assumption was embarrassingly validated when Gary Bald, the head of the FBI's National Security Branch (which included the Counterterrorism Division), had been unable to explain the difference between Sunni and Shia Islamic sects.[21] While seemingly esoteric, these philosophies are embraced by—respectively—al-Qaeda and Hezbollah. Not only did Bureau counterterrorism officials lack subject-matter expertise, but they also did not even believe it was important to possess such expertise.[22]

Even more problematic than management being unfamiliar with areas that they were supervising was the inadequacy and lack of continuity at headquarters. Management seemed to be perpetually in flux, with the average tenure of a senior executive service member at headquarters being thirteen months. As of 2005, the Counterterrorism Division, which the FBI had established only in 1999, had gone through six different chiefs.[23] The problem was not just with executives but also with the entire work force. Although Mueller was determined to make headquarters the center—rather the coordinator—of the FBI, he was unable to effectively staff it. For instance, in 2008 a unit responsible for international counterterrorism had only 62 percent of its full staffing level.[24] Rather than finding ways to mitigate the churn, Mueller simply institutionalized it. In 2005, the FBI advised Congress that it had developed the FBI HQ Term Temporary Duty Pilot Program, under which special agents would apply for eighteen-month tours at headquarters.[25] The seemingly perpetual churn at headquarters left the field bewildered. For instance, field personnel told the 9/11 Commission that they no longer had any idea of who their primary point of contact in the Counterterrorism Division was.[26]

Arguably, rapid turnover decreased accountability and allowed elements of the Bureau to make careers out of climbing the ranks, rather than doing the work. In 2001, a former FBI agent testified to the US Senate Judiciary Committee that there was a group of senior executive service officials, referred to by special agents as "The Club," who were "motivated by self-preservation and self-interest."[27] These senior executive service figures sought to impose "excessive headquarters control over field operations."[28] More recently, former FBI special agent James Gagliano confirmed that callous careerists exploited Mueller's expansion of headquarters to move rapidly through the ranks, while leaving legacies devoid of substance. As Gagliano explained, Mueller's headquarters enlargement drew junior agents, some with as little as three years in the organization and no significant case experience, to fill vacancies.[29] Andrew McCabe—the disgraced former deputy director—was among these climbers and bounced between headquarters and the Washington, DC, field division, a pattern that Gagliano assessed was "commonplace for ladder-climbers interested in hastening their ascent in the midlevel and senior executive ranks."[30]

Mueller's emphasis on building up headquarters demonstrated a lack of comprehension about the organization's dynamics. For instance, headquarters could not conduct analysis in a vacuum. (This was assuming that headquarters could conduct analysis at all. After all, according to Amy Zegart, a draft report on the terrorist threat to the United States, submitted in 2001, was of such poor quality that it was of no use. The report never addressed the likelihood of a terrorist attack, provided no assessment about different terrorist groups' capabilities, did not provide intelligence requirements, and did not make a single recommendation to FBI management about how to develop a counterterrorism strategy or how to allocate resources.[31]) In 2000, the FBI had assessed that the intelligence research specialists located in the field—not at headquarters—were the closest to raw information and were in the optimal position to establish intelligence collection requirements. Therefore, according to the Bureau, it was actually necessary to increase the number of intelligence research specialists within field offices.[32] Even as Mueller continued to emphasize the dominance of headquarters, he acknowledged that the knowledge that he wanted at headquarters had been "largely resident" in FBI field offices.[33] Mueller did not indicate how he was going to transfer this knowledge resident in the field to headquarters. Did he expect the experts to pack up and relocate? Did he think that walking through the door at headquarters invested an individual with previously unpossessed aptitude?

As Mueller settled into his term, he seemed to become more cognizant that the Bureau was composed of distributed expertise. In 2004 he acknowledged that "to the extent that you divorce the analysts or those who are making judgements from the underlying information . . . the ultimate judgements that are made in the intelligence arena may not be as good as you want them to be."[34] Furthermore, as the FBI advised Congress in 2004, the Bureau was a "geographically dispersed enterprise that performs distributed intelligence production."[35] In 2011, Mueller admitted that the physical location of an analyst did not determine whether their analysis was of a strategic or tactical nature, and that special expertise was distributed around the country and could contribute to a case coordinated by headquarters.[36] However, Mueller's growing insights about a distributed FBI were not reflected in the Bureau's organization. As of 2011, nearly half of the Directorate of Intelligence's resources were still located at FBI headquarters.[37]

Creation of New FBI Headquarters Components

Following 9/11, the FBI attempted to create a new headquarters intelligence infrastructure. After dismantling the Investigative Services Division, the FBI created an Office of Intelligence (not to be confused with the short-lived Office of Intelligence that the Bureau had established in the late 1990s) under the auspices of the Counterterrorism Division, in late 2001.[38] According to the FBI, this office was focused on aligning intelligence production efforts with national priorities and with developing standards for analyst performance.[39] However, according to journalist Garrett Graff, the reality was far less ambitious. Although the Office of Intelligence contained a Strategic Intelligence Unit, this function was "more in name only."[40] It "existed only as a sketch on a few pages of a legal pad."[41] The few analysts in the unit were "being forced to balance management and executive briefing responsibilities with actually conducting strategic analysis."[42]

In 2003, the FBI elevated intelligence to program status, putting it on par with national security and criminal investigations.[43] According to the Bureau, the FBI's intelligence program was created by the president and Congress "to provide centralized management of the nation's domestic intelligence efforts."[44] Mueller advised Congress that the FBI was "taking the steps necessary to strengthen [the capability to produce intelligence] by establishing a national intelligence program that is on a level equal to that of our traditional investigator programs."[45] However, this approach to intelligence institutionalized a fundamental misconception. Mueller—as previously discussed—contributed to the FBI's bifurcated nature through his inability to integrate law enforcement and intelligence into a cohesive enterprise. Splitting intelligence from the programs through which the FBI collected information exacerbated the dichotomy that the Bureau desperately needed to eliminate. Relatedly, stacking up the intelligence program alongside of, in competition with, and apart from the FBI's other programs made no sense, since—without collection resources—the intelligence program was a vacuum.

Consistent with this new status, the Bureau moved the Office of Intelligence out from under the Counterterrorism Division and applied the office's concept of intelligence across all FBI programs. According to a witness from the National Academy of Public Administration (NAPA) in testimony to Congress, the new Office of Intelligence was supposed to be a focal point of intelligence management across all of the FBI's key operational directorates. However, speaking in 2003, the NAPA witness cautioned that "plans for this office's functions and responsibilities are only beginning to be developed, and are far from being realized."[46]

The FBI continued to build up its intelligence architecture with the creation of an executive assistant director of intelligence in 2003. In May of that year, the FBI hired Maureen Baginski, a former National Security Agency official, to fill the position. Although the Bureau's Office of Intelligence had been in existence since late 2001, Baginski was underwhelmed by what she encountered, telling one reporter that "there was nothing there." Baginiski's approach to running the Office of Intelligence was to treat it, innovatively, as a "start-up company."[47] However, Baginski became a casualty of cultural momentum and, after clashing with entrenched bureaucrats, departed from the FBI.[48] It did not bode well for the Bureau's intelligence apparatus that a bona fide intelligence official was defeated by elements opposed to reform.

Passage of the Intelligence Reform and Terrorism Prevention Act (IRTPA) in 2004 required the FBI to convert the Office of Intelligence into a Directorate of Intelligence. On paper the Directorate of Intelligence consisted of six units: Career Intelligence, which worked to develop career paths for intelligence analysts; Strategic Analysis; Oversight (which was responsible for managing the Field Intelligence Groups [FIGs]); Intelligence Requirements and Collection Management; Administrative Support; and Executive Support.[49] However, according to the Commission on the Intelligence Capabilities of the United States (the WMD Commission), which delivered its report in 2005, "the Directorate of Intelligence itself [had] no authority to direct any of the Bureau's intelligence investigations, operations, or collections. It . . . [performed] no analysis, [commanded] no operational resources, and [had] little control over the 56 Field Intelligence Groups." Based on the recommendations of the WMD Commission, the FBI established a new National Security Branch and subordinated the Directorate of Intelligence to the new NSB. This reorganization placed an assistant director, who reported to the NSB's executive assistant director, over the Directorate of Intelligence and eliminated the position of executive assistant director of intelligence.

This did not bode well for the Bureau's struggling intelligence enterprise. In 2006, the Bureau explained to Congress that the Directorate of Intelligence's functions were carried out by embedded elements in the operational divisions of FBI headquarters.[50] This was an untenable situation if the FBI hoped to become a true intelligence service with a strategic perspective. The assistant director of the Directorate of Intelligence—downgraded from the executive assistant director of intelligence—was now only on par with the heads of the operational divisions, meaning that the assistant director would be contending—under the same executive assistant director—with multiple divisions rooted in a reactive approach. Furthermore, Directorate of Intelligence resources were located within these reactive divisions, providing an additional opportunity for operational components to co-opt the resources supposed to help the Bureau transcend its pre-9/11 blindly tactical culture.

Nearly a decade later—in 2014—the FBI moved the Directorate of Intelligence out from under the NSB and installed it under a new Intelligence Branch. The Bureau reestablished the position of executive assistant director of intelligence to lead this new branch. According to the FBI, the Intelligence Branch would manage the planning and direction of the Bureau's intelligence work, regardless of the programmatic area or threat issue that the work addressed.[51] The Intelligence Branch was supposed to drive the integration of intelligence and operations—employing a matrix management relationship with operational components—as well as engage the Bureau's partners across the intelligence community and law enforcement communities. Additionally, the Intelligence Branch was supposed to coordinate the management of resources of the FBI's national intelligence program. The executive assistant director of intelligence would serve as the focal point for the FBI's engagement with the Office of the Director of National Intelligence (ODNI).[52]

Office of Intelligence

The FBI headquarters intelligence component grew, in a few years, from an office to an entire directorate (see Figure 5.2). However, larger did not necessarily equate to better, given the continuing deficiencies in the Bureau's analytic program.

Figure 5.2 Office of Intelligence

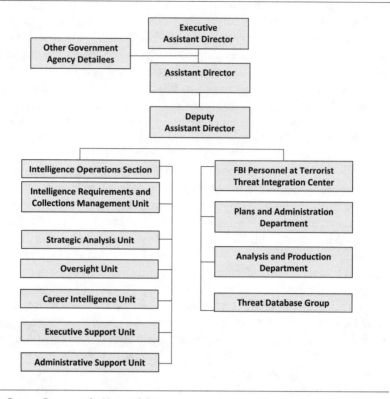

Source: *Report to the National Commission on Terrorist Attacks upon the United States* (Washington, DC: Federal Bureau of Investigation, 2004).

The newly constituted Intelligence Branch—comprising the Directorate of Intelligence, the Bureau Intelligence Council, the Office of Partner Engagement, and the Office of Private Sector—is supposed to manage "the planning and direction of the entire organization's intelligence work, regardless of . . . programmatic area or threat issues."[53] However, the Bureau's intelligence work force is still susceptible to co-optation by the FBI's reactive elements and culture. Directorate of Intelligence resources remain matrix-managed with operational components.[54] Additionally, as described by Comey, the executive assistant director "looks across the entire enterprise and drives integration."[55] The ability to do this depends on the perspective of the individual filling the position. So far, the executive assistant director has been an agent—a career steeped in the nuances of deductive analysis but not in the inductive analysis essential to a functioning intelligence service. For instance, in 2016, Comey appointed Joshua Skule as executive assistant director of intelligence, despite Skule's investigative background in violent crime and public corruption.[56] Comey caveated his decision to appoint an agent to this position, explaining in 2015 that the "role should be someone who came up through the intelligence career service."[57]

Agnostic Elements: Cyber and WMD

In the decade after the 9/11 attacks, the FBI created two entities—the Cyber Division and the WMD Directorate—that have struggled to find a mission in their own right. Unlike the Counterterrorism, Counterintelligence, and Criminal Investigative Divisions, these new elements focus on environments and capabilities, rather than actors. This approach is problematic, especially in an agency that has defined itself by disrupting threat actors and, at its best, identifies entities from which it can collect foreign intelligence information. Heretical as it might sound, these FBI components are more in line with the DHS's monitoring functions—surveying the landscape for changes in actors that enter and exit it, as well as assessing vulnerabilities—and the possibility of moving these components, wholesale, from the former agency to the latter makes national security sense.

Cyber Division

The FBI's Cyber Division is part of the Criminal, Cyber, Response, and Services Branch and took responsibility for a mission that had most recently belonged to the National Infrastructure Protection Center. However, the creation of the DHS split up the NIPC's functions between the FBI and DHS, suggesting that Bureau ownership of cybersecurity was not necessarily the optimal solution and certainly not a sacrosanct foregone conclusion. The Bureau created the Cyber Division, in 2002, as part of a broader reorganization.[58]

Upon creation, CyD, because of its inconsistency with the FBI's threat-focused approach, immediately overlapped with other divisions' missions. By the description of its assistant director, the Cyber Division combated cyber-based terrorism, hostile foreign intelligence operations that had a nexus to the internet, and cyber crimes.[59] Despite the nature of cyber as an environment, rather than a threat, the FBI made it an independent national priority—in the same ranking rubric as counterterrorism and counterintelligence—apart from the threats that operated within cyberspace.[60]

The Cyber Division's inconsistency with the FBI's structure has arguably left it searching for an identity. Even Mueller, who apparently lacked the vision to transform the Bureau into a coherent intelligence service, acknowledged that, "internally, the structure of the FBI does not lend itself to easily addressing cyber."[61] By the second decade of the twenty-first century, the division's focus had shifted from targeting "computer-enabled" traditional crimes, to focusing on "sophisticated cyber threats."[62] This evolution included restructuring of the Cyber Division to focus solely on computer intrusions and moved nonintrusion crimes that had a cyber nexus (i.e., the cyber crime program, the Innocent Images National Initiative, intellectual property rights, internet fraud, internet extortion, identify theft, internet money laundering, and internet gambling) to the Criminal Investigative Division.[63] The ongoing malleability of the Cyber Division's mission was apparent in the 2017 remarks by the Cyber Division's assistant director, who told a conference that the division was moving toward a "predictive" approach to the issues it covered.[64]

However, none of the changes resolved the fundamental failing that undermined the Cyber Division from its inception: cyber is not an actor; it is an agnostic environment. Paring down the set of activities on which the division focused did not give the division a unique identity; it simply reduced the number of divisions with which the Cyber Division overlapped. Furthermore, making the division more predictive was simply a new way of talking about old threats, since state and nonstate actors conducted the activities on which the division was predicating its identity.

If the Cyber Division was going to have unique relevance to the FBI, it would be in offering expertise to—rather than usurping—the intelligence activities within existing threat-oriented divisions. Initially, this seemed to be an aspect of the division's mission. For instance, the division's assistant director noted that the division had "significantly increased the hiring of technically trained agents, analysts, and forensic specialists."[65]

However, the government writ large has struggled to attract a skilled cyber-related work force, which can make far more money in private industry. The FBI, consequently, attempted to grow its own expertise. In 2007, the FBI established a Cyber Development Plan, which included twelve core courses, as well as optional courses with a more specialized focus. The Bureau expected its agents to complete the training in five to seven years.[66] Then, in 2012, the FBI introduced its Next Generation Cyber Initiative, which included increasing the capability of the cyber work force.[67] The new cyber training initiative included the High Technology Environment Training, which was directed at improving the technical skills and baseline technological knowledge of the entire FBI work force; commercially available training courses for cyber personnel so that they could maintain their skills; and opportunities for FBI personnel to earn a master of science degree in information technology.[68] The takeaway is that the FBI is no more uniquely postured to provide expertise in the cyber field than any other agency.

Rather than struggling to create a separate cyber work force, the FBI should draw on the capabilities of other agencies, with which it already collaborates, to create an efficiency of resources and encourage further interagency integration. The DHS, which has a core function of identifying network vulnerabilities, is already a member of the FBI's National Cyber Investigative Joint Task Force (NCIJTF).[69] The Bureau has demonstrated that it is able to work, operationally, with the DHS. For instance, it waged a successful joint campaign with the DHS Industrial Control Systems–Cyber Emergency Response Team (ICS-CERT) to combat cyber intrusions against the natural gas pipeline–sector companies.[70] This suggests that further integration is possible. Furthermore, the NCIJTF includes representation from the National Security Agency—the participation of which is presidentially mandated.[71] The NSA—and Cyber Command—for which the director of the NSA is responsible—present another pool of expertise upon which the FBI's cyber mission could draw.

The FBI's siloed approach to cyber has defined how the issue is worked at the field level. Whereas, pre-9/11, cyber-related squads were supposed to serve as resources, the Bureau has created cyber investigative squads. In 2006, the FBI told Congress that individual field offices had developed cybersecurity programs "tailored to their individual circumstances and threats."[72] By 2011, the FBI had established cyber squads in each of its fifty-six field offices and had deployed more than a thousand advanced cyber-trained FBI agents, analysts, and forensic examiners to staff these squads.[73]

Weapons of Mass Destruction Directorate

The Weapons of Mass Destruction Directorate is similar to the Cyber Division in several ways. Like the Cyber Division, it does not look at dynamic threat actors but instead at the implements that have a meaning only for national security once actors use, or attempt to use, those implements. Furthermore, both are structured as repositories of subject-matter expertise but attempt to be operational—against what is unclear, since their focus is on inert items—rather than analytical. As a result, the WMDD—like CyD—impinges on other divisions' missions.

Weapons of mass destruction have been of concern to the FBI since they were introduced (one need only think of the Bureau's investigation of espionage against the US atomic program to understand that the Bureau, by necessity, has evolved in parallel with the development of the WMD field). The FBI's National Security Branch—in response to Mueller's direction in 2005—established the WMDD in fiscal year 2006.[74] Creation of the directorate represented an effort to align and consolidate the Bureau's various counterproliferation initiatives, which multiple divisions had managed.[75]

It is in the WMDD's investigative functions that the directorate overlaps with existing operational divisions. The cases, which the directorate manages, fall into two primary categories: WMD terrorism and WMD proliferation.[76] Terrorism—which by definition overlaps with Counterterrorism Division's mission—includes nonattributed instances that involve the threat or use, or attempted use, of a WMD.[77] Cases that are categorized as proliferation involve instances when a state or non-state actor attempts to acquire material and expertise relevant to a WMD program.[78] The actor aspect, again, means that these cases are within the bailiwick of divisions handling counterterrorism, counterintelligence, and even criminal investigations.

The second aspect of the WMD Directorate's mission is developing preparedness for a WMD incident. Preparedness, according to the assistant director for the WMDD, "involve[d] the development of comprehensive plans and policy at the strategic and operational levels that specify responsibilities and courses of action."[79] Furthermore, the directorate engaged in training and exercises to ensure that the FBI and the US government were postured to address WMD threats.[80] However, this preparedness function is a duplication of the preparedness and first-responder missions for which the DHS is responsible.

Finally, the WMDD has a countermeasures and safeguard component to its mission. According to the then–assistant director for the WMDD, in 2012, "countermeasures bolster policy, and include outreach activities, identification of key indicators, and other measures to counter or eliminate the WMD threat."[81] For instance, the directorate identifies vulnerabilities in the biological agent exploitation process and develops corresponding countermeasures and prevention initiatives to mitigate these vulnerabilities. A specific example of an initiative is the Biological Sciences and Academic Biosecurity Workshop, a partnership between the FBI and the academic research community that facilitates the reporting of suspicious activities at research locations.[82]

However, the DHS has pursued overlapping preparedness projects that, given its status as an agency with significant first-responder functions, should absorb many of the WMDD's functions, to the point of rendering the directorate a nonentity. Following 9/11, the DHS inherited the National Domestic Preparedness Office—which focused on equipping personnel to deal with WMD incidents—as well as management of the Domestic Emergency Support Teams from the FBI. Furthermore, the DHS, through its Science and Technology Directorate, has pursued the development of countermeasures technologies such as radiation detection equipment (before—and after—absorbing the functions briefly under the auspices of the Domestic Nuclear Detection Office). Finally, the DHS Office of Intelligence and Analysis, which complements the DHS's responsibilities for safeguarding critical infrastructure, is the appropriate location for assessing vulnerabilities, as opposed to the actor-oriented FBI.

In field offices, WMD coordinators represent the WMD program. These coordinators are responsible for developing relationships with federal, state, and local crisis and consequence management agencies.[83] (However, this function seems to be well within the DHS's area of responsibility given this agency's responsibility for state and local liaison through fusion centers and its responsibility—notably through the Federal Emergency Management Agency—for consequence management.) Additionally, the WMD coordinator conducts outreach to local companies, state and local laboratories, and academia. This is another area of overlap with the DHS, which manages the Chemical Facility Anti-Terrorism Standards (CFATS) program and thus must also liaise with industry on WMD-related issues.

Intra-FBI Fusion

The FBI has tacitly admitted that separating out cyber and WMD issues from collection of intelligence against the actors who weaponize these implements is an unworkable idea. This acknowledgment takes the form of multiple intra-Bureau efforts to reintegrate the functions of the Cyber Division and the WMD Directorate with other operational divisions.

One such example of reintegration is the Counterproliferation Center (CPC). The FBI created the CPC in 2011 by bringing together the Counterintelligence Division's counterproliferation mission, with subject-matter expertise resident in the WMDD, with the Directorate of Intelligence's analytical resources.[84] CPC-managed investigations include all efforts directed at preventing the acquisition of information and technologies (missile delivery systems, advanced conventional weapons and components, etc.) that would enhance a foreign government's ability to create, use, or share WMD.[85]

The FBI also created the Cyber-Counterintelligence Coordination Section, which brought together elements from CyD and the Counterintelligence Division.[86] According to then–FBI director James Comey, this section focused on the identification, pursuit, and defeat of hostile intelligence services when those services used cyber means to penetrate or disrupt US government entities or economic interests.[87]

Multiple indictments against foreign actors illustrate the necessity of integrating cyber and counterintelligence capabilities. In 2014, the US Department of Justice charged five Chinese military hackers with cyber espionage against US corporations.[88] US politics remain in disarray in the aftermath of the 2016 hack by Russian cyber threat actors FANCY BEAR and COZY BEAR of the Democratic National Committee.[89] Then, in 2017, the United States charged Russian Federal Security Service (FSB) officers with hacking Yahoo and millions of email accounts.[90] Iran has also been implicated in activities that bridge the FBI's cyber and counterintelligence responsibilities. In 2018, the US Department of Justice charged nine Iranians with conducting a massive cyber theft campaign—directed against universities and the private sector—in order to benefit the Iranian Revolutionary Guard Corps.[91] All of these incidents illustrate that, although cyber awareness is necessary, the significance of these events for national security is largely in the nature of the actor (e.g., Iran) and the objective (e.g., technology) rather than the specific tool that the actor used to achieve the objective.

CyD and the WMD Directorate are both elements that do not fit with the FBI's structure and (increasingly) its mission. At present, both CyD and the WMDD are alternate universes that collide with intelligence efforts focused on threat actors by looking at the implements that a threat actor exploits. This primes the United States for another strategic intelligence failure, as separate entities work different parts of the same threat, thereby obfuscating the complete picture of how a US adversary or competitor operates against America's interests.

Scientific acumen is certainly necessary for understanding how threat actors exploit new technologies to degrade US elements of national power. However, the repositories of talent (ostensibly CyD and the WMDD) should not exist apart from the FBI's other operational divisions. Instead, the human capital should be matrixed from CyD and the WMDD to the Counterintelligence, Counterterrorism, and Criminal Investigations Divisions. By doing this, the Bureau could use both CyD and the WMDD to cultivate subject-matter expertise, while deploying it in a coordinated campaign against threat actors, alongside counterparts from other divisions.

However, the reality is that the FBI is no longer the only game in town. Its current capabilities—in the areas of both cyber and WMD—intersect with and at times duplicate the functions for which the DHS is responsible. Rather than creating redundant sets of expertise and competing initiatives, the DHS and the FBI need to identify areas of overlap and assign missions accordingly in order to create areas of comparative advantage that are of service to the broader domestic security community. For instance, the FBI should relinquish its WMD preparedness functions, given the DHS's significant role in mitigating vulnerabilities to US infrastructure and in facilitating first-responder activities. Furthermore, instead of developing a cyber work force, the Bureau should draw on the expertise available in partner agencies—such as the DHS and NSA—to help it understand how threat actors exploit new technologies and to monitor developments in this area.

Foreign Intelligence: An Unmet Challenge

The FBI, in the post-9/11 era, demonstrated that it was capable of collecting information of foreign intelligence value. Foreign intelligence collection fell under two distinct types of initiatives. The first of these consisted of the Bureau's debriefing of diaspora populations in order to obtain actionable information prior to the start of hostilities abroad. Foreign intelligence collection was also the objective of the Office of the Director of National Intelligence's Foreign Intelligence Collection Program (FICP). However, as was the case throughout the twentieth century, the FBI was unable to establish an effective apparatus to consolidate, or at least coordinate, foreign intelligence collection.

Interview Projects

In an effort to support US efforts in Iraq, the FBI, in 2003, began collecting information from individuals who had previously spent a significant amount of time in that country. During the pre-invasion of Iraq,
the FBI launched Operation Darkening Clouds.[92] This project drew on
more than 130,000 immigration records that the US Citizenship and
Immigration Service's Fraud Detection and National Security Unit,
under the DHS, had compiled.[93] In 2003, Mueller told Congress that the
FBI had established Iraqi task forces in each field office.[94] As a result of
voluntary interviews—which included engineers, scientists, and even
former leaders of the Iraqi government—the Bureau was able to provide
the US military with approximately 250 reports to assist with locating
weapons production and storage facilities, underground bunkers, fiber
optic networks, and Iraqi detention and interrogation facilities.[95]

The FBI reportedly undertook a similar project in relation to Libya.
In 2011, the *Wall Street Journal* reported that the Bureau was inter-
viewing Libyans residing in the United States to acquire information
that might assist allied military operations.[96] The Bureau's initial interviews focused on individuals with personnel or professional ties to
Libya, with a particular interest in Libyans who were residing in the
United States on visas.[97]

Foreign Intelligence Collection Program

The FBI received tasking from the Office of the Director of National
Intelligence to establish the Foreign Intelligence Collection Program. In
2006, the ODNI directed the FBI to use its collection authorities in furtherance of developing information responsive to the National Intelligence Priorities Framework and pursuant to the National HUMINT Collection Directives.[98] As of fiscal year 2009, the FBI was the primary or
supporting collector on ninety-eight of the topics associated with the
NIPF.[99] The Bureau explained to Congress that "prior to the establishment of the FICP, the FBI collected intelligence tangential to its existing
cases. There were no concerted efforts by the FBI to collect intelligence
exclusively."[100] The FICP was supposed to fill this gap and specifically
avoid duplicating counterintelligence and counterterrorism programs.
As of 2009, the FBI continued to insist that its intelligence program
"must acquire the capacity to establish and carry out a positive foreign
intelligence collection and reporting effort that allows the FBI to be
responsive to taskings received by the [ODNI]."[101]

Desk Officer News

A network of desk officers would have administered the FBI's Foreign Intelligence Collection Program (see Figure 5.3). The FBI has historically been unable to comprehensively exploit opportunities for the collection of foreign intelligence within the domestic setting. It has instead treated foreign intelligence as a by-product of reactive investigations, rather than as an objective in its own right.

Figure 5.3 Collaborative Desk Officer Network

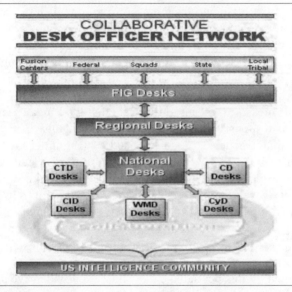

Source: *FY 2009 Budget Request Summary* (Washington, DC: Federal Bureau of Investigation), https://www.justice.gov/sites/default/jmd/legacy/2014/08/02/fy09-fbi.pdf.

Administration of the FICP

The FBI proposed the establishment of a bureaucratic infrastructure to manage the FICP. Through the Foreign Intelligence Collection and Oversight Unit, the FBI would oversee the FICP.[102] The Bureau would manage the FICP within the context of a Desk Officer Program (DOP) that would have four levels—national, regional, divisional, and Field

Intelligence Groups. In the field, each field office would have desk offices organized by country. Operational division desks would be aligned with their programs' priority targets. Through the DOP, the FBI envisioned leveraging the existing collection within its operational divisions and directing collection activities in response to national requirements. The scope of this project is indicated by the FBI's personnel request to staff the FICP. According to the Bureau, it would need thirty-five special agents, sixty-seven intelligence analysts, and twenty-seven support personnel. Out of the intelligence analysts, forty-two would be assigned to the field, while twenty-five would be assigned to FBI headquarters.[103] Additionally, the FBI planned to reassign 200 agents to work on foreign intelligence issues in the field.[104] However, discussion of the FICP and DOP disappeared, completely, from discussion in congressional testimony and budget submissions after 2009.

To its credit, the FBI did attempt to ensure that it was disseminating products that addressed NIPF requirements. According to congressional testimony, from 2009, the percentages of FBI headquarters and field office–finished intelligence products that addressed an NIPF topic were performance measures, meant to illustrate that the Bureau's intelligence program was responsive to the intelligence community.[105]

Unfortunately, the FBI also imposed a meaningless metric on its production of raw intelligence. According to the Bureau, at least 25 percent of its Intelligence Information Reports (IIRs) were supposed to be on purely foreign intelligence topics.[106] This was not a realistic approach to doing business. If a field office did not have foreign intelligence information within its area of responsibility, it could not be reasonably expected to devote 25 percent of its IIRs to these topics. Similarly, an office that had access to a wealth of information should not be constrained by this percentage and consequently deprive policymakers of significant information. Finally, the arbitrary figure meant that a field office could claim it was doing its job as soon as it hit the mark, rather than exploiting the full extent of intelligence within its domain.

The Demise of Foreign Intelligence

The FBI appears to have never gotten what seems to have been an ambitious foreign intelligence collection program past the planning stages. Even if it had progressed beyond the 2009 explanation, it would not have resolved the Bureau's split personality into a coherent identity. Mueller, as he typically did, talked in terms of bifurcation when he discussed foreign intelligence. Speaking in 2003, he called for the FBI to establish a "national intelligence program that is on a level equal to that of [the FBI's] traditional [investigative] programs."[107] Any hope of establishing the FBI as a functioning foreign intelligence producer would disappear in fiscal year 2010, when the Bureau started designing a new rubric for allocating resources—known as the Threat Review and Prioritization process—which utterly failed to account for the need to serve external customers.

Reorganization of the FBI's Field Office Structure and Creation of Field Intelligence Groups

The FBI reorganized its field office structure to emphasize intelligence. Unfortunately, the Field Intelligence Groups, which were the outcome of this reorganization, rode a bureaucratic merry-go-round and within a decade had experienced full-circle reinvention that took them back to where they had started. This episode illustrated the Bureau's short institutional memory, a factor that has arguably impeded lasting reform.

In October 2003, the Bureau established FIGs in each of its fifty-six field offices. As described by a Congressional Research Service report, FIGs were "stand alone entities comprised largely of intelligence analysts, linguists, and surveillance specialists."[108] The FIGs sequestered analytic resources from the rest of the office. According to the FBI, it had created FIGs because analysts assigned to field operational squads had been conducting data management (e.g., checking databases) and clerical assignments, rather than performing analysis. The FBI expected FIGs to progress through three phases: the first was to bring together analysts and conduct necessary hiring of new analysts (it is not known to what extent analytic skills, rather than simply allocated bodies, were assessed prior to making determinations about new hiring); second, the FIG would become responsible for managing the analysis and dissemination of intelligence; and third, the FIG would then task agents to collect against intelligence gaps that analysis demonstrated exist.[109]

The creation of FIGs exacerbated the Bureau's atomization by doubling down on the concept of fifty-six field offices with resources owned by those field offices. Field offices implemented the FIG structure inconsistently, highlighting that the FBI continued to operate as a collection of offices, rather than as a corporate entity. The 9/11 Commission discussed the problems inherent in field-level leadership, pointing out that "management . . . still [could] allocate people and resources to local concerns that diverge[d] from the national security missions," which could result in "a focus on lower-priority criminal justice cases over national security requirements."[110] In a 2005 report, the National Academy of Public Administration reported that the field offices received substantial latitude on how to structure FIGs. While some offices consolidated most of their analysts, reports officers, and intelligence specialists into a centrally managed pool, others opted for a consolidated analytic and reporting pool composed of virtually all analysts—including financial analysts, who were generally associated with support for investigations of white-collar crime—and reports officers. Still others decentralized intelligence specialists to support individual counterterrorism squads and more immediately involve intelligence personnel in collection operations.[111] As independent audits and visits of the Senate Select Committee on Intelligence staff to field offices determined, as of 2007, FIGs continued to lack clear guidance.[112]

Furthermore, the imposition of the FIG structure did nothing to standardize or improve how offices used analysts. According to the Congressional Research Service, following interviews of field personnel, "each office handled the three analytic work functions differently—for example, some wanted analysts cross-trained in each of the three work roles, and others had individual analysts allocated to one of the three functions."[113] Similarly, the WMD Commission noted that the FIG structure was not enhancing FBI analysis and stated that "although we are sympathetic to the FBI's particular analytic needs, we remain concerned that the current structure of the FBI's intelligence program and the relationship between analysis and field operations, will not encourage analysts to rise above individual investigations, develop subject matter expertise, or drive—and not merely inform, counterintelligence, counterterrorism, and foreign intelligence collections, investigations, and operations."[114]

The FBI then proceeded to do an about-face within its structuring of the FIGs. Five years after the FBI established the FIG concept, the Bureau acknowledged that "one of the biggest problems impeding our progress is poor information flow between the agents collecting information and Intelligence Analysts (IAs) on the FIG."[115] This was hardly surprising. After all, the Bureau had created the FIGs, in part, to cordon off its analysts from co-optation by investigators. The FBI attempted to remedy this breakdown by embedding analysts on operational squads, while keeping the supervision of those analysts under the auspices of the FIG.[116] Within a few years, the Bureau was back where it started.

However, resituating analysts with FBI programs did not prove to be the solution. According to a 2011 DoJ report, FBI agents were not receiving tactical analytical assistance from embedded analysts. The report identified this as inconsistent with the Field Intelligence Model that the FBI had introduced in 2008. Rather, "contrary to the [model], intelligence analysts [whom the OIG] interviewed stated that their role [was] to provide a strategic overall threat analysis and not to provide tactical or case-specific support."[117] Coming complete circle in less than a decade may have created at least some of this confusion. The Bureau then did something that could only make matters worse when it decided to transfer intelligence analysts from FBI headquarters to the field.[118] Although FBI headquarters was not an ideal location for analysts, hurling bodies at a confused field environment was far from an optimal solution.

The creation—or at least the implementation—of FIGs, along with other Mueller reforms, had unintended consequence for the FBI's transformation into an intelligence service. Field offices, which had a long tradition of maintaining control over their resources, were probably not thrilled by suddenly being told that these new, unproven FIGs were suddenly in charge of managing intelligence production and dissemination. Furthermore, the analytic human capital that was responsible for this process had a legacy that did not exactly inspire confidence. Even as the FIGs tried to find their footing, they made additional demands on field office resources. In 2010, the Bureau explained that the FIGs, as part of the collection management business process, would evaluate and prioritize collection taskings.[119] Again, the FIGs—which had still not found their footing—were nevertheless making a bid for field offices' operational resources. In 2015, the Bureau described its FIGs as "centralized intelligence components in the field that serve to integrate the intelligence cycle" and insisted that it was "the responsibility of the FIG to coordinate, guide, and support the field office's operational activities."[120] Ultimately this collision between the field office culture and the FIGs' insistence on—but inability to demonstrate—the essentiality of intelligence likely left field office personnel outside of the FIGs with a rather dim view of the intelligence cycle.

Attempts to Overcome Field Office Stovepiping

FIGs reinforced the Bureau's antiquated, field office–centric organizational model. Creating intelligence bodies controlled by field offices did little to develop a strategic picture that transcended field offices' geographic jurisdictions—arbitrary demarcations that threat actors do not politely respect. Two projects, both of which disappeared into the ether, were attempts to overcome this problem but seemed anchored to the Bureau's underlying organizational shortcomings. The first effort was the proposed network of desk officers, which perpetuated the field office silos, by arranging for information to travel upward to headquarters, but not horizontally—which would have encouraged the integration of stovepipes. A second attempt, the Joint Regional Intelligence Groups (JRIGs), attempted to push the horizons of geographically distributed resources beyond their individual field offices. However, the JRIGs were still linked to geographic distinctions—they simply changed the scope of territory covered.

Although the FBI's JRIGs, from their outset, pushed geographic delimitations beyond the confines of field office parochialism, they did not surmount the conceptual problem of geographic boundaries as a framework for organization. In 2009, Congress learned that the FBI needed personnel to establish a regional management structure that would consolidate individual field offices' understanding of their domains into six regional domain pictures.[121] The six-region structure was supposed to "tie together field offices' assessments and their discrete threats and vulnerabilities," which would improve the understanding of potential indicators about criminal and national security issues.[122] In 2012, the FBI established a pilot program that consisted of JRIGs.[123] The JRIGs appear to have been the implementation of the previously expressed desire to establish a regional structure. However, the pilot program envisioned twelve such entities, rather than the suggested six. The JRIGs, the first of which was created in Chicago, were supposed to establish regional priorities and provide focus for the field office–based FIGs.[124] However, according to the 9/11 Review Commission, the FBI had terminated the JRIG concept by 2015.[125] The FBI had smartly reverted to a structure that emphasized the analytical capability that existed within field office intelligence programs.[126] Of course, the efficacy of this approach was contingent on a proper structure at headquarters emphasizing coordination rather than top-down direction and implementing this role by leveraging human capital as a corporate resource, wherever that human capital might be located.

Models for a Corporate Approach

The FBI has established business models in specific disciplines that if encouraged, tweaked, and expanded could provide paths to greater organizational success. The Office of Origin—revisited in concept, if not in name—as part of the Cyber Threat Team model, is the first structure worth reexamining to inform a new approach. Furthermore, various FBI entities, which bring expertise to specific investigations and crises, make human capital a corporate, rather than a parochial field office, asset. Both of these approaches have elements that would help to leverage ground-level, distributed expertise on behalf of the FBI writ large.

The Office of Origin concept was not a terrible one. Prior to 9/11, the FBI had a long-established protocol by which the field office, which initiated an investigation, was known as the office of origin. Under this model, the office of origin maintained control over the investigation. This could extend to entire intelligence programs. For instance, the New York field office was the office of origin for the FBI's al-Qaeda program.[127] Similarly, the Chicago field office was the office of origin for investigations pertaining to the Weather Underground Organization.[128] Offices that provided assistance with specific investigative tasks were known as auxiliary offices. The office of origin provided instruction to the auxiliary offices by setting a "lead." (Auxiliary offices could also set leads to another auxiliary office.)

After 9/11, Mueller turned the FBI on its head by consolidating control of investigations at headquarters and effectively abolishing the Office of Origin model. The 9/11 Commission drove another nail into the Office of Origin coffin by assessing that the model allowed the field to establish its own priorities with little direction from FBI headquarters.[129] However, it is important to recall that the investigative breakdowns prior to 9/11 were actually headquarter failures to share information and to grant authority for intelligence collection. The Office of Origin concept—although not the name—reemerged under then-director James Comey in the form of the Cyber Threat Teams (CTTs). Each CTT consisted of a lead field office, known as a Strategic Threat Execution Office, and as many as five field offices, known as Tactical Threat Execution Offices, which assisted with specific aspects of the issue on which the Strategic Threat Execution Office was focused.[130]

The Office of Origin/CTT approach to the FBI's mission brings field-level expertise to bear on national-level issues. Certainly the Office of Origin approach was imperfect and there was room for breakdowns in communication. However, in the current technological climate, leveraging distributed subject-matter expertise—regardless of where it is located—would unlock a resource of which the Bureau does not make sufficient use. The role of headquarters in this would be one of facilitation—bringing the right people together and securing the necessary resources for collaborative, field-based, nationally focused work.

Distributed expertise is not a new concept to the FBI, and the Bureau has established a number of mobile groups to address specialized problems. In 1998, the FBI established rapid deployment teams capable of dispatching investigators to sites of terrorist attacks.[131] Furthermore, in 2004, the FBI established a rapid deployment Art Crimes Team.[132] Similarly, in 2005, the Bureau created a Child Abduction Rapid Deployment Team, which comprised sixty agents assigned to multiple field offices.[133] However, the FBI has not fully adopted the idea of distributed expertise. For instance, following 9/11, it established headquarters-based "flying squads."[134] The underlying false assumption was that headquarters was where the expertise resided (when, actually, headquarters had been the site of multiple missteps that contributed to the 9/11 attacks).

Furthermore, the FBI has made use of distributed expertise in its language program. The FBI's translators are assigned across fifty-two field offices and headquarters. These translators are connected to secure networks, which allow a translator in any FBI office to work on projects for any other office.[135] According to then-director Mueller, the FBI could push cuts of intercepted conversations around the country to a language specialist who had a particular skill set.[136]

Notes

1. *Reforming the FBI in the 21st Century,* Before the Committee on the Judiciary, Senate, 107th Cong., S. Doc. 107-971 (2002).

2. *Report of the Joint Inquiry into the Terrorist Attacks of September 11, 2001,* House Permanent Select Committee on Intelligence and Senate Select Committee on Intelligence (2002).

3. *Reforming the FBI in the 21st Century.*

4. *Departments of Commerce, Justice, and State, the Judiciary, and Related Agencies Appropriations for 2005,* Before a Committee of the Committee on Appropriations, House of Representatives, 108th Cong., pt. 10 (2004).

5. *Joint Inquiry into Intelligence Community Activities Before and After the Terrorist Attacks of September 11, 2001,* Before the Select Committee on Intelligence, Senate, and the Permanent Select Committee on Intelligence, House of Representatives, S. Doc. 107-1086, vol. 2 (2002).

6. *Reforming the FBI in the 21st Century.*

7. *Science, the Departments of State, Justice, and Commerce, and Related Agencies Appropriations for 2007,* Before a Subcommittee of the Committee on Appropriations, House of Representatives, 109th Cong., pt. 2 (2006).

8. *Departments of Commerce, Justice, and State, the Judiciary, and Related Agencies Appropriations for 2004,* Before a Subcommittee of the Committee on Appropriations, House of Representatives, 108th Cong., pt. 10 (2003).

9. *Ten Years After 9/11: 2011,* Before the Committee on Homeland Security and Governmental Affairs, Senate, 112th Cong. (2012).

10. *Joint Inquiry into Intelligence Community Activities Before and After the Terrorist Attacks of September 11, 2001,* vol. 2.

11. National Commission on Terrorist Attacks upon the United States, *The 9/11 Commission Report* (New York: Norton, 2004).

12. Ibid.

13. Department of Justice, *A Review of the FBI's Handling of Intelligence Information Related to the September 11 Attacks* (Washington, DC, 2004).

14. Ibid.

15. *Departments of Commerce, Justice, and State, the Judiciary, and Related Agencies appropriations for 2004,* pt. 10.

16. *Departments of Commerce, Justice, and State, the Judiciary, and Related Agencies Appropriations for 2005,* pt. 10.

17. *Joint Inquiry into Intelligence Community Activities Before and After the Terrorist Attacks of September 11, 2001,* vol. 2.

18. *Departments of Commerce, Justice, and State, the Judiciary, and Related Agencies Appropriations for 2005,* pt. 10.

19. *Commerce, Justice, Science, and Related Agencies Appropriations for 2009,* Before a Subcommittee of the Committee on Appropriations, House of Representatives, 103rd Cong., pt. 1 (2009).

20. 9/11 Commission, "Reforming Law Enforcement, Counterterrorism, and Intelligence Collection in the United States," Staff Statement no. 12, Undated. http://govinfo.library.unt.edu/911/staff_statements/staff_statement_12.pdf.

21. *FBI Oversight,* Before the Committee on the Judiciary United States Senate, 109th Cong. (2006); Roger Z. George and James B. Bruce, eds., *Analyzing Intelligence* (Washington, DC: Georgetown University Press, 2014), p. 284.

22. *Federal Bureau of Investigation Oversight,* Before the Committee on the Judiciary, Senate, 109th Cong., S. Doc. 109-763 (2005).

23. Ibid.

24. *Oversight of the Federal Bureau of Investigation,* Before the Committee on the Judiciary, Senate, 111th Cong., S. Doc. 111-115 (2009).

25. *Federal Bureau of Investigation Oversight.*

26. 9/11 Commission, "Reforming Law Enforcement, Counterterrorism, and Intelligence Collection."

27. *Oversight of the FBI,* Before the Committee on the Judiciary, Senate, 107th Cong., S. Doc. 107-447 (2001).

28. Ibid.

29. James Gagliano, "Andrew McCabe Owes Us Some Answers," *The Hill,* January 30, 2018.

30. Ibid.

31. Amy Zegart, *Spying Blind* (Princeton: Princeton University Press, 2007).

32. *Departments of Commerce, Justice, and State, the Judiciary, and Related Agencies Appropriations for 2001,* Before a Subcommittee of the Committee on Appropriations, House of Representatives, 106th Cong., pt. 2 (2000).

33. *Departments of Commerce, Justice, and State, the Judiciary, and Related Agencies appropriations for 2004,* pt. 10.

34. *Departments of Commerce, Justice, and State, the Judiciary, and Related Agencies Appropriations for 2005,* pt. 6.

35. Ibid.

36. *Oversight of the Federal Bureau of Investigation,* Before the Committee on the Judiciary, Senate (2011).

37. Ibid.

38. *Departments of Commerce, Justice, and State, the Judiciary, and Related Agencies Appropriations for 2005*, pt. 10.

39. Ibid.

40. Alfred Cumming and Todd Masse, *FBI Intelligence Reform Since September 11, 2001: Issues and Options for Congress* (Washington, DC: Congressional Research Service, 2004).

41. Garrett Graff, *The Threat Matrix* (New York: Back Bay, 2011), p. 424.

42. Cumming and Masse, *FBI Intelligence Reform Since September 11, 2001.*

43. *Departments of Commerce, Justice, and State, the Judiciary, and Related Agencies Appropriations for 2005*, pt. 2.

44. *Commerce, Justice, Science, and Related Agencies Appropriations for 2010*, Before a Subcommittee of the Committee on Appropriations, House of Representatives, 111th Cong., pt. 1 (2009).

45. *Departments of Commerce, Justice, and State, the Judiciary, and Related Agencies Appropriations for 2004*, pt. 10.

46. Ibid.

47. Elsa Walsh, "Learning to Spy," *The New Yorker*, November 8, 2004.

48. Scott Shane and Lowell Bergman, "F.B.I. Struggling to Reinvent Itself to Fight Terror," *New York Times*, October 10, 2006.

49. Alfred Cumming and Todd Masse, *Intelligence Reform Implementation at the Federal Bureau of Investigation: Issues and Options for Congress* (Washington, DC: Congressional Research Service, 2005).

50. *Science, the Departments of State, Justice, and Commerce, and Related Agencies Appropriations for 2007*, pt. 2.

51. *Commerce, Justice, Science, and Related Agencies Appropriations for 2017*, Before a Subcommittee of the Committee on Appropriations, House of Representatives, 114th Cong., pt. 2B (2016).

52. Ibid.

53. Ibid.

54. Ibid.

55. Department of Justice, Statement of James B. Comey, Director, Federal Bureau of Investigation, Before the Committee on Homeland Security, House of Representatives, at a Hearing Entitled "World Wide Threats and Homeland Security Challenges," October 21, 2015.

56. Federal Bureau of Investigation, "Joshua Skule Named Executive Assistant Director for the Intelligence Branch," June 23, 2016, https://www.fbi.gov/news/pressrel/press-releases/joshua-skule-named-executive-assistant-director-for-the-intelligence-branch.

57. *Commerce, Justice, Science, and Related Agencies Appropriations for 2016*, Before a Subcommittee of the Committee on Appropriations, House of Representatives, 114th Cong., pt. 6 (2015).

58. "Panel Chairman Seeks Study of FBI Reorganization; Rep Wolf Cites Concerns on Impact of Shifting Agents to Counterterrorism Effort," *Washington Post*, June 5, 2002.

59. Statement of Joseph M. Demarest Jr., Assistant Director, Cyber Division, Federal Bureau of Investigation, Before the Subcommittee on Crime and Terrorism, Committee on Judiciary, Senate, Entitled "Cyber Threat: Law Enforcement and Private Sector Responses," May 8, 2013.

60. Ibid.

61. *Oversight of the Federal Bureau of Investigation*, Before the Committee on the Judiciary, Senate, S. Doc. 112-405 (2011).

62. John P. Carlin, *Detect, Disrupt, Deter: A Whole-of-Government Approach to National Security Cyber Threats* (Cambridge: Harvard University Press, 2016).

63. Department of Justice, *Audit of the Federal Bureau of Investigation's Implementation of Its Next Generation Cyber Initiative* (Washington, DC, 2015).

64. Chris Bing, "FBI Is 'Moving Towards' Predictive Cybercrime-Fighting Tools, Assistant Director Says," February 16, 2017, https://www.fedscoop.com/fbi-moving-towards-predictive-cybercrime-fighting-tools-assistant-director-says.

65. Statement of Demarest, "Cyber Threat."

66. Department of Justice, *The Federal Bureau of Investigation's Ability to Address the National Security Cyber Intrusion Threat* (Washington, DC, 2011).

67. Statement of Demarest, "Cyber Threat."

68. Department of Justice, *Audit of the Federal Bureau of Investigation's Implementation of Its Next Generation Cyber Initiative.*

69. Department of Justice, *The Federal Bureau of Investigation's Ability to Address the National Security Cyber Intrusion Threat.*

70. *Federal Bureau of Investigation,* Before the Committee on the Judiciary, House of Representatives, H.R. 113-77 (2014).

71. Department of Justice, *The Federal Bureau of Investigation's Ability to Address the National Security Cyber Intrusion Threat.*

72. *FBI Oversight,* Before the Committee on the Judiciary, Senate, 109th Cong., S. Doc. 109-921 (2006).

73. *Cyber Security: Responding to the Threat of Cyber Crime and Terrorism,* Before the Subcommittee on Crime and Terrorism of the Committee on the Judiciary, Senate, 112th Cong., S. Doc. 112-167 (2011).

74. *FBI FY 2015 Budget Justification, 35; Ten Years After 9/11: 2011,* Before the Committee on Homeland Security and Governmental Affairs, Senate, 112th Cong. (2012).

75. *Commerce, Justice, Science, and Related Agencies Appropriations for 2010,* pt. 1.

76. *Commerce, Justice, Science, and Related Agencies Appropriations for 2017,* pt. 2B.

77. Ibid.

78. Ibid.

79. *Ten Years After 9/11: 2011.*

80. Ibid.

81. Ibid.

82. Ibid.

83. *Federal Bureau of Investigation Oversight,* Before the Committee on the Judiciary, Senate, 109th Cong., S. Doc. 109-76 (2005).

84. *Commerce, Justice, Science, and Related Agencies Appropriations for 2014,* Before a Subcommittee of the Committee on Appropriations, House of Representatives, 113th Cong., pt. 2B (2013).

85. Ibid.

86. Statement of James B. Comey, Director, Federal Bureau of Investigation, Before the House Committee on the Judiciary, House of Representatives, at a Hearing Entitled "Oversight of the Federal Bureau of Investigation," October 22, 2015.

87. Ibid.

88. Department of Justice, "U.S. Charges Five Chinese Military Hackers for Cyber Espionage against U.S. Corporation and a Labor Organization for Commercial Advantage," May 19, 2014, https://www.justice.gov/opa/pr/us-charges-five-chinese-military-hackers-cyber-espionage-against-us-corporations-and-labor.

89. "Bears in the Midst: Intrusion into the Democratic National Committee," June 15, 2016, https://www.crowdstrike.com/blog/bears-midst-intrusion-democratic-national-committee.

90. Department of Justice, "U.S. Charges Russian FSB Officers and Their Criminal Conspirators for Hacking Yahoo and Millions of Email Accounts," March 15, 2017, https://www.justice.gov/opa/pr/us-charges-russian-fsb-officers-and-their-criminal-conspirators-hacking-yahoo-and-millions.

91. Department of Justice, "Nine Iranians Charged with Conducting Massive Cyber Theft Campaign on Behalf of the Islamic Revolutionary Guard Corps," March 23, 2018,

https://www.justice.gov/opa/pr/nine-iranians-charged-conducting-massive-cyber-theft-campaign-behalf-islamic-revolutionary.

92. Graff, *The Threat Matrix*.

93. *New York Civil Liberties Union v. United States Department of Justice*, June 24, 2008.

94. *Departments of Commerce, Justice, and State, the Judiciary, and Related Agencies Appropriations for 2004*, pt. 6.

95. *The FBI's Counterterrorism Program Since September 2001*, report to the National Commission on Terrorist Attacks upon the United States (2004)

96. *Commerce, Justice, Science, and Related Agencies Appropriations for 2012*, Before a Subcommittee of the Committee on Appropriations, House of Representatives, 112th Cong., pt. 7 (2011).

97. Devlin Barrett, "FBI Questioning Libyans—Agency Aims to Prevent Revenge Attacks in America, Help Military Campaign," *Wall Street Journal*, April 5, 2011.

98. *Commerce, Justice, Science, and Related Agencies Appropriations for 2009*, Before a Subcommittee of the Committee on Appropriations, House of Representatives, 103rd Cong., pt. 1 (2009).

99. "FBI FY 2009 Budget Request," https://www.justice.gov/sites/default/files/jmd/legacy/2014/08/02/fy09-fbi.pdf.

100. *Commerce, Justice, Science, and Related Agencies Appropriations for 2009*, pt. 1.

101. Ibid.

102. "FBI FY 2009 Budget Request."

103. Ibid.

104. *Commerce, Justice, Science, and Related Agencies Appropriations for 2009*, pt. 1.

105. Ibid.

106. Ibid.

107. *Departments of Commerce, Justice, and State, the Judiciary, and Related Agencies appropriations for 2004*, pt. 10.

108. Cumming and Masse, *Intelligence Reform Implementation at the Federal Bureau of Investigation*.

109. Ibid.

110. Ibid.

111. National Academy of Public Administration, *Transforming the FBI: Progress and Challenges* (Washington, DC, 2005).

112. *The Federal Bureau of Investigation's Strategic Plan and Progress on Reform*, Before the Select Committee on Intelligence, Senate, 110th Cong., S. Doc. 110-793 (2007).

113. Cumming and Masse, *Intelligence Reform Implementation at the Federal Bureau of Investigation*.

114. Commission on the Intelligence Capabilities of the United States Regarding Weapons of Mass Destruction, *Report to the President of the United States* (2005).

115. Federal Bureau of Investigation, *The New Field Intelligence: March 2008—March 2009*, version 1.5 (Washington, DC, 2009).

116. Ibid., pp. 7, 9.

117. Department of Justice, *The Federal Bureau of Investigation's Ability to Address the National Security Cyber Intrusion Threat*.

118. Government Accountability Office, *FBI Counterterrorism: Vacancies Have Declined but FBI Has Not Assessed the Long-Term Sustainability of Its Strategy for Addressing Vacancies* (Washington, DC, 2012).

119. *Commerce, Justice, Science, and Related Agencies Appropriations for 2011*, Before a Subcommittee of the Committee on Appropriations, House of Representatives, 111th Cong., pt. 1A (2010).

120. *Commerce, Justice, Science, and Related Agencies Appropriations for 2016*, Before a Subcommittee of the Committee on Appropriations, House of Representatives, 114th Cong., pt. 2B (2015).

121. *Commerce, Justice, Science, and Related Agencies Appropriations for 2010,* Before a Subcommittee of the Committee on Appropriations, House of Representatives, 111th Cong., pt. 1 (2009).

122. Ibid.

123. *Reviewing the Department of Homeland Security's Intelligence Enterprise,* House Homeland Security Committee, Majority Staff Report (Washington, DC, 2016).

124. Michael P. Dowing and Matt A. Mayer. *The Domestic Counterterrorism Enterprise: Time to Streamline* (Washington, DC: Heritage Foundation, 2012).

125. 9/11 Review Commission, *The FBI: Protecting the Homeland in the 21st Century* (Washington, DC, 2015).

126. Ibid.

127. 9/11 Commission, "Law Enforcement, Counterterrorism, and Intelligence Collection in the United States Prior to 9/11," Staff Statement no. 9, undated, http://govinfo.library.unt.edu/911/staff_statements/staff_statement_9.pdf.

128. *FBI Oversight,* Before the Subcommittee on Security and Terrorism of the Committee on the Judiciary, Senate, 97th Cong. (1982).

129. 9/11 Commission, "Law Enforcement, Counterterrorism, and Intelligence Collection in the United States Prior to 9/11."

130. 9/11 Review Commission, *The FBI: Protecting the Homeland in the 21st Century;* Department of Justice, *Audit of the Federal Bureau of Investigation's Cyber Threat Prioritization* (Washington, DC, 2016).

131. *Oversight of the FBI,* Before the Committee on the Judiciary, Senate, 107th Cong., S. Doc. 107-447 (2001).

132. Federal Bureau of Investigation, "Art Theft," https://www.fbi.gov/investigate/violent-crime/art-theft.

133. Federal Bureau of Investigation, "Investigating Child Abductions," https://www.fbi.gov/news/stories/investigating-child-abductions1.

134. *Departments of Commerce, Justice, and State, the Judiciary, and Related Agencies Appropriations for 2005,* pt. 10.

135. Ibid.

136. *FBI Oversight: Terrorism and Other Topics,* Before the Committee on the Judiciary, Senate, 108th Cong., S. Doc. 108-804 (2004).

6

The FBI's
Human Capital Issues

The FBI, despite the smoke and noise of its reform efforts, failed to address existing human capital problems and managed to create new ones. Prior to 9/11 the Bureau's structure had not encouraged the development of expertise, and its reforms—particularly in the field of analysis—failed to account for this shortcoming and instead perpetuated entrenched problems. In the field of collection, the Bureau did not do much better. Although any FBI agent who develops sources is a collector of human intelligence, Mueller's watch included the creation of specific HUMINT squads—a development that needlessly ran counter to creating a common intelligence-oriented corporate culture.

Intelligence Analysis at the FBI After 9/11

Following 9/11, the FBI made another bid to establish a distinct intelligence component, which would replace the Investigative Services Division. The successive iterations of this component (the Office of Intelligence, the Directorate of Intelligence, and the Intelligence Branch) have fluctuated in their stature vis-à-vis the rest of the Bureau. The FBI's intelligence component has demonstrated an inability to maintain a strategic perspective and has instead been repeatedly co-opted by the reactive, tactical approach ingrained in the Bureau's institutional DNA. In addition to the structural deficiencies, the FBI continues to suffer from an underwhelming analytic work force, which demonstrates the legacy of pre-9/11 human capital deficiencies.

The decision, by Comey, to appoint an individual with an operational rather than analytical background as the head of the Bureau's intelligence component is forgivable. Unfortunately, Comey's options were constrained by the hobbled state of analytical capital, in which there was a dearth of viable candidates (and from which appropriate individuals will unlikely come anytime soon). The FBI's experience with creating an analytic work force after 9/11 was crippled by the legacy of "analysis" (little more than glorified data entry and other clerical tasks) prior to the attacks. Despite at least one attempt, the Bureau never successfully extirpated the placeholders who passed as analysts and who established a cultural DNA that will carry on their malignant legacy long after these individuals have retired with more-than-deserved benefits.

By 2000, the FBI had started to come to terms with the fundamentally flawed nature of its analytic work force. In 1998, the Bureau had published an internal study identifying that two-thirds of the FBI's analysts were not qualified to fill the positions they held.[1] According to a study by the Department of Justice, analysts who had started their employment with the FBI prior to fiscal year 2002 were thirty times more likely to have less than a bachelor's degree compared to the analysts who joined the organization between fiscal years 2002 and 2004.[2] In order to cull the intellectual dead weight represented by uncredentialled analysts, the Office of Intelligence, following the creation of the position of executive assistant director of intelligence in 2003, made an attempt to "improve the quality of the FBI's analytical corps by requiring a college degree for the intelligence analyst position . . . also mandating that analysts reapply for their current jobs." This was "canceled before the process was completed."[3] Furthermore, the Bureau's standards for hiring new analysts continued to be insufficiently stringent. For instance, in 2005 the FBI advised Congress that over the previous two years, less than 40 percent of the analysts hired possessed advanced degrees.[4] Even more troubling, in 2004 the FBI acknowledged that it would no longer require new analysts to have a bachelor's degree from an accredited college or university.[5] Once analysts were on board, there was no mechanism for quality control. The 9/11 Commission expressed concern that no process existed for evaluating and reassigning unqualified analysts.[6]

Once the FBI began focusing on improving analysis, it should have at least closed the watertight doors and put a stop to the flood of internal hires. Instead, the Bureau persisted in this practice. The number of employees who transferred into the analyst position from the distinctly unintellectual General Administrative, Clerical, and Office Services Group actually increased each year between fiscal years 2002 and

2004.[7] Even when the Bureau recruited from the outside, its approaches to attracting talent were dubious. In 2005, the Bureau told Congress that its "special effort" to attract applicants for analyst positions included a television ad that aired during the Super Bowl,[8] an appeal unlikely to attract the best and brightest of candidates.

The FBI's hiring process was distorted by the presence of these legacy analysts. In 2004, the Bureau introduced a new rubric to assess candidates that used a weighted question–based system. These weighted questions were the concoction of a group of "senior intelligence analysts and intelligence analyst managers."[9] Considering the lackluster intellectual provenance of the Bureau's analytical human capital prior to 9/11, allowing entrenched analysts—whose careers progressed under less-than-rigorous standards—to serve as gatekeepers was a recipe for perpetuating conditions that had already proved not only untenable but also dangerous to national security. These legacy analysts remained in positions to undermine reform, since, as of 2003, the FBI planned to start from the bottom by hiring individual at lower grade levels first.[10] By this logic, the underqualified pre-9/11 ranks would be shaping the perceptions (and careers) of the analysts who were entering the organization specifically to change its culture. There would be no clean break from the dysfunctional analytical culture that had pervaded the Bureau prior to 9/11.

These dynamics created a culture that discouraged both prospective analysts and current employees. In 2004, Congress gave the FBI special authority to hire twenty-four senior intelligence analysts. By 2007, the Bureau had filled only two of these positions.[11] Once the FBI had hired analysts, it had difficulty with retention. According to the Department of Justice's Office of the Inspector General, analysts who have earned advanced degrees are the most likely to leave the Bureau within two years of being hired.[12] This is consistent with a broader trend of frustration within the analytic intelligentsia. According to the office of the DoJ inspector general, "analysts with advanced degrees [were] less satisfied than those without advanced degrees."[13] Unfortunately, the FBI, despite being an agency that prides itself on its ability to collect information, has not endeavored to establish a feedback loop to better understand why it is hemorrhaging talent. In a response to Congress, the Bureau indicated that it did not conduct specific exit interviews of departing intelligence analysts.[14]

Received wisdom has attributed the problems with analysis in the FBI to the agent/analyst divide. One oft-repeated maxim was that if you were not an agent, you were furniture.[15] Even the DoJ inspector general highlighted the supposed divide between analysts and agents. According to the inspector general's 2007 report, "many intelligence analysts believe that some special agents . . . continue to view intelligence analysts as administrative staff rather than equal professional partners."[16] However, this rift is equally attributable—if not even more attributable—to the expectations that analysts' pre-9/11 predecessors (who were allowed to remain in place and skew reform) established through their work, which was analytic in name only. One is left to wonder how much of this narrative is the work of analysts—discussed in the Joint Congressional Inquiry, the *9/11 Commission Report,* and in Lawrence Wright's *The Looming Tower*—who proved incompetent prior to 9/11 and propagated the agent/analyst split canard as a smokescreen for their inability to meet new expectations.[17]

Legacy analysts and their intellectual ilk were not producing meaningful analytic products prior to, or after, 9/11. For instance, in 2000 the Bureau acknowledged that the FBI must improve its analytical capability in the field of counterintelligence. This capability should produce "intelligence of broader scope and improved timeliness" as well as "long-range, strategic" studies that addressed the intelligence collection plans, methods, intentions, capabilities, and personnel of foreign powers.[18] Similar deficiency was apparent in the field of counterterrorism, for which the Bureau's only strategic assessment of the terrorist threat to the United States was considered too shoddy to be of any use and failed to address the likelihood of a terrorist attack or the capabilities of different terrorist groups.[19] Even in 2004, the Bureau's analytic apparatus—perhaps because of the lingering influence of pre-9/11 analysts—continued to issue assessments such as one that Senator Dianne Feinstein described as "a combination of older intelligence data and random comments on ongoing investigations."[20] More than a decade later, intelligence scholar John A. Gentry identified that the FBI periodically published reports that contained structured analytic techniques that were not appropriate for the format and message that the reports presented, a trend that "damage[ed] the effectiveness of its products."[21]

Analytical Roles

Consistent with the Mueller-era ethos of papering over entrenched problems with new terminology, the Bureau, in 2003, introduced the position of intelligence analyst to replace the roles of intelligence research specialist and intelligence operations specialist.[22] Within the analyst position there were three work roles: reports officer, operations specialist, and all-source analyst.[23] The collection and reporting position was essentially the collection management officer role that the Bureau had proposed creating prior to 9/11; the strategic analyst function was the intelligence research specialist all over again; and the tactical analyst was simply the old intelligence operations specialist. Once analysts reached the GS-11 level of seniority, they were supposed to decide whether to develop expertise in a specific program area, gain broader experience that would prepare them to work in a broader number of program areas, or work toward becoming a manager in the Intelligence Program.[24] (The GS-11 level, according to the US Office of Personnel Management, requires an incoming employee to possess a PhD or equivalent doctoral degree; or 3 years of progressively higher-level graduate education leading to such a degree; or an LLM, if related to the job position. Employees with lower levels of education can reach this threshold through multiple years of government service.[25]) Then, in 2011, the FBI decided to create three distinct career paths—collection and reporting, tactical analysis, and strategic analysis—out of these intelligence analyst roles.[26]

Mandating that the Bureau include formal tactical and strategic perspectives was a smart decision. During previous attempts to establish an analytical apparatus, the Bureau's tactical corporate culture had co-opted strategic resources. (One need only look at the pre-9/11 dynamic of intelligence operations specialist and intelligence research specialist for evidence of dysfunction.) However, the desiccation of the Investigative Services Division was a cautionary tale that even if resources were, ostensibly, allocated for strategic analysis, they could still too easily become sidelined. In addition to the threat of a tactical tsunami that would sweep analysts out of strategic roles, the conceptualization of the intelligence analyst position around functions did not create incentives for the development of deep subject-matter knowledge (e.g., awareness about specific threat actors) among the analytical work force.

Furthermore, Mueller almost immediately began to undermine the Bureau's fragile analytical capability by promoting a plug-and-play approach that did not encourage (and arguably discouraged) analysts' development of deep subject-matter expertise. Almost as soon as the Bureau made its decision, in 2003, to consolidate all analytic roles under the title of intelligence analyst, critics correctly assessed that this one-size-fits-all approach could work against cultivating analytic human capital with deep functional, geographic, and target-specific knowledge.[27] Perversely, the FBI did not recognize the shortcoming inherent to this approach as a problem and instead viewed it as a desirable objective.

According to a 2005 DoJ inspector general report, "one purpose of this consolidation of roles was to provide for much greater flexibility in assigning analysts, who could perform any of the three functions." Furthermore, analysts were interchangeable not only with other analysts but also with the full panoply of support staff. The same report assessed that "if an intelligence analyst resigned, FBI management could decide to replace the intelligence analyst with a financial analyst or some other category of support staff."[28] Mueller only confirmed this assumption of interchangeability when, in 2008, he claimed that, due to the standardization of Field Intelligence Groups, an "analyst working on the FIG in the Atlanta office could easily transition to the FIG in the Albany office."[29]

Finally, the establishment of intelligence analyst management positions exacerbated existing problems. Prior to 2009, the FBI had first-line analytic supervisors—known as supervisory intelligence analysts. Then, in 2009, the Bureau established the position of senior supervisory intelligence analyst.[30] These responsibilities of the latter analysts included managerial and liaison functions as well as strategic planning and personnel matters. The Bureau trotted out the position as an indication of its commitment to creating an analytic enterprise. For instance, Comey described the position as filling a role that had traditionally been performed by agents and thus "demonstrating that [the FBI was] promoting effective integration throughout the organization."[31]

However, timing suggests that the slots for senior supervisory intelligence analysts institutionalized the legacy culture. The FBI created these positions less than a decade after it had started to muck out the morass that legacy analysts had created prior to 9/11. Because the Bureau had focused its post-9/11 hiring efforts on entry-level positions, the senior analysts, who would be qualified for a second-rung management job, were from—or at least perilously close to—the pre-9/11 "analytic" cadre. If the Bureau were indeed to allow individuals of suspect aptitude not only to fill, but also to define, the roles of the senior supervisory intelligence analysts, the pre-9/11 culture may very well continue on, zombie-like, into at least the third decade of the twenty-first century.

HUMINT Collection After 9/11

Although the FBI has, from the moment it recruited its first informant, had a significant capacity for human intelligence, it has been ambivalent about developing sources purely to address intelligence requirements rather than to disrupt criminal activity. Although programs such as TOP HOODLUM did focus on the development of informants who would develop an ongoing intelligence picture of a specific milieu (e.g., the criminal underworld), the FBI has also pushed back against using agents to seek out sources who could supply intelligence rather than close investigations. For instance, as early as 1946, the FBI's Executive Conference was "opposed to specific instructions that Agents be assigned exclusively in each office to the development of confidential informants. . . . [W]ith the shortage of Agent personnel and the amount of important work pending throughout the field the Bureau cannot afford to devote the exclusive services of a large number of Agents to this one program."[32]

However, the FBI revisited the issue of source development in the decade following 9/11. In 2004, the FBI created a new special agent career path that allowed agents to focus on one of four tracks: counterterrorism/counterintelligence, criminal investigations, cyber, and intelligence.[33] According to Mueller, the introduction of this career path would guarantee that agents obtain experience in intelligence investigations and with intelligence processes.[34] (Whether the career path approach is creating more qualified collectors is debatable, given that, as of 2011, 36 percent of field agents who were handling national security cyber-related investigations admitted to lacking the necessary networking and counterintelligence expertise.[35])

The process of specialization provided the context for the Bureau's creation of the position of the HUMINT collector special agent. These individuals were supposed to develop, recruit, and exploit sources in order to fill field office collection gaps.[36] According to the 9/11 Review Commission, the Bureau, in 2008, directed these HUMINT-focused agents to focus on developing long-term sources who had "placement and access to strategic threat issues in support of critical national intelligence issues," including those defined by the National Intelligence Priorities Framework, "rather than in support of cases."[37] Also in 2008, the FBI announced that it would create squads responsible for focusing solely on developing HUMINT sources and intelligence collection in each field office.[38] However, by 2015, the 9/11 Review Commission discovered that there was confusion about how to divide labor between HUMINT squads and traditional, investigative squads.[39] In fact, each field office that the commission visited had developed a different approach to HUMINT collection.[40]

The FBI's discussion of HUMINT, after 9/11, was another example of how Mueller's Bureau adopted intelligence buzzwords but failed to follow through on those terms' implications. HUMINT, for instance, was nothing new—any agent and any squad that recruited sources was effectively a HUMINT squad. Rather than starting from this premise, Mueller treated HUMINT as a separate and novel concept—in competition with the existing Bureau institutions—rather than demonstrating how this expansion of HUMINT collection grew organically from one of the FBI's core competencies. Mueller compounded this error by never fully committing to using these squads to collect on topics according to the National Intelligence Priorities Framework and instead defined the function of these agents as filling "the spaces between the cases."[41] This meant that the FBI's traditional investigators were providing the overarching outline, while HUMINT collectors were coloring within the lines.

Despite these shortcomings, the FBI's approach to HUMINT at least stressed interagency integration. According to Intelligence Community Directive 304, the director of the CIA is the intelligence community's national HUMINT manager. In this capacity, the CIA director, among other tasks, manages the national HUMINT collection capability; issues on an annual basis "an integrated national HUMINT plan with associated goals and performance objectives"; and ensures that "the most effective use is made of resources and appropriate account is taken of the risks to the United States and to those involved in HUMINT collection operations and activities."[42] Additionally, the CIA director, in their capacity as HUMINT manager, is responsible for developing, promulgating, and overseeing the implementation of "core common standards for clandestine and overt HUMINT, including human source validation, training, intelligence collection requirements, evaluation, intelligence reporting, source description lexicon, cover support, and other HUMINT tradecraft practices."[43] Consistent with this guidance, the FBI announced, in 2004, that it would begin sending special agent collectors to the CIA's thirty-two-week case-agent training course and that the Bureau would add modules from the CIA to the FBI's own training programs.[44] Additionally, the FBI's HUMINT agents would "leverage relationships with external partners in order to collect intelligence."[45]

However, the FBI subsequently indicated that, rather than continuing to integrate with the CIA in training collectors, it would instead attempt to create its own course. In late 2006, the Bureau launched the first iteration of its Domestic Human Intelligence Collection Course (DHCC).[46] According to the Bureau, creation of the DHCC addressed the previous absence of a single HUMINT training program—comparable to those offered by other agencies—in the FBI. The Bureau believed that its dual law enforcement and intelligence missions necessitated a program unique to the FBI's needs.[47] To create this new training regimen, the FBI drew relevant elements from other agencies' courses and combined these into a comprehensive curriculum that aligned with the Bureau's top three strategic priorities of counterterrorism, counterintelligence, and intelligence.[48] As of 2008, the FBI also planned to develop a DHCC follow-on course that would specifically focus on developing sources that targeted terrorist organizations.[49] Unfortunately, the divergence in training retreats from an opportunity to develop a common, interagency understanding that would facilitate more fluid collaboration.

Strategic Execution Team:
The Midcourse Correction That Ran Aground

Mueller had been struggling to institutionalize intelligence for half a decade when, in a course correction, not entirely at the FBI's choosing, he launched the Strategic Execution Team (SET) initiative. SET was never going to be a panacea—Mueller's fundamentally flawed conceptualization of a bifurcated Bureau ensured this—but it was certainly less effective than it might have been due to a number of factors. Chief among these was a lack of institutional knowledge: those who were responsible for the SET initiative failed to understand where the FBI was coming from as an intelligence service and thus were incapable of helping it get where it needed to go.

Although the FBI's culture is insular, it is not introspective. Consequently, the Bureau does not so much evolve as careen from initiative to initiative, discarding ideas wholesale, only to reinvent them a few years later. The structure of the FIGs, which came full circle by degrees in approximately a decade, is one example of this. Other programs have also encountered similar unnecessarily disruptive fits and starts. For example, counterintelligence outreach has gone from the Plant Security Program, to Development of Espionage, Counterintelligence, and Counterterrorism Awareness (DECA), to Awareness of National Security Issues and Response (ANSIR), to strategic partnerships, to the Office of Private Sector.

In the wake of September 11, the FBI Science and Technology Board, which convened in 2003, offered a proposal that may have facilitated real progress, rather than change driven by failure. The board's proposal was the establishment of an FBI Federally Funded Research and Development Center (FFRDC)—an organization akin to the Rand Corporation and the Mitre Corporation—which, among other tasks, would perform independent and objective analysis and interpretation with particular attention to the application of such information to strategic planning, assessment, forecasting, and organizational management; human capital planning; work force structure and resource management; and initiating studies and analysis for ensuring the long-term capacity of the FBI to identify, assess, develop, and implement strategic concepts for dealing with current and emerging challenges.[50] This unique FFRDC would have provided a hub for knowledge and intellectual transformer, translating insights—from private industry; institutions of higher education; nonprofit institutions; and federal, state, and local government agencies—into concepts applicable to the Bureau's work.[51] The FFRDC proposal disappeared from the public record and, with it, a body that could have helped the Bureau maintain a steady hand on the tiller, rather than lurching from reacting to crisis after crisis.

In the absence of ongoing introspection about how the Bureau could operate efficiently and effectively as an intelligence service (with law enforcement capabilities), the FBI's reform attempts quickly began to founder. Mueller acknowledged, that, by 2007, "intelligence had not yet become central in FBI operations."[52] In response to this failing transformation, the President's Foreign Intelligence Advisory Board (PFIAB) provided recommendations about how the Bureau might accelerate its efforts.[53] In May 2007, the FBI initiated a comprehensive self-assessment of its intelligence program and concluded that it needed to move "further and faster to enhance [its] capabilities."[54]

From its earliest stages, SET was primed for failure, as it combined outside consultants with an internal work force that was not unified in its understanding of mission or desired outcomes. In conjunction with the PFIAB's recommendations, the Bureau engaged the consulting firm McKinsey and Company. Through its work with McKinsey, the FBI identified areas where it could accelerate progress.[55] However, Mueller's bifurcated Bureau (and the implications that this had for the rest of the Bureau's self-perception) meant that a fundamental question—progress toward *what?*—remained unanswered. Unlike the private sector, the Bureau has no financial bottom line toward which reform can be oriented. In the absence of this, it needed a strong vision toward which to drive, and Mueller did not offer that vision.

Although the introduction that Mueller provided for the SET manual called for "one FBI" that was not stovepiped by field office, region, or program, he never articulated what this one FBI was supposed to look like.[56] SET emphasized a more fluid flow of information, shifting the Bureau's culture from one of "limited internal information sharing" to "internal/external information sharing with [the] intelligence community."[57] However, SET never answered the question of how the FBI brought value to its customers. Was it in collecting on NIPF-defined topics? Was it in providing tactical intelligence that helped the cop on the street? The follow-on from this identification of value would have been to ask how the FBI could collect and analyze in order to systematically fulfill the role that its customers wanted. Mueller, unfortunately, never got much further than endorsing information sharing as being good for its own sake.

The Strategic Execution Team initiative, which started in September 2007, included—in addition to McKinsey consultants—approximately ninety special agents, intelligence analysts, and other professionals from FBI headquarters and twenty-seven field offices.[58] Arguably, twenty-seven field offices, less than half of the FBI's fifty-six, was an insufficient sampling, given the demonstrated extreme differentiation in field offices' approaches to intelligence. Each office had handled the analytic work roles differently.[59] Furthermore, offices had received "substantial latitude," according to a NAPA study, in how they structured the FIGs.[60] According to Mueller, SET was supposed to rectify this lack of consistency by identifying "best practices" and "decide what works and what does not."[61] However, there was no guarantee that the personnel who composed SET were coming from offices that had successful intelligence programs or who had the acumen (given the lingering influence of "legacy" analysts) to make such significant decisions.

SET focused heavily on functions but fudged on objectives. It developed a standardized model for field intelligence that was adaptable to account for the size and complexity of small, medium, and large offices; it established core intelligence tasks for special agents and defined their intelligence career path; and it refined the intelligence analyst career path by identifying training, experiences, and roles that were necessary for the development of the Bureau's analytic work force.[62] However, so long as Mueller dithered about whether the FBI was fish or fowl (or at least found a way to turn the organization into a flying fish), these functional improvements were meaningless.

That SET failed, under these circumstances, was unsurprising. According to the *Wall Street Journal,* FBI officials referred to the results of SET—which was introduced to the field in April 2008—as vague and consisting of pages of "consultant speak."[63] Given that SET established functions while leaving the purpose of those functions murkily defined, this was about the best that could be expected.

Furthermore, SET suffered from cultural blowback. According to a former assistant director for the FBI's Directorate of Intelligence, SET did not anticipate how much communication would be necessary to educate the field about these new approaches.[64] (However, no amount of bloviating could have communicated what was not there: a conceptualization of the Bureau's role, beyond vague talk of "threats"—which was still mired in the reactive world of investigations—that would have informed the development of capabilities.)

SET also blithely walked into a buzz-saw when it failed to account for the FBI's culture. The initiative elicited a negative reaction by referring to agents as "intelligence collectors."[65] According to a former assistant director, agents viewed SET's description as diminishing their legacy.[66] However, FBI agents were intelligence collectors, and the Bureau's own storied history validated this statement. Mueller and his SET initiative, whether due to ignorance or arrogance, failed to use this context to their advantage. There was no indication that they attempted to show the continuity between current agents' work and the roles of their predecessors, such as those agents who had staffed the Bureau's Special Intelligence Service and those who handled the SOLO operation, to demonstrate that, indeed, FBI agents had always been significant intelligence collectors, whether at home or abroad, in the service of US strategic interests.

Even if SET had been a well-thought-out initiative capable of putting the Bureau on a solid footing as an intelligence service, there are indications that it might still have failed to achieve its objectives. According to one assistant special agent in charge, who actually believed that SET was a "great concept," people began doubting the concept because SET's execution was flawed.[67] By 2011, three years after the FBI introduced SET to the field, the Department of Justice reported that the intelligence program, in the field, was already beginning to break down. According to the DoJ's inspector general, analysts, contrary to the Field Intelligence Model—which SET had introduced—claimed that their role was to provide a strategic threat analysis rather than to provide "tactical or case-specific support."[68]

Overextension of the FBI and
Implications for Its Human Capital

Even before 9/11 it was clear that the FBI's range of missions required more resource than the Bureau could consistently dedicate to each area of responsibility. Consequently, the organization had to regularly shift personnel, potentially disrupting effectiveness in newly impoverished programs and undercutting the formation of long-term subject-matter expertise on topics the FBI was supposed to address.

Once counterterrorism, following the September 11 attacks, became the most high-visibility issue for the Bureau, personnel allocations followed suit. Mueller moved 2,000 agents from FBI criminal programs to national security missions.[69] Out of these 2,000, 1,200 were reassigned to counterterrorism, 400 went to counterintelligence, and 400 went to intelligence.[70] According to Mueller, in 2011, prior to September 11, approximately 7,000 agents in the field had been working criminal cases, while less than half that number—3,000—had been working on national security matters.[71] By 2011, criminal and national security issues were roughly even in the number of agents assigned to these topics.[72] In addition to formal reallocations, the Bureau unofficially reassigned resources as needed. In 2006, the DoJ inspector general advised Congress that "the actual number of agents used to investigative criminal matters was significantly less than the FBI had allocated."[73]

This movement of personnel compounded an existing problem. Within the criminal investigative field, the FBI had already been surging resources from one threat to the next. According to Mueller, the Bureau had handled emerging criminal threats by transferring personnel within the criminal branch.[74] However, the hollowing out of the criminal investigative work force meant that even this whack-a-mole approach was too much for the FBI. In 2008, Mueller acknowledged that the FBI had failed to replace nearly 2,400 agents who had moved to counterterrorism squads.[75]

The post 9/11 personnel deficits in criminal investigative matters had a disproportionate impact on several programs. Counternarcotics work—into which the FBI had been a reluctant entrant but had not extricated itself even after its concurrent jurisdiction with the DEA ended in 1987—was an early area of cannibalization. Mueller pointed to the special agents in charge of field offices as believing that counternarcotics was the program from which these special agents could reassign agents to counterterrorism.[76] According to Mueller, these agents may not have been working on issues that warranted the Bureau's involvement. In 2009, he characterized a majority of the counternarcotics agents as having been focused on "smaller drug cases."[77] Furthermore, Mueller noted that many of the reassigned agents had been assigned to violent crime and gang squads.[78] Like small-ball narcotics cases, violent crime and violent gangs are often well within the bailiwick of state and local authorities.

In order to compensate for the shift in resources away from criminal investigative matters, the FBI has attempted to leverage the capabilities of its federal and subfederal partners. After the initial reallocation of agents from counternarcotics to counterterrorism, Bureau officials both at headquarters and in field offices conferred with DEA counterparts to ensure continued coverage of counternarcotics matters.[79] Furthermore, as of 2010, the FBI advised Congress that it had also relied on participation in the Organized Crime Drug Enforcement Task Forces, as well as the High Intensity Drug Trafficking Area initiatives, to address counternarcotics issues.[80]

The Bureau has also used this approach of delegation to address other criminal investigative programs. For instance, in 2006, the FBI announced the formation—in conjunction with state and local law enforcement agencies—of twenty-four Violent Crime Task Forces throughout the United States.[81] Similarly, in 2010, the Bureau noted its participation with 143 Violent Gang and Safe Streets Task Forces as a countermeasure to criminality.[82] The FBI, in 2011, emphasized the leveraging of external resources, stating that it had "successfully maximized its resources and relationships with its law enforcement partners domestically and internationally, to address its priority criminal investigative responsibilities."[83]

Despite its admitted inability to cover all of the programs that it has accumulated over more than a century—and the indications that other agencies might be better positioned to assume some of these functions—the FBI has clung to its missions, even as it has acknowledged that is incapable of affording sufficient attention to all of the responsibilities with which it has been entrusted. According to testimony for Congress, the FBI explained that its reallocation of agents "did not diminish the FBI's commitment to criminal matters, but it did reduce the number of FBI [agents] available to prevent and respond to crime."[84]

Mueller insisted on keeping programs under the Bureau's purview even though he also acknowledged that the FBI could not fully address them. As early as 2003, Mueller told Congress that he had "looked for areas where there [was] an overlap with other law enforcement or intelligence entities that [could] undertake the responsibilities before [he moved] individuals from some other program."[85] In 2011, he told Congress that the Bureau could not "afford to do the same number of bank robberies and embezzlements that [the FBI had] done in the past," due to the other priorities.[86]

With these comments, Mueller underlined the reality that the Bureau was overextended. Unfortunately, as with his relentless arguing that the FBI should not be split, Mueller's rationalizations and excuses for the Bureau's inability to fulfill its missions warded off discussions of fundamental reform. Rather than simply leveraging other entities to do the Bureau's work, Mueller should have given serious consideration to making the case for scoping the FBI's identity and determining which missions it could relinquish to other agencies, whether federal or subfederal in nature.

Notes

1. *Federal Bureau of Investigation Oversight,* Before the Committee on the Judiciary, Senate, 109th Cong., S. Doc. 109-76 (2005).
2. Department of Justice, *The Federal Bureau of Investigation's Efforts to Hire, Train, and Retain Intelligence Analysts* (Washington, DC, 2005).
3. Ibid.
4. *Federal Bureau of Investigation Oversight.*
5. *Departments of Commerce, Justice, and State, the Judiciary, and Related Agencies Appropriations for 2005,* Before a Subcommittee of the Committee on Appropriations, House of Representatives, 108th Cong., pt. 10 (2004).
6. 9/11 Commission, "Reforming Law Enforcement, Counterterrorism, and Intelligence Collection in the United States," Staff Statement no. 12, http://govinfo.library.unt .edu/911/staff_statements/staff_statement_12.pdf.
7. Department of Justice, *The Federal Bureau of Investigation's Efforts to Hire, Train, and Retain Intelligence Analysts.*
8. *Federal Bureau of Investigation Oversight,* Before the Committee on the Judiciary, Senate, 109th Cong., 1st sess., S. Doc. 109-763 (2005).
9. Department of Justice, *A Review of the FBI's Handling of Intelligence Information Related to the September 11 Attacks* (Washington, DC, 2004), appendix 3.
10. Department of Justice, *The Federal Bureau of Investigation's Efforts to Improve the Sharing of Intelligence and Other Information.*
11. *Oversight of the Federal Bureau of Investigation,* Before the Committee on the Judiciary, Senate, 111th Cong., S. Doc. 111-115 (2009).
12. Congressional Research Service, *Intelligence Reform Implementation at the Federal Bureau of Investigation: Issues and Options for Congress* (Washington, DC, 2005).
13. Department of Justice, *The Federal Bureau of Investigation's Efforts to Hire, Train, and Retain Intelligence Analysts.*
14. *Departments of Commerce, Justice, and State, the Judiciary, and Related Agencies Appropriations for 2005,* pt. 10.
15. *Federal Bureau of Investigation Oversight,* S. Doc. 109-763.

16. Department of Justice, *Follow Up Audit of the Federal Bureau of Investigation's Efforts to Hire, Train, and Retain Intelligence Analysts* (Washington, DC, 2007).

17. *Joint Inquiry into Intelligence Community Activities Before and After the Terrorist Attacks of September 11, 2001,* Before the Select Committee on Intelligence, Senate, and the Permanent Select Committee on Intelligence, House of Representatives, S. Doc. 107-1086, vol. 2 (2002); Lawrence Wright, *The Looming Tower* (New York: Knopf, 2006).

18. *Departments of Commerce, Justice, and State, the Judiciary, and Related Agencies Appropriations for 2001,* Before a Subcommittee of the Committee on Appropriations, House of Representatives, 106th Cong., pt. 2 (2000).

19. Amy Zegart, *Spying Blind* (Princeton: Princeton University Press, 2007).

20. *FBI Oversight: Terrorism and Other Topics.*

21. John A. Gentry, "Has the ODNI Improved U.S. Intelligence Analysis?" *International Journal of Intelligence and Counterintelligence* (November 8, 2015), 19:17.

22. Department of Justice, *The Federal Bureau of Investigation's Efforts to Hire, Train, and Retain Intelligence Analysts.*

23. *Departments of Commerce, Justice, and State, the Judiciary, and Related Agencies Appropriations for 2005,* pt. 10.

24. Ibid.

25. Office of Personnel Management, "Classification & Qualification: General Schedule Qualification Standards, https://www.opm.gov/policy-data-oversight/classification-qualifications/general-schedule-qualification-standards/#url=Group-Standards.

26. Government Accountability Office, *FBI Counterterrorism: Vacancies Have Declined but FBI Has Not Assessed the Long-Term Sustainability of Its Strategy for Addressing Vacancies* (Washington, DC, 2012).

27. Alfred Cumming and Todd Masse, *FBI Intelligence Reform Since September 11, 2001: Issues and Options for Congress* (Washington, DC, Congressional Research Service, 2004).

28. Department of Justice, *The Federal Bureau of Investigation's Efforts to Hire, Train, and Retain Intelligence Analysts.*

29. Statement of Robert S. Mueller III, Director, Federal Bureau of Investigation, United States Department of Justice, Before the Senate, Committee on the Judiciary, Concerning "Oversight of the Federal Bureau of Investigation," September 17, 2008.

30. *Ten Years After 9/11: 2011,* Before the Committee on Homeland Security and Governmental Affairs, Senate, 112th Cong. (2012).

31. Statement of James B. Comey, Director, Federal Bureau of Investigation, Before the House Committee on the Judiciary, House of Representatives, at a Hearing Entitled "Oversight of the Federal Bureau of Investigation," October 22, 2015.

32. Federal Bureau of Investigation, Executive Conference to the Director, April 16, 1946.

33. *Departments of Commerce, Justice, and State, the Judiciary, and Related Agencies Appropriations for 2005,* pt. 10.

34. Statement of Robert S. Mueller III, Director, Federal Bureau of Investigation, to the National Commission on Terrorist Attacks upon the United States, April 14, 2004.

35. Department of Justice, *The Federal Bureau of Investigation's Ability to Address the National Security Cyber Intrusion Threat* (Washington, DC, 2011).

36. *Commerce, Justice, Science, and Related Agencies Appropriations for 2010,* Before a Subcommittee of the Committee on Appropriations, House of Representatives, 111th Cong., pt. 1 (2009).

37. 9/11 Review Commission, *The FBI: Protecting the Homeland in the 21st Century* (Washington, DC, 2015); Department of Justice, *Audit of the Federal Bureau of Investigation's Cyber Threat Prioritization* (Washington, DC, 2016).

38. Federal Bureau of Investigation, "The FBI on Track with Its Intelligence Mission," press release, September 29, 2008.

39. 9/11 Review Commission, *The FBI: Protecting the Homeland in the 21st Century;* Department of Justice, *Audit of the Federal Bureau of Investigation's Cyber Threat Prioritization.*

40. Ibid.

41. Statement of Mueller, "Oversight of the Federal Bureau of Investigation."

42. Office of the Director of National Intelligence, *Intelligence Community Directive 304: Human Intelligence* (Washington, DC, 2009).

43. Ibid.

44. *Departments of Commerce, Justice, and State, the Judiciary, and Related Agencies Appropriations for 2005,* pt. 10.

45. *Commerce, Justice, Science, and Related Agencies Appropriations for 2010,* Before a Subcommittee of the Committee on Appropriations, House of Representatives, 111th Cong., pt. 1 (2009).

46. Ibid.

47. Ibid.

48. *Commerce, Justice, Science, and Related Agencies Appropriations for 2009,* Before a Subcommittee of the Committee on Appropriations, House of Representatives, 110th Cong., pt. 1 (2008).

49. Ibid.

50. *Departments of Commerce, Justice, and State, the Judiciary, and Related Agencies Appropriations for 2005,* pt. 10.

51. Ibid.

52. *Ten Years After 9/11: 2011.*

53. *The Federal Bureau of Investigation's Strategic Plan and Progress on Reform,* Before the Select Committee on Intelligence, Senate, 110th Cong., S. Doc. 110-793 (2007).

54. *Commerce, Justice, Science, and Related Agencies Appropriations for Fiscal Year 2009,* Before a Subcommittee of the Committee on Appropriations, Senate, 110th Cong., S. Doc. 110-628 (2008); *Commerce, Justice, Science, and Related Agencies Appropriations for 2010,* pt. 1.

55. *The Federal Bureau of Investigation's Strategic Plan and Progress on Reform.*

56. Federal Bureau of Investigation, *The New Field Intelligence: March 2008–March 2009,* version 1.5, https://assets.documentcloud.org/documents/402530/doc-35-new-field-intel.pdf.

57. *Commerce, Justice, Science, and Related Agencies Appropriations for 2011,* Before a Subcommittee of the Committee on Appropriations, House of Representatives, 111th Cong., pt. 1A (2010).

58. *Commerce, Justice, Science, and Related Agencies Appropriations for Fiscal Year 2009; Commerce, Justice, Science, and Related Agencies Appropriations for 2010,* pt. 1.

59. National Academy of Public Administration, *Transforming the FBI: Progress and Challenges* (Washington, DC, 2005); Cumming and Masse, *Intelligence Reform Implementation at the Federal Bureau of Investigation: Issues and Options for Congress* (Washington, DC, 2005).

60. National Academy of Public Administration, *Transforming the FBI.*

61. *Oversight of the Federal Bureau of Investigation,* Before the Committee on the Judiciary, Senate, 110th Cong., S. Doc. 110-910 (2008).

62. *Commerce, Justice, Science, and Related Agencies Appropriations for 2011,* pt. 1A.

63. Siobhan Gorman and Evan Perez, "FBI Wrestling with Remake as Intelligence Agency," *Wall Street Journal,* September 16, 2008.

64. Jan W. Rivkin, Michael Roberto, and Ranjay Gulati, *Federal Bureau of Investigation 2009* (Cambridge: Harvard Business School, 2010).

65. Ibid.

66. Ibid.

67. Ibid.

68. Department of Justice, *The Federal Bureau of Investigation's Ability to Address the National Security Cyber Intrusion Threat;* Federal Bureau of Investigation, *The New Field Intelligence: March 2008–March 2009,* version 1.5.

69. *Oversight of the Federal Bureau of Investigation,* S. Doc. 111-115.

70. *Oversight of the Federal Bureau of Investigation,* S. Doc. 110-910.

71. *Commerce, Justice, Science, and Related Agencies Appropriations for 2012,* Before a Subcommittee of the Committee on Appropriations, House of Representatives, 112th Cong., pt. 7 (2011).

72. Ibid.

73. *FBI Oversight,* Before the Committee on the Judiciary, Senate, 109th Cong., S. Doc. 109-706 (2006).

74. *Federal Bureau of Investigation Oversight,* S. Doc. 109-763.

75. *Oversight of the Federal Bureau of Investigation,* S. Doc. 110-910.

76. *Departments of Commerce, Justice, and State, the Judiciary, and Related Agencies Appropriations for 2004,* Before a Subcommittee of the Committee on Appropriations, House of Representatives, 108th Cong., pt. 10 (2003).

77. *Oversight of the Federal Bureau of Investigation,* S. Doc. 111-115.

78. *Oversight of the Federal Bureau of Investigation,* S. Doc. 110-910.

79. *Departments of Commerce, Justice, and State, the Judiciary, and Related Agencies Appropriations for 2004,* pt. 6.

80. *Oversight of the Federal Bureau of Investigation,* Before the Committee on the Judiciary, Senate, 111th Cong., S. Doc. 111-1001 (2010).

81. *FBI Oversight,* S. Doc. 109-706.

82. *Oversight of the Federal Bureau of Investigation,* S. Doc. 111-1001.

83. *Oversight of the Federal Bureau of Investigation,* Before the Committee on the Judiciary, Senate, 112th Cong., S. Doc. 112-173 (2011).

84. *Oversight of the Federal Bureau of Investigation,* Before the Committee on the Judiciary, Senate, 110th Cong., S. Doc. 110-881 (2007).

85. *Departments of Commerce, Justice, and State, the Judiciary, and Related Agencies Appropriations for 2004,* pt. 6.

86. *Oversight of the Federal Bureau of Investigation,* Before the Committee on the Judiciary, Senate, S. Doc. 112-405 (2011).

7

The Intelligence Enterprise at the Department of Homeland Security

An intelligence apparatus has grown within the Department of Homeland Security since the establishment of the DHS in 2002. Originally, the DHS Information Analysis and Infrastructure Protection Directorate, under the undersecretary for information analysis and infrastructure protection, had the bailiwick for intelligence analysis.[1] As part of Secretary Chertoff's DHS Second Stage Review, the Office of Intelligence and Analysis became separate from the IAIP and took the directorate's analysts with it.[2] That review also designated the assistant secretary for information analysis—who would lead the new OI&A—as the department's chief intelligence officer.[3] (The position of assistant secretary became elevated to an undersecretary as a result of the 9/11 Commission Act of 2007.)[4] The designation of the CINT as a direct reporter to the DHS secretary heightened the visibility of intelligence within the DHS. The OI&A serves as one of two DHS conduits (the other is the intelligence component of the Coast Guard) to the intelligence community and as an intelligence community conduit to subfederal entities.[5]

However, the DHS, like the FBI, is composed of disparate components and missions. Intelligence does not fit neatly within just one of these entities. The DHS has, consequently, described this broader network as the DHS intelligence enterprise.[6] This enterprise includes the OI&A—as well as two headquarter elements that the OI&A supports—and the intelligence elements of US Customs and Border Protection; US Immigration and Customs Enforcement, which includes Homeland Security Investigations; US Citizenship and Immigration Services; the Transportation Security Administration; the US Coast Guard; and the US Secret Service.[7] Former CINT Charles Allen established the first strategic plan for the DHS intelligence enterprise, which addressed requirements, collection, dissemination and information sharing, analysis, and warning, in an attempt to "create the overall DHS intelligence culture that is supported by solid business practices."[8] Allen made these comments in 2006 and it is troubling that, as of 2014, Secretary Johnson found himself needing to jump-start analytic integration. Johnson planned to "harness a number of existing planning and analytic cells throughout DHS" as part of a "collective DHS Headquarters strategy, planning, and analytic capability." Johnson also noted that the analytic "capability must be integrated into, not created and employed in isolation from, existing Departmental functions that are critical day-to-day mission execution and mission support activities."[9] A juxtaposition of Allen's and Johnson's statements, made almost a decade apart, suggests that the DHS intelligence enterprise has not been particularly successful in becoming an integrated part of the department.

The unwieldy DHS intelligence enterprise is managed by several entities. Key members—including the heads of DHS intelligence elements—of the enterprise constitute the Homeland Security Intelligence Council (HSIC).[10] Through the intelligence council, the DHS addresses crosscutting intelligence issues including recruitment, training, analytic standards, and budgetary topics.[11] Although the HSIC, which was created in 2005, serves as the DHS intelligence enterprise's decisionmaking and implementation oversight body, the heads of DHS intelligence components are required to advise and coordinate with the CINT, who is responsible for integrating and standardizing the DHS intelligence enterprise.[12]

Delays and disorganization have plagued the enterprise. For instance, only in 2006 was the CINT able to tell Congress that the DHS had completed the first review of component intelligence programs.[13] Furthermore, it took until 2011 for the DHS intelligence enterprise to produce a unified program of analysis that would prevent redundancies, identify opportunities for collaboration across components, and ensure that all mission requirements are adequately covered.[14] However, the DHS's one-foot-in, one-foot-out relationship with the intelligence community (only the US Coast Guard and OI&A fall under the director of national intelligence) has made establishment of a unified intelligence enterprise a difficult task. While the OI&A is subject to intelligence community directives and standards, component intelligence programs are not obligated to comply with those guidelines, unless the DHS institutionalizes the guidance in its own policies.[15] Considering these deficiencies, it is not surprising that, according to a 2017 report by the inspectors general for the intelligence community, DHS, and DoJ, there continued to be a "lack of unity among [intelligence and analysis] and other DHS component intelligence programs."[16]

The DHS Intelligence Landscape

Although the DHS intelligence enterprise is the textbook answer to how the DHS functions as an intelligence agency, the department's intelligence role is more accurately apparent in an assessment of the DHS's functions, independent of the intelligence enterprise framework. Reviewing the DHS through this lens avoids forcing an intelligence framework on existing entities and instead looks at components to comprehend how they contribute to intelligence collection and analysis. This assessment highlights the competencies and comparative advantages around which future DHS growth should center (a much stronger way to build a corporate, crosscutting identity than Napolitano's moratorium on separate component logos). By first identifying the department's de facto—rather than desired—foundation, the DHS can then shape its intelligence enterprise to complement the department's strengths. Furthermore, an assessment of how the DHS has developed its capabilities provides US policymakers with a roadmap for making course corrections in developing the domestic setting's overarching intelligence enterprise. If the responsibility for a certain function is primarily within the DHS, policymakers would be wise to consolidate that function, by moving similar capabilities and resources from other agencies into the department (e.g., the FBI's Criminal Justice Services Division—a component with significant responsibilities for information sharing with state and local entities—should be moved to the DHS, in order to complement the DHS's responsibility for interaction with fusion centers). Similarly, if the DHS is clinging to certain functions that other agencies are exercising more robustly, DHS capabilities and resources should be transferred to the identified agencies (e.g., Homeland Security Investigations—an Immigration and Customs Enforcement component—should move to the FBI).

The DHS currently has significant collection, analytical, and information dissemination functions, which are distributed across multiple components. Its collection activities are primarily passive—gleaning information as entities cross US physical and electronic borders. Active intelligence collection (e.g., investigation) is an outlier, limited primarily to Immigration and Customs Enforcement. Analytically, the DHS focuses on the implications of specific threats and on identifying vulnerabilities, rather than developing awareness of state and nonstate threat actors. Finally, the DHS has a significant role in information sharing with sub-federal governments, through the fusion center network, and with the private sector. The department can make a good case for consolidating the range of programs and entities, involved with similar activities, that are currently spread across multiple agencies.

Passive HUMINT Collection

Multiple DHS components engage in passive collection—they do not seek out information but instead glean it through encounters for which department components are responsible (e.g., Customs and Border Protection does not proactively chase drug traffickers; it identifies them as they cross into US territory). Passive collection can result from a variety of techniques, including traditional human intelligence collection by a Customs and Border Protection officer; imagery intelligence (IMINT) collection by an unmanned aerial vehicle patrolling an area; measures and signatures intelligence (MASINT) collection by a sensor directed at sniffing the air for indicators of a biological attack; and even signals intelligence (SIGINT) collection by DHS components that monitor the internet for threats and vulnerabilities.

Much of the DHS's passive HUMINT collection is located within Customs and Border Protection. The creation of the protection combined multiple passive collection agencies into one entity. It consists of elements from the Immigration and Naturalization Service, the Border Patrol, the Customs Service, and the Department of Agriculture's Animal and Plant Health Inspection Service.[17] With nearly 60,000 employees, Customs and Border Protection is the largest law enforcement agency in the United States and the primary federal law enforcement agency for border issues.[18] It is responsible for disrupting multiple threats that may transit US borders, including terrorists, weapons of mass effect, smugglers of humans and narcotics, and agricultural diseases.[19] As part of their border inspection activities, Customs and Border Protection officers have an opportunity to glean intelligence information by examining printed material and electronic media such as computer disks and hard drives.[20] Customs and Border Protection's Border Patrol component is a significant law enforcement collector of HUMINT and generates intelligence reports based on the apprehensions it makes.[21] However, as the then-head of Customs and Border Protection, Robert Bonner, explained in 2004, Customs and Border Protection is an interdicting agency that is not responsible for following up on investigations.[22]

Although Customs and Border Protection is the DHS's most prominent passive HUMINT collector, it is not the only one in the department. The DHS is also responsible for the Transportation Security Administration, which incorporates several passive collection components. Transportation security officers (i.e., TSA screeners) are the most visible aspect of TSA collectors. However, they are not the TSA's only element evaluating travelers. TSA behavior detection officers work to identify passengers who exhibit behavior that may indicate a threat to aviation security and who, consequently, warrant additional screening.[23] Finally, the Federal Protective Service, currently part of the DHS National Protection and Programs Directorate (NPPD), is responsible for vigilance, as the law enforcement provider for various federal facilities.[24] Interestingly, the Federal Protective Service originally entered the DHS (from the General Services Administration) as part of the Directorate of Border and Transportation Security, which aligned it with the DHS's other passive collectors: Customs and Border Protection and the Transportation Security Administration.

Passive SIGINT Collection

The DHS has passive SIGINT-related functions, as part of its responsibility for monitoring systems and identifying responsibilities, in the cyber field. The National Cybersecurity and Communications Integration Center (NCCIC)—part of the National Protection and Programs Directorate—has the most prominent role in maintaining vigilance about ongoing cyber activities. The DHS established the NCCIC, in 2009, to serve as the principal hub for organizing US cyber response efforts and maintaining the cyber and communications common operating picture.[25] The National Cybersecurity Protection Act of 2014 statutorily established the NCCIC's role as the federal civilian interface for information sharing on cybersecurity risks, incidents, analysis, and warnings with federal and nonfederal entities, within the DHS.[26] The NCCIC consists of four subordinate entities: the US Computer Emergency Readiness Team (US-CERT); the Industrial Control Systems Cyber Emergency Response Team (ICS-CERT); the National Coordinating Center for Communications (NCC); and NCCIC Operations and Integration (NO&I). The first three of these entities have a SIGINT nexus, while the last is a coordinating body. US-CERT analyzes data about emerging cyber threats and responds to incidents; ICS-CERT analyzes and responds to control systems–related incidents; the NCC is responsible for assisting the US government, private industry, and international partners to share and analyze threat information about, assess the operating status of, and understand the risk posture of the communications infrastructure.[27]

The DHS's original cybersecurity function was the National Cyber Security Division, under the Information Analysis and Infrastructure Protection Directorate.[28] As part of the DHS Second Stage Review, Chertoff created the position of assistant secretary for cyber and telecommunication security, as part of the newly created Preparedness Directorate.[29] The DHS transferred its cybersecurity functions to the NPPD upon the directorate's creation in 2007.[30]

Passive IMINT Collection

Customs and Border Protection, with a vast territory—along the southern and northern borders of the United States—to cover, has turned to IMINT, especially unmanned aerial vehicles (drones), as a means to maintain visibility on a wide area of responsibility. With the exception of the Department of Defense, Customs and Border Protection possesses the largest drone fleet of any federal agency.[31] In 2005, Customs and Border Protection's Air and Marine Operations began flying Predator drones along the southwest border of the United States and expanded the use of Predators, in 2009, to the northern border.[32] Customs and Border Protection drones, among other functions, provide intelligence data to the agency's Office of Intelligence and Investigative Liaison for analysis.[33]

In addition to drones, the agency has also deployed other IMINT capabilities, directed at maintaining awareness of activities that enter into specific locations. As of 2006, Customs and Border Protection had deployed a license plate reader system that automatically identified and communicated license plate information to the Treasury Enforcement Communication System (TECS), which automatically queried its database for law enforcement information associated with the license plate.[34] (Immigration and Customs Enforcement, another DHS component, attempted to take this one step further, in 2014, when it solicited bids for a national license plate recognition database, which would compile data from every vehicle that passed a scanner.)[35] Furthermore, Treasury Enforcement Communication System, as part of its America's Shield Initiative (ASI), deployed video surveillance equipment along the northern and southern land borders of the United States.[36] According to a 2005 report by the Electronic Privacy Information Center, ASI included a remote video surveillance system that integrated multiple color cameras and thermal infrared images into a single remote system.[37] As of 2015, Customs and Border Protection used the remote system along both the southwest and northern borders to conduct short-, medium-, and long-range persistent surveillance.[38]

Passive MASINT Collection

Several DHS components make use of measures and signatures intelligence to identify illicit human activities as well as the presence of airborne threats. Customs and Border Protection and the TSA both employ sensors to identify, via MASINT, individuals who might pose a threat to US interests. The BioWatch initiative, for which the DHS's Office of Health Affairs is responsible, monitors the air in specific locations to identify the presence of pathogens. Despite the integral role of MASINT to DHS efforts to maintain awareness of threats that pass through US areas of responsibility, the DHS—as indicated by the brief history of the Domestic Nuclear Detection Office (DNDO)—has not always been able to ensure that its collectors have adequate technology to identify MASINT indicators of threats.

With its need for tripwires to identify violation of US borders, Customs and Border Protection is a natural user of MASINT collection that can identify trespass into a specific geographic area. As early as 2005, the America's Shield Initiative included radar, seismic, motion, magnetic, and heat detectors.[39] Customs and Border Protection makes use of unattended ground sensors for short-range surveillance. These sensors have a variety of capabilities including collection of seismic and acoustic information.[40] The agency also engages in airborne MASINT collection. For instance, Customs and Border Protection outfitted drones with technology for electronic signals interception and human identification.[41] Its tethered aerostat radar system uses these stationary airborne platforms to detect and monitor low-altitude aircraft and vessels along the US-Mexico border and the Florida straits.[42]

Similar to Customs and Border Protection, the Transportation Security Administration collects intelligence as individuals pass into and through its area of responsibility. Transportation security officers use x-ray equipment, magnetometers, and advanced imaging technology to screen passengers.[43] The TSA, in accordance with the Aviation and Transportation Security Act of 2001, also uses explosives detection systems and explosives trace detection to screen all checked baggage departing from US commercial airports.[44] However, the best technology available is still susceptible to human error and, in 2011, a review of the TSA's explosives detection systems found that some of these systems were set to comply only with 1998 standards.[45]

The DHS's BioWatch program uses passive MASINT collection to ensure that biological threats are not present in specific locations. BioWatch, which began operation in 2003, is a project of the DHS's Office of Health Affairs. Through this program—which is managed federally and implemented locally—high-risk metropolitan areas throughout the United States receive aerosol collection devices and analytical support, in furtherance of identifying the presence of a biological agent before people who have been exposed develop symptoms of illness.[46] However, in 2011, the Institute of Medicine and the National Research Council of the National Academies identified significant problems with BioWatch and determined that there was a need for better technical and operational testing.[47] Furthermore, in 2013, a US congressional committee noted that the program had been imposed on state and local health departments without increases in funding.[48]

In 2005, the DHS announced the establishment of the new Domestic Nuclear Detection Office to coordinate US efforts at developing improved radiation detection technologies. Creation of this office was part of the DHS Second Stage Review initiative.[49] Although the DNDO did not have a role as a collector of intelligence, it was envisioned as having a significant MASINT role, as a developer of technologies that other agencies—notably Customs and Border Protection—could deploy to detect radiological/nuclear material.[50]

The DNDO, at the time of its creation, subsumed the DHS Science and Technology Directorate's radiological/nuclear programs as well as the associated staff.[51] Three directorates within DNDO focused on technological research and development (R&D). The Transformational and Applied Research Directorate focused on long-term R&D to address architectural and technical challenges that did not have near-term solutions.[52] The DNDO's Systems Engineering and Evaluation Directorate was responsible for establishing performance requirements and specifications and for assessing commercial off-the-shelf systems and next-generation technologies.[53] Finally, the Production, Acquisition, and Development Directorate attempted to handle the development, production, procurement, and deployment of current and next-generation nuclear detection systems.[54] This final directorate's functions became sources of significant embarrassment for the DNDO.

Development of nuclear detection technology proved to be an area where the DNDO would experience high-profile mismanagement. The Radiation Portal Monitor Program—which the DNDO had taken over from Customs and Border Protection and on which it continued to collaborate with the latter agency—put an early focus on devices known as advanced spectroscopic portals. Although the DHS had completed a cost-benefit analysis of the technology in May 2006, the General Accounting Office cast doubts on the results of that analysis when, in October 2006, it reported that the analysis was methodologically flawed.[55] In an especially egregious misstep, the DNDO conducted numerous preliminary runs of nearly all the materials that the advanced spectroscopic portals were supposed to detect and then allowed the contractors responsible for this system to collect test data and adjust their systems to identify the materials.[56] This defeated the objective of developing a system to scan for unknown and potentially deadly contraband. When the DNDO finally began field-testing the advanced spectroscopic portals at ports, in 2009, the monitors registered an unacceptably high number of false alarms and also experienced a critical failure, during which the scanner simply shut down without notifying the operator.[57] Not surprisingly, the DNDO announced, in early 2010, that it had ceased pursuing advanced spectroscopic portals as a primary scanning technology.[58]

The Cargo Advanced Automated Radiography System (CAARS) was another large-scale DNDO gaffe. The DNDO began working on the CAARS program, in 2005, as a means for Customs and Border Protection to automatically detect and identify highly shielded nuclear material at US ports of entry. In 2006, the DNDO awarded a contract for research, development, acquisition, and deployment of CAARS. However, the DNDO seems to have planned the acquisition and deployment of CAARS machines with no understanding of Customs and Border Protection's logistical requirements. Only after completing several years' worth of work on CAARS did the DNDO learn that Customs and Border Protection did not want the machines for the simple reason that they would not fit in the primary inspection lanes and would consequently slow the flow of commerce and produce significant delays.[59]

As the DNDO stumbled in its key missions and drew scrutiny, worried overseers began to reduce the office's scope of responsibilities, until a new office finally subsumed the DNDO's functions entirely. In 2011, a US Senate committee strongly endorsed transferring radiological and nuclear research and development back to the DHS's Directorate of Science and Technology (the same directorate from which DNDO had acquired these missions several years earlier).[60] The DNDO's R&D activities also shifted from government-sponsored development of material solutions to an emphasis on existing, commercially available capabilities.[61] Congress went even further when it directed the DHS secretary to provide a plan, in 2014, for consolidation of the DNDO and the DHS's Office of Health Affairs, into an Office of Weapons of Mass Destruction Defense.[62] In 2016, the DHS identified the Office of Chemical, Biological, Radiological, Nuclear, and Explosives as the primary entity of the US government to further develop, acquire, and support the deployment of an enhanced system for detection and reporting on attempts to import, possess, store, transport, develop, or use an unauthorized nuclear explosive device, fissile material, or radiological material in the United States.[63] In 2017, Kirstjen Nielsen, the then–newly confirmed DHS secretary, described the DHS's Office of Countering Weapons of Mass Destruction as the entity that would "elevate and streamline DHS efforts to prevent terrorists and other national security threat actors from using harmful agents, such as chemical, biological, radiological, and nuclear material and devices."[64]

As of late 2017, the DHS characterized the DNDO as a jointly staffed office within the Office of Countering Weapons of Mass Destruction office. The DNDO remained "the primary entity in the U.S. government for implementing domestic nuclear detection efforts for a managed and coordinated response to radiological and nuclear threats, as well as integration of federal nuclear forensics program."[65] Additionally, the DNDO was responsible for "coordinating the development of the global nuclear detection and reporting architecture, with partners from federal, state, local, and international governments and the private sector."[66]

Proactive HUMINT Collection

The DHS, although primarily a passive collector, does include several elements that engage in proactive, investigatively driven intelligence collection. These elements are Homeland Security Investigations, of Immigration and Customs Enforcement, and the nonprotective activities of the US Secret Service. Other elements of the DHS also engage in aspects of HUMINT collection. For instance, in 2016, the OI&A established an Overt Human Intelligence Collection Program.[67] Previously, DHS officials made use—albeit it constrained—of fusion centers for HUMINT collection. Although DHS officials could be present at interviews of subjects, they could only ask questions that were directed at clarifying information which had already been solicited.[68] However, in 2014, the DHS stated that it was training intelligence officers in major urban fusion centers (an OI&A project), which would increase HUMINT by an addition 50–60 percent.[69]

Immigration and Customs Enforcement

Immigration and Customs Enforcement is the DHS's most significant HUMINT collector. This agency is the result of a merger between functions of the former Immigration and Naturalization Service (including its intelligence operations), the US Customs Service, and the Federal Protective Service. It functions as the DHS's principal investigative arm.[70] Immigration and Customs Enforcement has an extensive—arguably overextensive—mandate that includes identifying national security threats, including weapons of mass destruction and potential terrorists; identifying criminal aliens; investigating immigration-related document and benefit fraud; investigating work-site immigration violations; detaining and ensuring the departure of illegal immigrants; exposing alien and contraband smuggling operations; and interdicting narcotics shipments.[71]

Immigration and Customs Enforcement's collection component is known as Homeland Security Investigations. This element resulted from a 2010 structural realignment that consolidated Immigration and Customs Enforcement elements involved with criminal investigations.[72] Probably to the annoyance of the FBI, DEA, and several other entities, Homeland Security Investigations claims to "set the standard for federal law enforcement/intelligence agencies." The agency contains eight headquarters-level divisions: Domestic Operations; National Security Investigations Division; Office of Intelligence; Investigative Programs; Intellectual Property Rights Coordination Center; International Operations; Mission Support; and the Information Management Directorate.[73] Three Homeland Security Investigations divisions are of greatest relevance to the intelligence collection architecture in the domestic setting. These are the National Security Investigations Division, the Investigative Programs Division, and the Domestic Operations Division.

The National Security Investigations Division (NSID), of Homeland Security Investigations, is responsible for the pursuit of terrorists and criminals as well as facilitating liaison and interagency cooperation. The division is composed of multiple components. The first of these is the National Security Integration Center, which facilitates interagency partner coordination in the fields of information sharing and intelligence. The National Security Unit supports law enforcement and intelligence counterterrorism operations.[74] Additionally, the NSID contains two visa security-related units (the Overstay Analysis Unit and the Counterterrorism and Criminal Exploitation Unit) and the Human Rights Violators and War Crimes Unit as well as the Student and Exchange Visitor Program.[75] Finally, the NSID hosts the Export Enforcement Coordination Center—the primary forum within the federal government for executive departments and agencies to coordinate and enhance their export control enforcement efforts.[76]

The NSID clearly overlaps with a mission area in which the FBI has an established legacy. Its Counter Proliferation Investigations Program (CPIP) handles investigations related to countering terrorist acquisition of US military technology, weapons of mass destruction, and chemical, biological, radiological, and nuclear materials.[77] The Bureau addresses these issues through its WMD Directorate as well as through its Counterterrorism Division. The CPIP also enforces US laws involving the export of controlled materials to sanctioned or embargoed countries.[78] The FBI's Counterproliferation Center similarly focuses on this issue. Redundancies in counterproliferation and counter-WMD capabilities warrant examination for consolidation, as duplication of functions in these areas is not only an inefficient use of resources but also a preventable point of failure in establishing comprehensive awareness of developments that could result in catastrophic consequences.

The second Homeland Security Investigations division of particular interest is the Investigative Programs Division. This division is responsible for the Homeland Security Investigations components that handle planning and operational initiatives. The financial, narcotics, and special operations component addresses contraband smuggling, illicit finance and criminal proceeds, and bulk cash smuggling; the transnational crime and public safety component supports investigations directed at human smuggling and trafficking, identity theft and benefit fraud, and transnational street gangs; and the cyber crimes component focuses its efforts on cyber crime threats and online child exploitation.[79]

The Investigative Programs Division, like the Counterproliferation Investigations Program, addresses multiple mission sets for which other members of the US domestically oriented intelligence enterprise have already established legacies. The FBI has devoted resources to human smuggling and trafficking. Its Cyber Division as well as aspects of its Criminal Investigative Division focus on illicit activities facilitated by the internet. (The DHS writ large also has a significant cyber aspect, but this capacity is consolidated around passive monitoring of networks to ensure security.) Both the FBI and the ATF have directed resources at the problem of transnational street gangs. The DEA and the FBI are both engaged in counternarcotics work.

This current overlap is not an argument for the Investigative Programs Division to remove itself from these functions. Rather, it is simply an indication that there is substantial fragmentation—with an attendant waste of resources and unnecessary potential points of failure—in certain mission sets. The FBI has acknowledged, to congressional overseers, that its resources are currently stretched thin—to the point that the Bureau has had to draw down personnel from specific areas of responsibility and instead rely on other agencies' activities in these areas (even though the Bureau has refused to divest itself of mission ownership). The willingness of Homeland Security Investigations to assume missions should be a starting point for discussion of how the Bureau can rationalize its mandate and hand off specific enforcement responsibilities.

Homeland Security Investigations has an extensive field presence throughout the United States. At headquarters, this presence—of twenty-six principal field offices—is overseen by the Domestic Operations Division.[80] The field offices investigate violations at the US border—Immigration and Customs Enforcement special agents receive notification from Customs and Border Protection of all narcotics discoveries—and within the interior of the United States.[81]

Its investigative/intelligence collection mission makes Immigration and Customs Enforcement an outlier in the primarily passive DHS intelligence enterprise. Homeland Security Investigations comes across as an agency desperate to prove its value in the domestic setting, particularly vis-à-vis the FBI. In addition to its claims of standard-setting, Immigration and Customs Enforcement (pre–Homeland Security Investigations) made it clear that it was "the second largest team in Federal law enforcement, with only the FBI being larger."[82] More recently, Immigration and Customs Enforcement has asserted its role as the DHS's "leading producer" of DHS homeland intelligence reports.[83] However, the braggadocio of Homeland Security Investigations is not always matched by its accomplishments. For instance, in 2013 the *New*

York Times reported "Federal Officials Return Looted Afghan Artifacts"; in 2014 the *New York Times* reported "Two Men, Long on N.F.L.'s Radar Are Charged with Making Counterfeit Tickets"; also in 2014, the *New York Times* reported that "Authorities to Seize a Roman Statute in Queens That They Say Was Stolen." It seems that 2014 was a banner year for Homeland Security Investigations embarrassments. According to one account, two Homeland Security Investigations agents entered a women's lingerie store in Kansas City, Missouri, purchased pairs of women's underwear that featured a logo similar to that of the Kansas City Royals, and then announced their presence to the store's owners, flashing their badges and pointing out that the merchandise infringed on Major League Baseball copyrights. The agents then seized the store's eighteen other pairs of women's underwear.[84]

Proactive SIGINT-Related Collection

Both Homeland Security Investigations and the US Secret Service have elements focused on computer (SIGINT)–related crimes. The US Secret Service, which obtained authority to investigate computer crimes in 1984, established a Cyber Investigations Branch—focused on financial crimes (a long-standing Secret Service mission), as part of its Criminal Investigative Division.[85] A technological investigate milestone for the Secret Service known as Operation Firewall involved the Secret Service hosting an established website that had been a portal for online fraud. The investigation culminated with twenty-six search warrants.[86] The focus of Homeland Security Investigations has been on "cyber-enabled" crimes (i.e., traditional crimes that are substantially facilitated by the use of computers and computer networks).[87] Immigration and Customs Enforcement, even before the creation of Homeland Security Investigations, had established a Cyber Crimes Center, which monitored the internet for the solicitations to purchase or sell prohibited or export-controlled items.[88] Despite these efforts, Stewart Baker, a former DHS assistant secretary for policy, assessed that neither Immigration and Customs Enforcement nor the Secret Service prioritized investigations strategically based on guidance from the DHS cybersecurity office.[89] Furthermore, as of 2015, the Secret Service appeared to be dedicating limited resources to cyber crime enforcement investigations.[90]

Despite their seemingly scattershot approaches, both Immigration and Customs Enforcement and the Secret Service have developed specialized cyber-related expertise. The Secret Service established its Electronic Crimes Special Agent Program, which develops computer investigative specialists who are qualified to conduct examinations on electronic evidence including computers, personal data assistant devices, telecommunications devices, and electronic organizers.[91] Immigration and Customs Enforcement has similarly made it clear that it intends to provide computer forensics support for investigations of domestic and international illicit activities.[92] This commitment of human capital to functions about which Immigration and Customs Enforcement and the Secret Service are lukewarm, at best, raises questions of whether these functions should be reassigned and consolidated under a single agency, in order to create a comparative advantage that multiple federal, subfederal, and even private-sector partners could leverage.

The third DHS entity—and a statutory member of the intelligence community—with a significant SIGINT responsibility is the US Coast Guard. The Coast Guard, while it can trace its intelligence history to 1915, and established a headquarters-level intelligence division in 1936,[93] did not become a formal member of the intelligence community until late 2001.[94] The Coast Guard has SIGINT responsibilities via its Cryptologic Group. The Cryptologic Group provides a maritime cryptologic presence to the intelligence community (the US Coast Guard, prior to World War II, developed what might be seen as the first SIGINT intercept ship for the United States). It responds to validated SIGINT requirements that also address US Coast Guard and DHS needs.[95] Through its Service Cryptologic Component, the Coast Guard provides personnel to the National Security Agency and Central Security Service.[96]

Notes

1. Richard A. Best Jr., *Homeland Security Intelligence Support* (Washington, DC: Congressional Research Service, 2004), https://fas.org/irp/crs/RS21283.html.

2. Stephen R. Vina, *Homeland Security: Scope of the Secretary's Reorganization Authority* (Washington, DC: Congressional Research Service, 2005), https://fas.org/sgp/crs/homesec/RS21450.pdf.

3. Harold C. Relyea and Henry B. Hogue, *Department of Homeland Security Reorganization: The 2SR Initiative* (Washington, DC: Congressional Research Service, 2005), https://fas.org/sgp/crs/homesec/RL33042.pdf.

4. *The DHS Intelligence Enterprise: Past, Present, and Future,* Before the Subcommittee on Counterterrorism and Intelligence of the Committee on Homeland Security, House of Representatives, 112th Cong. (2011).

5. Inspectors General of the Intelligence Community, Department of Homeland Security, and Department of Justice, *Review of Domestic Sharing of Counterterrorism Information* (Washington, DC, 2017).

6. Mark A. Randol, *The Department of Homeland Security Intelligence Enterprise: Operational Overview and Oversight Challenges for Congress* (Washington, DC: Congressional Research Service, 2010), https://fas.org/sgp/crs/homesec/R40602.pdf.

7. Ibid.

8. *The Progress of the DHS Chief Intelligence Officer,* Before the Subcommittee on Intelligence, Information Sharing, and Terrorism Risk Assessment of the Committee on Homeland Security, House of Representatives, 109th Cong. (2006) (testimony of Charles Allen).

9. Department of Homeland Security, *Strengthening Departmental Unity of Effort* (Washington, DC, 2014), http://www.hlswatch.com/wp-content/uploads/2014/04/DHS UnityOfEffort.pdf.

10. *The DHS Intelligence Enterprise: Past, Present, and Future.*

11. *The Progress of the DHS Chief Intelligence Officer.*

12. Inspectors General, *Review of Domestic Sharing of Counterterrorism Information.*

13. *The Progress of the DHS Chief Intelligence Officer* (testimony of Charles Allen).

14. *The DHS Intelligence Enterprise: Past, Present, and Future.*

15. Inspectors General, *Review of Domestic Sharing of Counterterrorism Information.*

16. Ibid.

17. Jennifer E. Lake, *Department of Homeland Security: Consolidation of Border and Transportation Security Agencies* (Washington, DC: Congressional Research Service, 2003).

18. *Department of Homeland Security Appropriations for 2005,* Before the Subcommittee of the Committee on Appropriations, House of Representatives, 108th Cong., pt. 6 (2004).

19. *The DHS Intelligence Enterprise: Past, Present, and Future.*

20. Randol, *The Department of Homeland Security Intelligence Enterprise.*

21. *Drugs and Security in a Post–September 11 World: Coordinating the Counternarcotics Mission at the Department of Homeland Security,* Before the Subcommittee on Criminal Justice, Drug Policy, and Human Resources of the Committee on Government Reform and the Subcommittee on Infrastructure and Border Security of the Committee on Homeland Security, House of Representatives, 108th Cong., H. Rep. 108-285 (2004).

22. Ibid.

23. *Ten Years After 9/11: 2011.*

24. Government Accountability Office, *National Protection and Programs Directorate: Factors to Consider When Reorganizing* (Washington, DC, 2015).

25. *Ten Years After 9/11: 2011.*

26. Government Accountability Office, *Cybersecurity: DHS's National Integration Center Generally Performs Required Functions but Needs to Evaluate Its Activities More Completely* (Washington, DC, 2017).

27. Ibid.; "About the Industrial Control Systems Cyber Emergency Response Team," https://ics-cert.us-cert.gov/About-Industrial-Control-Systems-Cyber-Emergency -Response-Team; US-CERT, "About Us," https://www.us-cert.gov/about-us.

28. General Accounting Office, *Critical Infrastructure Protection: Department of Homeland Security Faces Challenges in Fulfilling Cybersecurity Responsibilities* (Washington, DC, 2005).

29. Relyea and Hogue, *Department of Homeland Security Reorganization.*

30. *Homeland Security Department's Budget Submission for Fiscal Year 2012,* Before the Committee on Homeland Security and Governmental Affairs, Senate, 112th Cong., S. Doc. 112-196 (2011).

31. Craig Whitlock and Craig Timberg, "Drones Increasingly Used by Law Enforcement," *Washington Post,* January 15, 2014.

32. Customs and Border Protection, "Unmanned Aircraft System: MQ-9 Predator B," https://www.cbp.gov/sites/default/files/documents/FS_2015_UAS_FINAL_0.pdf.

33. *Department of Homeland Security Appropriations for 2016,* Before a Subcommittee of the Committee on Appropriations, House of Representatives, 114th Cong., pt. 1A (2015).

34. *Department of Homeland Security Appropriations for 2007,* Before a Subcommittee of the Committee on Appropriations, House of Representatives, 109th Cong., pt. 1A (2006).

35. Ellen Nakashima and Josh Hicks, "Homeland Security Is Seeking a National License Plate Tracking System," *Washington Post,* February 18, 2014.

36. *Department of Homeland Security's Budget Submission for Fiscal Year 2006,* Before the Committee on Homeland Security and Governmental Affairs, Senate, 109th Cong., S. Doc. 109-8 (2005).

37. Electronic Privacy Information Center, "Spotlight on Surveillance: Surveillance at Our Borders," March 2005, https://epic.org/privacy/surveillance/spotlight/0305.

38. *Department of Homeland Security Appropriations for 2016,* pt. 1A.

39. Electronic Privacy Information Center, "Spotlight on Surveillance."

40. *Department of Homeland Security Appropriations for 2016,* pt. 1A.

41. *The Future of Drones in America's Law Enforcement and Privacy Considerations,* Before the Committee on the Judiciary, Senate, 113th Cong. (2013).

42. Department of Homeland Security, "Border Surveillance Systems," 2014, https://www.dhs.gov/sites/default/files/publications/privacy_pia_CBP_BSS_August2014.pdf.

43. Transportation Security Administration, *Progress and Challenges Faced in Strengthening Three Key Security Programs* (Washington, DC: Government Accountability Office, 2012).

44. Government Accountability Office, *Aviation Security: TSA Has Enhanced Its Explosives Detection Requirements for Checked Baggage but Additional Screening Actions Are Needed* (Washington, DC, 2011).

45. Senator Tom Coburn, *A Review of the Department of Homeland Security's Missions and Performance* (Washington, DC: Senate, 2015).

46. *Ten Years After 9/11: 2001; Homeland Security Department's Budget Submission for Fiscal Year 2010,* Before the Committee on Homeland Security and Governmental Affairs, Senate, 111th Cong., S. Doc. 111-980 (2009).

47. Senator Tom Coburn, *A Review of the Department of Homeland Security's Missions and Performance.*

48. "Supplemental Memorandum Re: Committee Investigation of the Department of Homeland Security BioWatch Program," Committee on Energy and Commerce, House of Representatives (2013).

49. Congressional Research Service, *Organization and Mission of the Emergency Preparedness and Response Directorate: Issues and Options for the 109th Congress* (Washington, DC, 2005).

50. *Department of Homeland Security Appropriations for 2009,* Before a Subcommittee of the Committee on Appropriations, House of Representatives, 110th Cong., pt. 1B (2008).

51. Government Accountability Office, *Combating Nuclear Smuggling: DHS Has Made Progress Deploying Radiation Detection Equipment at U.S. Ports of Entry but Concerns Remain* (Washington, DC, 2006).

52. Domestic Nuclear Detection Office, "DNDO Overview," Summer 2008, https://nsarchive2.gwu.edu/nukevault/ebb270/20.pdf.

53. Ibid.

54. Ibid.

55. Government Accountability Office, *Combating Nuclear Smuggling: DNDO Has Not Yet Collected Most of the National Laboratories' Test Results on Radiation Portal Monitors in Support of DNDOs Testing and Development Program* (Washington, DC, 2007).

56. Ibid.

57. Ibid.

58. *Nuclear Terrorism: Strengthening Our Domestic Defenses,* Before the Committee on Homeland Security and Governmental Affairs, Senate, 111th Cong., S. Doc. 111-1096, pts. 1–2 (2010).

59. Government Accountability Office, *Combating Nuclear Smuggling: Inadequate Communication and Oversight Hampered DHS Efforts to Develop an Advanced Radiography System to Detect Nuclear Materials* (Washington, DC, 2010).

60. Jennifer E. Lake, *Homeland Security Department: FY2011 Appropriations* (Washington, DC: Congressional Research Service, 2011).

61. *Department of Homeland Security Appropriations for 2018,* Before a Subcommittee of the Committee on Appropriations, House of Representatives, 115th Cong., pt. 1C (2017).

62. William L. Painter, *Department of Homeland Security: FY2013 Appropriations* (Washington, DC: Congressional Research Service, 2013).

63. *Department of Homeland Security Appropriations for 2017,* Before a Subcommittee of the Committee on Appropriations, House of Representatives, 114th Cong., pt. 1C (2016).

64. Nick Miroff, "New Anti-Terrorism Office to Focus on Countering Weapons of Mass Destruction," *Washington Post,* December 8, 2017.

65. See website of the Domestic Nuclear Detection Office, https://www.dhs.gov /domestic-nuclear-detection-office.

66. Ibid.

67. Inspectors General, *Review of Domestic Sharing of Counterterrorism Information.*

68. *Federal Support for and Involvement in State and Local Fusion Centers,* Senate Committee on Homeland Security and Government Affairs, Majority and Minority Staff Report (Washington, DC, 2012), pp. 11–14, 21.

69. Federation of American Scientists, "DHS Seeks Increase in Domestic HUMINT Collection," *Secrecy News,* April 6, 2015, https://fas.org/blogs/secrecy/2015/04/dhs-humint.

70. Chad C. Haddal, *Border Security: Key Agencies and Their Missions* (Washington, DC: Congressional Research Service, 2010).

71. Ibid.

72. Jerome P. Bjelopera, *Homeland Security Investigations: A Directorate Within U.S. Immigration and Customs Enforcement—In Brief* (Washington, DC: Congressional Research Service, 2015).

73. Ibid.

74. Ibid.

75. Ibid.

76. See website of the Export Enforcement Coordination Center, https://www.ice .gov/eecc.

77. See website of the National Security Investigations Division, https://www.ice .gov/national-security-investigations-division January 3, 2018.

78. Ibid.

79. Bjelopera, *Homeland Security Investigations.*

80. Ibid.

81. *Drugs and Security in a Post–September 11 World;* Bjelopera, *Homeland Security Investigations.*

82. *Department of Homeland Security Transition: Bureau of Immigration and Customs Enforcement,* Before the Subcommittee on Immigration, Border Security, and Claims of the Committee on the Judiciary, House of Representatives, 108th Cong. (2003).

83. *The DHS Intelligence Enterprise: Past, Present, and Future.*

84. Tom Coburn, *A Review of the Department of Homeland Security's Missions and Performance* (Washington, DC: Senate, 2015), p. 72.

85. *Cyber Security: Responding to the Threat of Cyber Crime and Terrorism,* Before the Subcommittee on Crime and Terrorism of the Committee on the Judiciary, Senate, 112th Cong., S. Doc. 112-167 (2011); Randol, *The Department of Homeland Security Intelligence Enterprise,*

86. *Department of Homeland Security Appropriations for Fiscal Year 2007,* Before a Subcommittee of the Committee on Appropriations, Senate, 109th Cong., S. Doc. 109-305, pt. 2 (2006).

87. Coburn, *A Review of the Department of Homeland Security's Missions and Performance.*

88. *Department of Homeland Security Appropriations for 2005,* Before a Subcommittee of the Committee on Appropriations, House of Representatives, 108th Cong., pt. 3 (2004).

89. *The Department of Homeland Security: An Assessment of the Department and a Roadmap for Its Future,* Before the Committee on Homeland Security, House of Representatives, 112th Cong. (2012).

90. Coburn. *A Review of the Department of Homeland Security's Missions and Performance.*

91. *Department of Homeland Security Appropriations for Fiscal Year 2007,* pt. 2.

92. *Department of Homeland Security Appropriations for 2013,* Before a Subcommittee of the Committee on Appropriations, House of Representatives, 112th Cong., pt. 2 (2012).

93. *Final Report of the Select Committee to Study Governmental Operations with Respect to Intelligence Activities,* Supplementary Reports on Intelligence Activities, Senate, 94th Cong., S. Doc. 94-755 (1976).

94. Jeffrey Richelson, *The U.S. Intelligence Community,* 6th ed. (Boulder: Westview, 2011), p. 102.

95. Coast Guard, *Intelligence,* Publication no. 2.0 (Washington, DC, 2010), p. 20.

96. Randol, *The Department of Homeland Security Intelligence Enterprise.*

8

DHS Intelligence Analysis

The Department of Homeland Security's intelligence enterprise includes a variety of headquarter and individual agency analytic components. Most significant is the Office of Intelligence and Analysis—one of two DHS agencies that is part of the formal intelligence community (the US Coast Guard's intelligence element is the other). In addition to OI&A, multiple DHS components, including Immigration and Customs Enforcement, Customs and Border Protection, and the Transportation Security Administration, have their own analytic components. Furthermore, analysis is not limited to traditional intelligence analysis but rather includes scientific disciplines that help to comprehend and mitigate threats and harden vulnerabilities.

From the outset, the DHS has had a significant analytical component. The Homeland Security Act of 2002 made the Directorate of Information Analysis and Infrastructure Protection responsible for receiving, analyzing, and integrating law enforcement and intelligence information (a dichotomy similar to the FBI's erroneous bifurcation of missions).[1] As originally envisioned, the IAIP would identify and assess the nature and scope of terrorist threats to the homeland; detect and identify threats of terrorism against the United States; and understand such threats in light of actual and potential vulnerabilities of the homeland.[2] However, the establishment of the interagency Terrorist Threat Integration Center effectively stripped the IAIP of the first two functions. The TTIC assumed the primary responsibility, within the US government, for terrorism analysis (with the exception of solely domestic terrorism).[3]

The introduction of the TTIC curtailed the IAIP's analytic mission to the third item: assessing threats in the context of actual and potential homeland vulnerabilities. As described in the fiscal year 2005 DHS budget submission, the IAIP became the primary agency for "matching the assessments of the risk posed by identified threats and terrorist capabilities to [US] vulnerabilities."[4] Based on its analysis of threat-related information received from the intelligence community, the TTIC, and other DHS components, the IAIP became a warning entity—providing products to state and local officials and the private sector once the IAIP had matched terrorist threats and intentions to US vulnerabilities.[5]

However, it was not at all clear whether this truncated role was ideal or effective. Making separate agencies responsible for identifying and communicating terrorist threats introduced one more potential point of failure. Although "information sharing" was the buzzword following 9/11, there was no need to create more opportunities for communication breakdowns. There was also the problem of duplication of effort. For instance, in 2004, the DHS told Congress that its analysts would "take a different 'cut' at a similar universe of information" that the TTIC was examining.[6] The other cause for concern was the IAIP's apparent inability to distinguish between critical infrastructure and less important entities. The Homeland Security Act directed the IAIP to recommend measures necessary to protect critical infrastructure—a key step in this process was development of the National Asset Database.[7] (This was the continuation of a function for which the FBI had originally been responsible—starting in 1988 with the Infrastructure Vulnerability/Key Asset Program—and that shifted to the DHS when the latter entity absorbed the National Infrastructure Protection Center.)[8] The effectiveness of the IAIP's approach to this task was questionable, at best, given that its National Asset Database eventually grew to include over 77,000 entities, including such distinctly unnecessary locations as a kangaroo conservation center, a flea market, and a popcorn purveyor.[9]

Intelligence analysis rose in prominence with Chertoff's DHS Second Stage Review changes. In 2005, the IAIP's information analysis resources became part of a stand-alone office—the Office of Intelligence and Analysis (OI&A)—which would report directly to the Secretary of the Department of Homeland Security.[10] Whereas the information analysis element of the IAIP had been overseen by the undersecretary of homeland security for information analysis and infrastructure protection, the OI&A would be led by the assistant secretary (later undersecretary) for information and analysis.[11] This position was dual-hatted as the DHS's chief intelligence officer.[12] As part of the Second Stage Review, the OI&A became responsible for ensuring that intelligence within DHS was coordinated, fused, and analyzed, to provide a common operational picture.[13] The OI&A draws on information collected by individual DHS components developed as part of those components' functions; foreign intelligence from the intelligence community; law enforcement information; private-sector data; and open source research.[14] It also became the primary connection between the DHS and the intelligence community—a task that would prove to be more easily assigned than implemented—as well as the primary source of information for subfederal and private-sector entities.[15] The OI&A has focused its analysis around five key themes or "analytic thrusts": border security (including trafficking of narcotics and people as well as money laundering); radicalization and extremism; the entrance into the United States of groups that could be exploited by terrorists or criminals; critical infrastructure; and weapons of mass destruction and health-related threats.[16]

The OI&A, as of 2016, has seven elements that contribute to the DHS's informational advantage (an advantage that ultimately benefits customers in the federal, subfederal, and private sectors). The deputy undersecretary for intelligence operations oversees eight of these elements: the Collection Division; the Watch, Warning, and Watchlisting Division; the Homeland Threats Division; the Field Operations Division; the Borders Security Division; the Cyber Division; the Partner Engagement Branch; and the Planning, Products, and Standards Division (see Figure 8.1).[17] In addition to these elements, the Counterintelligence Division—established as a program office in 2008—reports directly to the undersecretary for intelligence and analysis.[18]

Despite its responsibilities to the intelligence community and to subfederal and private-sector actors, the OI&A has not been fully successful in serving its customers. The OI&A has defined its customer groups, in descending order of importance, as the DHS leadership; state, local, tribal, and territorial partners; operational components; intelligence community members; and private critical infrastructure sectors.[19] Unfortunately, state and local entities have criticized the DHS's intelligence as being "irrelevant" to states and localities because the intelligence has lacked timeliness and added little value to local counterterrorism efforts.[20] Similarly, the Office of the Director of National Intelligence has stated that it does not perceive the members of the intelligence community to be customers of the OI&A's products because the products are not targeted at intelligence community elements, and intelligence community agencies rely on other sources for analysis.[21]

Figure 8.1   Organization of DHS Office of Intelligence and Analysis as of 2016

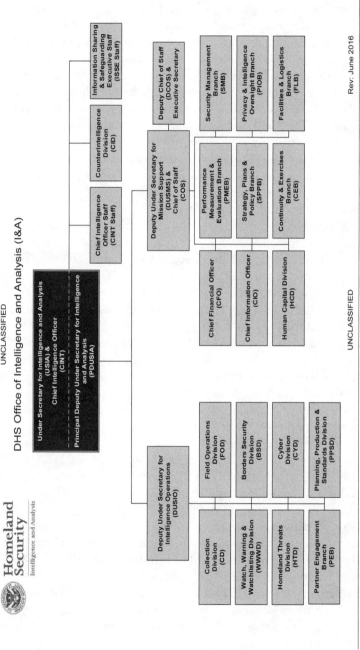

UNCLASSIFIED

DHS Office of Intelligence and Analysis (I&A)

Rev: June 2016

UNCLASSIFIED

Source: DHS Office of Intelligence and Analysis, https://www.dhs.gov/sites/default/publications/Current%20I%26A%20Organizational%20Chart.pdf.

The DHS Intelligence Enterprise Beyond the OI&A

Although it is the keystone of the DHS's intelligence enterprise, the OI&A is not the enterprise's only component. According to the DHS's generalized definition, the component intelligence programs are those organizations whose significant purposes are processing, analyzing, production, or dissemination of intelligence, or whose employees perform "national or departmental intelligence functions."[22] However, beyond this generalized conceptualization, there are differing explanations of which specific entities constitute the DHS intelligence enterprise. In 2015, the DHS chief intelligence officer's staff depicted the intelligence enterprise as consisting of the OI&A, the US Coast Guard, the National Protection and Programs Directorate, Customs and Border Protection, the Transportation Security Administration, Immigration and Customs Enforcement, the US Citizenship and Immigration Services, the Federal Emergency Management Agency, the US Secret Service, the Office of the Chief Security Officer, and the Office of Operations Coordination (OPS). On a different occasion, the CINT's staff claimed that the Secret Service, Office of Operations Coordination, and Office of the Chief Security Officer were not part of the DHS intelligence enterprise. If the DHS is unable to define its own intelligence enterprise, it is hardly surprising that other government agencies have been unable to definitively characterize the enterprise. For instance, in 2014, a GAO report characterized OPS and the Office of the Chief Security Officer as *ex officio* DHS intelligence enterprise members.[23] Given the lack of a definitive accounting, the intelligence enterprise, for purposes of discussion here, will assess the analytical intelligence enterprise using DHS's generalized definition.

Customs and Border Protection

The intelligence component of Customs and Border Protection—known as the Office of Intelligence and Operations Coordination (OIOC)—is under the direction of an assistant commissioner. Established in 2007, the OIOC provides intelligence support to Customs and Border Protection's counterterrorism, counter-WMD, and criminal disruption efforts (e.g., targeting alien smuggling, narcotics trafficking). The OIOC is engaged in the entire intelligence cycle (e.g., planning, collection, processing, production and dissemination of all-source information).[24] It functions as the coordinator and integrator of Customs and Border Protection's multiple intelligence-oriented elements.[25] The OIOC resulted from the merger between Customs and Border Protection's Office of Anti-Terrorism and Intelligence as well as elements drawn from the Office of Field Operations, Border Patrol, and Information Technology.[26] In 2016, Customs and Border Protection explained to Congress that the Office of Intelligence and Investigative Liaison—apparently the successor to the OIOC—was responsible for all-source analysis as well as the production and dissemination of strategic and tactical intelligence products to support DHS decisionmakers.[27] As of 2018, Customs and Border Protection characterized the Office of Intelligence as an integrator of its intelligence capabilities into a single, cohesive intelligence enterprise.[28] Customs and Border Protection develops a large amount of diverse data regarding persons and cargo inbound to the United States as well as information gained through the course of illegal alien apprehensions, narcotics seizures, and other border enforcement activities.[29]

The National Targeting Center (NTC) is an important element of Customs and Border Protection's capability for tactical analysis. The NTC is part of Customs and Border Protection's Office of Field Operations and supports all Customs and Border Protection field elements.[30] The origins of the NTC are in the pre-DHS Customs Service, which began developing targeting techniques at the port level to detect drug smuggling and currency violations.[31] It began around-the-clock operations on November 10, 2001, with a priority mission of providing tactical targeting and analytical research support to Customs and Border Protection's counterterrorism efforts.[32] Since then, the NTC has diversified its mission. This center develops information about targets—based on raw intelligence—that helps to interdict US-bound terrorists, criminals, and illicit or terrorism-related items.[33] The NTC consists of two entities: the National Targeting Center–Passenger and the National Targeting Center–Cargo. Analysts at NTC identify targets of interest or requiring interdiction.[34] Customs and Border Protection's Automated Targeting System—which is operated by the Customs and Border Protection's Office of Intelligence and Investigative Liaison—complements the analytic activity by screening travelers and goods against known patterns of illicit activity, which are generated from successful cases and other intelligence information.[35] Customs and Border Protection subject-matter experts develop these parameters.[36]

Finally, Customs and Border Protection operates the Air and Marine Operations Center (AMOC). This is a multiagency, around-the-clock coordination center, located in Riverside, California, that monitors air and marine tracks of interest—taking Customs and Border Protection's monitoring of borders from ground level to the skies. AMOC's analytic deliverable is a comprehensive air surveillance radar picture that fuses input from as many as 450 sensors, to provide a real-time picture that identifies anomalous, possibly hostile activities such as suspicious or noncooperative aircraft and marine vessels.[37] As described by Customs and Border Protection, AMOC combines its air and marine operations network with intelligence, law enforcement case work, and open source information to create domain awareness.[38]

The Transportation Security Administration

The TSA intelligence component is currently (as of 2017) known as the Office of Intelligence. According to TSA's assistant administrator for intelligence, the TSA has three primary aspects—indications and warning; predictive analysis; and incident response—to its intelligence program.[39] It consist of six divisions and an intelligence cell at the Transportation Security Operations Center. The Office of Intelligence has a unique role, being the only organization that analyzes threats specifically related to transportation.[40] It receives threat information—ranging from inputs by the intelligence community, law enforcement agencies, entities responsible for the ownership and operation of transportation systems, and the TSA's own collectors (e.g., transportation security officers and federal air marshals)—pertinent to transportation-related entities, and provides it to industry officials who have a transportation nexus, as well as to federal and subfederal government agencies. Disseminated information can take the form of reports, assessments, and briefings.[41]

The TSA's involvement with intelligence is not a new development. Prior to the creation of the DHS, the TSA (which was under the Department of Transportation) included a Transportation Security Intelligence Service (TSIS)—an organic capability for review, synthesis, and analysis of transportation-specific intelligence.[42] It was a warning agency—providing current and strategic awareness of threats to US transportation—and identified trends and changes in targeting by threat actors.[43] After the creation of the DHS, the Transportation Security Intelligence Service continued to produce a daily intelligence summary and a weekly report of suspicious incidents. It provided these products to federal security directors, federal air marshals, and federal and subfederal industry transportation stakeholders.[44] TSIS products provided a threat framework for the prioritization of security resources.[45]

The TSA's Office of Intelligence includes a field element that is integrated with a variety of federal, subfederal, and private-sector partners. Field intelligence officers are deployed to major US airports and serve as the principal advisers to federal security directors on intelligence matters.[46] These field intelligence officers provide direct support to personnel (e.g., airport security directors, transportation security officers) at the locations to which field intelligence officers are assigned, by providing intelligence data pertinent to daily operations. Field intelligence officers engage with stakeholders and partners at federal, subfederal, and private industry levels.[47]

Immigration and Customs Enforcement

The DHS's Immigration and Customs Enforcement—which sometimes seems to want to be the FBI—has a significant intelligence component (although, unlike the Bureau, it is not part of the intelligence community). Immigration and Customs Enforcement's Office of Intelligence is responsible for collecting, analyzing, and disseminating strategic and tactical intelligence.[48] Immigration and Customs Enforcement intelligence interests are, broadly, related to the movement of people, money, and materials into, within, and out of the United States, and the Office of Intelligence seeks to support investigative activities by identifying patterns, trends, routes, and methods of criminal activity; conducting anticipatory analysis of emerging and future threats; and assessing potential systemic vulnerabilities and measures to mitigate those vulnerabilities.[49]

Office of Intelligence headquarters is divided into issue and functional elements. The analysis subdivision is organized around criminal issues including illicit finance; illicit trade—which includes illegal sales, technology transfers, and the proliferation of technology and products that endanger public safety; and illicit travel. The office also guides efforts by Homeland Security Investigations to extract intelligence information from investigative activity; disseminates this information to DHS components; and manages Homeland Security Investigations intelligence training.[50]

In addition to its headquarters element, this Office of Intelligence has a field-based element. At headquarters, the Intelligence Operations Division provides intelligence support to Immigration and Customs Enforcement's twenty-six Field Intelligence Groups. These groups are aligned with Immigration and Customs Enforcement offices and are managed by a field intelligence director. They are staffed by a combination of intelligence and operational personnel who identify and analyze criminal trends, threats, methods, and systemic vulnerabilities—which align with Immigration and Customs Enforcement strategic priorities—in the areas of responsibility of the FIGs.[51]

Immigration and Customs Enforcement's scope of activities suggests that it may be overambitious in its intelligence work. Analytically, Immigration and Customs Enforcement appears to challenge the OI&A's role in fusing all-source intelligence. Not only does Immigration and Customs Enforcement leverage information developed by its operational activities, but it also draws on reporting from the intelligence community; other federal agencies; other DHS components; and subfederal agencies.[52] Immigration and Customs Enforcement also seems to usurp the OI&A's role as the DHS's conduit to the intelligence community by working with the National Security Agency and other intelligence units—at the Tactical Intelligence Center, in Mississippi—to integrate and analyze signals intelligence, human intelligence, and law enforcement information in furtherance of identifying new criminal organizations as investigative targets.[53] Furthermore, Immigration and Customs Enforcement's Joint Intelligence Operations Center, managed by the Collection Management and Requirement Division of its Office of Intelligence, maintains contacts with the NSA as well as the CIA, the FBI, other members of the intelligence community, and subfederal authorities.[54] Additionally, the Collection Management and Requirements Division articulates intelligence requirements to collection elements within the intelligence community to ensure that Immigration and Customs Enforcement receives information that it deems to be parochially necessary.[55] Finally, according to testimony provided to Congress in 2011, Immigration and Customs Enforcement also maintains intelligence liaisons with interagency partners in both the intelligence community and law enforcement.[56] Immigration and Customs Enforcement's analysis and interagency relationships may also impinge on the FBI's role as the primary intelligence service within the domestic setting.

In addition to its Office of Intelligence, Immigration and Customs Enforcement, as part of its Homeland Security Investigations element, has a Threat Analysis Section. With a specific focus on identifying individuals previously unknown to the US government and who may pose a potential threat to national security, the Threat Analysis Section uses unlimited access to immigration, law enforcement, and intelligence information to identify hidden links and associations between persons and events.[57] Based on this information, the Threat Analysis Section produces actionable leads for Immigration and Customs Enforcement field offices.[58] The Threat Analysis Section work force comprises agents and intelligence analysts.[59]

US Citizenship and Immigration Services

US Citizenship and Immigration Services (USCIS), which, like most other DHS entities, collects data as the data cross into the USCIS's area of responsibility, does have an intelligence component. The USCIS Intelligence Branch is located within the agency's Office of Fraud Detection and National Security (FDNS), which in turn is part of the USCIS's Directorate of National Security and Records Verification.[60] Products issued by the Intelligence Branch—which manages analysis, reporting, production, and dissemination—focus on the identification of fraud trends or vulnerabilities in the immigration process. The Intelligence Branch is also the conduit for information sharing, coordination, and collaboration with the intelligence community as well as various law enforcement agencies.[61]

The information to which the USCIS and its Intelligence Branch have access has potential value for national security efforts. For instance, by mining USCIS electronic databases, the branch's intelligence research specialists can identify previously unknown links, associations, emerging trends, correlations, anomalies, and indications and warnings. One example of this process is a classified report, which the Intelligence Branch produced, following the 2007 failed bombings in London and Glasgow, that identified individuals who had exact matches to national security–related database hits and individuals under investigation by federal law enforcement.[62]

Who Speaks for the DHS?

By necessity, DHS components liaise with their federal and subfederal counterparts through established, mission-oriented relationships. The TSA—through its field intelligence officers—works closely with members of the intelligence community; the FBI's Joint Terrorism Task Forces and Field Intelligence Groups; locally assigned National Counterterrorism Center analysts; and a variety of subfederal law enforcement agencies.[63] The predecessor of the TSA's Office of Intelligence, the Transportation Security Intelligence Service, even prior to creation of the DHS, assigned full-time liaison officers to the FBI and CIA in order to provide rapid analysis and notification of threats.[64] The TSA is not alone in usurping the OI&A's liaison role. Customs and Border Protection produces intelligence products not only for Customs and Border Protection operational customers and other DHS components, but also for other government agencies. Similarly, Immigration and Customs Enforcement develops intelligence products for external partners including the Department of State, FBI, DEA, and ATF as well as sub-federal entities.[65] According to a 2016 congressional report, almost every component had at least one unique product type.[66] This must seem confusing for external customers who might find themselves at a loss to identify what, exactly, corporate DHS thinks. Furthermore, starting in 2012, DHS components established their own intelligence reporting programs and the OI&A ceased producing intelligence reports based on components' information.[67] Customs and Border Protection has even vied to position itself on an equal footing, as a member of the intelligence community, with the OI&A. As of early 2018, Customs and Border Protection, which has its own intelligence component, had made a bid to become a formal member of the intelligence community.[68]

Who Does the DHS Speak For?

The DHS intelligence enterprise has also been the subject of criticism about whether its products add value for customers. According to a 2016 congressional report, although members of the DHS intelligence enterprise produced a vast array of finished intelligence products, these products were often nothing more than repackaged work of the intelligence community. For instance, according to the same congressional study, the OI&A's "Homeland Intelligence Daily" was frequently populated with analytical products copied from intelligence community agencies.[69] This problem is further illustrated by the TSA, which admitted that it often produced intelligence notes—products that are supposed to provide information or analysis on a specific issue or provide situation awareness of an ongoing or recent incident—that were completely devoid of DHS-component information.[70]

The OI&A has had a strained relationship with the DHS's broader intelligence enterprise. DHS elements have complained that directives from the CINT—who serves as the head of the OI&A—have on occasion not been coordinated and thought through, which has consequently made them unrealistic for the components on which these directives have been imposed. According to a 2016 congressional report, there was an "unhealthy disconnect" between OI&A and DHS intelligence enterprise components.[71] Furthermore, there is at least a perceived lack of experience within the OI&A about component-level operations, including collection capabilities and datasets.[72] This may be, in part, the OI&A's own doing. A 2015 report assessed that the OI&A was attempting to develop an independent analytic capability, rather than focusing on integrating the component intelligence entities.[73]

Despite these tensions, the CINT has engaged in multiple projects to integrate the DHS's far-flung intelligence enterprise. One way in which the OI&A has attempted to pull DHS intelligence threads together is through the formulation of department-wide intelligence products—including intelligence requirements. Forward deployment of OI&A personnel to component agencies has provided another opportunity for integration and enhancement of what DHS secretary Jeh Johnson referred to as "unity of effort." Finally, departmental fusion efforts have served a similar function as forward deployment, by bringing analysts and operators from different elements into coordination around a specific mission.

Oversight

The DHS intelligence enterprise has a steering committee, known as the Homeland Security Intelligence Council. Created in 2005, the HISC consists of the heads of DHS intelligence components as well as representation from other key members of the intelligence enterprise, including the National Protection and Programs Directorate.[74] Through the HSIC, the chief intelligence officer exercises authority over the DHS intelligence enterprise.[75] The HSIC serves as the intelligence enterprise's decision-making and implementation oversight body.[76] It addresses crosscutting DHS intelligence enterprise issues including recruitment, training, and analytic standards.[77] HSIC working groups are formed on an ad hoc basis to address systematic and programmatic issues, as well as substantive intelligence topics. These working groups, which are chaired by members of the DHS intelligence enterprise, are responsible for developing plans of action, based on HISC guidance.[78]

It took the DHS several years to take stock of the intelligence entities it had inherited. In 2006, Charles Allen, the DHS chief intelligence officer, advised Congress that the DHS had conducted the first-ever review of departmental component intelligence programs.[79] This review would result in the first time that the CINT made substantive inputs to the DHS Resource Allocation Decision. Allen assessed that this would be "a major step toward treating the budget resources the Department devotes to intelligence as a coherent program." Allen, also in 2006, approved the first strategic plan for the DHS intelligence enterprise, establishing clear objectives to address requirements, collection, dissemination, and information sharing, analysis and warning, and creation of a shared DHS intelligence culture.[80]

Analytic Coordination and Collaboration

Part of unifying the DHS involves getting its intelligence enterprise components to function in coordination. In 2010, the DHS intelligence enterprise produced its first program of analysis. The program articulated seventeen key intelligence questions and then identified how the DHS would produce analysis to address each of these questions. By developing its program of analysis, the DHS sought to prevent redundant work, identify opportunities for collaboration from the beginning of projects, and navigate overlap between DHS components' approaches to various issues.[81] Unfortunately, despite its ambitious objectives, the program has not produced the expected integration. According to the Government Accountability Office, in 2014, the DHS could not provide assurance that component intelligence analytic activities were aligned to support both strategic departmental intelligence priorities and component-specific missions.[82]

Operationally, the OI&A has engaged in specific collaborative projects with other DHS components. For instance, in 2008, the OI&A, in conjunction with Immigration and Customs Enforcement's Border Violence Integration Cell and Customs and Border Protection, produced an intelligence report on US southbound weapons smuggling.[83] Additionally, in 2010, the OI&A worked with Customs and Border Protection and Immigration and Customs Enforcement to establish the Border Intelligence Fusion Section at the DEA's El Paso Intelligence Center.[84] The OI&A also hosts the Immigration and Customs Enforcement–led DHS Threat Task Force—an interagency body that maintains situational awareness of the terrorist threat stream picture, allows Immigration and Customs Enforcement to glean information from other DHS intelligence components, and provides that information to

Immigration and Customs Enforcement special agents who are working with FBI Joint Terrorism Task Forces (JTTFs).[85] More recently, in 2015, the OI&A and Immigration and Customs Enforcement initiated a pilot program under which OI&A reports officers would author information intelligence reports containing Immigration and Customs Enforcement information, with both components receiving credit for the reports.[86] These projects, although limited, demonstrate that integrating components' intelligence entities with OI&A efforts is possible and should be pursued more robustly, in order to create a coherent approach to intelligence, something toward which the DHS has been actively striving since at least 2006.

The OI&A appears to be more comfortable in collaborative efforts that involve DHS nonintelligence enterprise components. Two prominent examples of this involve collaboration with centers related to infrastructure. This working relationship dates to the founding of founding of the DHS, when Information Analysis (the predecessor to the OI&A) and Infrastructure Protection (the predecessor to the NPPD) were under the same directorate.

A significant example of NPPD/OI&A collaboration is the Homeland Infrastructure Threat and Risk Analysis Center (HITRAC). This center—located within NPPD's Information Analysis and Strategy Division (IASD)—was a joint project of the OI&A and the NPPD's Office of Infrastructure Protection.[87] HITRAC's mission was the production and dissemination of timely and meaningful threat-and-risk informed analytic products that could inform the development of strategies for infrastructure protection.[88] The OI&A, through its analysts assigned to HITRAC, provided both ongoing and incident-specific briefings and reports to federal, subfederal, and private-sector entities responsible for critical infrastructure protection.[89] In 2014, the IASD became the Office of Cyber and Infrastructure Analysis, which built on HITRAC's legacy.

The OI&A has also been a long-standing contributor to the DHS's cyber-related mission, which is currently conducted under the NPPD's auspices. In 2003, the DHS established its National Cyber Security Division (NCSD) under the IAIP Directorate—the predecessor to both the OI&A and the NPPD.[90] The NCSD's role was that of a focal point for addressing cybersecurity issues. It was also the US government's lead for the US Computer Emergency Response Team, a public-private partnership.[91] The DHS's cyber mission evolved into its National Cybersecurity and Communications Integration Center, established in 2009 within the NPPD, which includes US-CERT. The OI&A's cyber intelligence analytic program supports the NCCIC, US-CERT, and the Industrial Control Systems Computer Emergency Response Team, another NCCIC component.[92]

Requirements

From its outset, what is now the OI&A has attempted to lead the DHS's engagement with the broader national security (federal and subfederal) community by providing intelligence requirements to elicit information that would advance the DHS's mission. The OI&A's Collection Requirements Division is the focal point for the department's collection requirements. It ensures that DHS components' and customers' intelligence needs have been articulated, assigned, and fulfilled. Additionally, this division represents the DHS at intelligence community collection requirement committees. The Collection Requirements Division also manages DHS's Open Source Program, which develops domestic open source intelligence.[93]

The DHS took nearly a decade to develop a unified approach to requirements-driven collection. Following the creation of the TTIC, then–DHS secretary Tom Ridge, in 2003, stated that the DHS would have intelligence requirements and would be able to task analysts at the TTIC to pull information from their respective agencies, and even include questions of unique significance to the DHS when conducting interviews.[94] In 2008, DHS chief intelligence officer Charles Allen advised Congress that, in coordination with the National HUMINT Requirements Tasking Center, the OI&A had developed National HUMINT Collection Directives in support of US southwest-border enforcement initiatives. These directives were a milestone, as they represented the first time that the DHS had led the development of a national collection strategy.[95] Only in 2010 did the OI&A announce that it had completed a comprehensive, department-wide set of standing information needs that provided a uniform documentation of continuing intelligence and information requirements.[96] In 2011, the DHS advised Congress that it had created a Homeland Security Intelligence Priorities Framework (HSIPF), which aggregated the intelligence enterprise's intelligence priorities and which served a similar function as the National Intelligence Priorities Framework.[97] The HSIPF reflects input collected by the CINT staff, from members of the DHS intelligence enterprise.[98] (The creation of separate frameworks is an unnecessary bifurcation of the foreign and domestic environments that—along with the FBI's artificial distinction between intelligence and law enforcement—hinders the creation of a unified approach to intelligence around which the federal and subfederal national security enterprise can collaborate.)

Geospatial Intelligence and the Domestic Setting

Satellite imagery is an area in which the United States has attempted to use resources, developed in furtherance of foreign intelligence collection, to better understand the domestic setting. These efforts, however, have encountered multiple impediments, ranging from classification to political controversy, and have not been fully realized.

The first effort to leverage satellite resources in furtherance of intelligence collection with a nexus to the homeland began in 1967, when the US government formed the Argo Committee.[99] Argo—which existed under the auspices of the president's science adviser and the White House Office of Science and Technology, with the concurrence and assistance of the director of central intelligence—focused on making member agencies aware of material that was derivable from reconnaissance satellites. It also organized pilot studies of civilian uses of coverage by the U-2 aircraft for special projects. Through this activity, the committee hoped to stimulate these non–intelligence community agencies to identify uses for photography and to collate the agencies' requirements for information for passage to the director of central intelligence for consideration during the tasking of satellites. Argo participants included the US Department of Agriculture, the Departments of Commerce and Interior, and the National Aeronautics and Space Administration (NASA), among others.[100]

Argo was less than successful because the intelligence community and non–intelligence community agencies could not easily share information. First, the Argo material was only usable in facilities and by personnel authorized to view TALENT KEYHOLE information.[101] (TALENT material is the product obtained from US reconnaissance operations from sensitive manned aircraft overflights, and KEYHOLE refers to products obtained from US reconnaissance operations from satellites.[102]) Furthermore, even when agencies did recognize the value of aerial photography, they had a limited understanding of reconnaissance systems' capabilities. There was also no formal mechanism by which agencies could pass their requirements to members of the intelligence community who had the authority to task satellite operations. Additionally, the intelligence community did not take an official interest in promoting the civilian sector's use of reconnaissance photography and had not assumed the responsibility for assisting civilian agencies with identifying new uses for this imagery.[103] Finally, even if non–intelligence community agencies had taken a more robust interest in the technologies, there were concerns about the possibility that use of imagery for civilian purposes might "compete with the collection or exploitation of satellite photography for intelligence purposes."[104]

Although civilian agencies did not adopt the use of imagery on a large scale, these early efforts did produce some limited successes. These included coverage of damage from natural disasters including the Santa Barbara, California, oil spill; route surveys for the Alaskan pipeline; inventories of national forests; extents of snowfall; and crop blights.[105]

The US executive and legislative branches' scrutiny of intelligence in the mid-1970s did not, for the most part, take aim at the use of aerial resources to develop information about the domestic environment and instead encouraged it, albeit gingerly. The 1975 report by the Commission on CIA Activities within the United States (also known as the Rockefeller Commission) acknowledged that, although a small percentage of imagery had been used for law enforcement purposes and thus was outside of the CIA's purview, the commission also assessed that the legislators who had placed prohibitions on the CIA in the National Security Act of 1947 could not have contemplated the complexities of the collection capabilities that had developed in the intervening years.[106] According to an October 1975 White House memorandum, the commission could "find no impropriety in continued civilian use of [overhead photography] and that economy dictates the use of the photographs for appropriate civilian purposes."[107]

With this encouragement, the White House, in late 1975, established the Committee for Civil Applications of Classified Overhead Photography of the United States—also known as the Civil Application Committee (CAC).[108] This new committee was intended to formalize the requirements mechanism for the exploitation of aerial photography on behalf of civil agencies.[109] The secretary of the interior was responsible for establishing this new committee, which would receive, evaluate, consolidate, standardize, and establish priorities, and transmit all civilian agencies' requests for photography to the director of central intelligence.[110] Voting members of the CAC included—aside from the Department of the Interior—the Departments of Agriculture, Commerce, Energy, and Transportation; the Environmental Protection Agency; the Federal Emergency Management Administration; the National Aeronautics and Space Administration; the National Science Foundation; and the US Army

Corps of Engineers. The CAC would be responsible for reaching compromises among requests and capabilities.[111]

The CAC, although leveraging intelligence community assets, would be minimally impacted by intelligence community agencies' demands. It included the National Imagery and Mapping Agency, the National Reconnaissance Office, the US Department of State, and the Environmental and Social Issues Center (the latter under the director of central intelligence) as nonvoting associate members. The director would not participate in judgments pertaining to civil agency needs or priorities. However, civil collection would remain incidental to foreign intelligence photography.[112]

Interest in the domestic potential for intelligence community imagery capabilities surged again, in the 1990s, with the Government Applications Task Force (GATF). According to intelligence historian Jeffrey Richelson, the GATF—established in the 1990s—existed to facilitate civil projects that required support from classified satellite imagery systems.[113] The intelligence community, in fiscal year 1996, funded eight GATF pilot projects involving wetland mapping for the Department of the Interior, estimates of crop yield of the Department of Agriculture, coastal management for the National Oceanic and Atmospheric Administration (NOAA), bilge oil monitoring for the US Coast Guard, waste site characterization for the Department of Energy, streams remediation for the Environmental Protection Agency, habitat characterization for the Department of Defense, and floodplain mapping for the Federal Emergency Management Administration.[114]

The next major inflection point in the progression of domestically oriented aerial imaging was in 2005, when the CAC Blue Ribbon Independent Study Group issued its final report. The deputy director of national intelligence for collection and the director of the US Geological Survey chartered the study group "to review the current operations and future role" of the CAC and to "study the current state of Intelligence Community support to homeland security and law enforcement entities."[115] This report, issued in the context of the first decade after 9/11, concluded that there was "an urgent need for action because opportunities to better protect the nation [were] being missed."[116] (During the same year, the National Geospatial Intelligence Agency—in conjunction with the CAC—had demonstrated the continued value of aerial imagery to domestic concerns when, in the aftermath of Hurricane Katrina, it provided graphics for relief efforts that depicted locations of major airports, police and fire stations, emergency operations centers, hazardous materials, highways, and schools.[117])

Interestingly, the CAC study group went even further than either Argo or the CAC in its recommendation that not only should aerial imagery be used for purposes with a domestic nexus but also domestic customers should take a larger role in developing US aerial reconnaissance capabilities. The study group assessed that domestic users should have influence on policy, research and development, and acquisition decisions. It also criticized the intelligence community's policies about the use of systems that discouraged domestic agencies' use of them, to the extent that cooperation to address domestic topics resembled a "pick-up game" rather than a "well-coordinated, focused, and repeatable process."[118]

The CAC study group opened the door—with its recommendation that the director of national intelligence establish a Domestic Applications Program—to improved uses of aerial assets. In 2006, the Department of the Interior and the Department of Homeland Security inked a memorandum of understanding that assigned responsibilities to the two departments for the creation and maintenance of geospatial information in support of homeland security.[119] During that same year, DHS secretary Michael Chertoff notified the director of national intelligence, John Negroponte, that Chertoff "fully agree[d] with the [CAC study group] panel's report recommendation to establish a Domestic Applications Office within DHS and to appoint DHS as Executive Agent."[120] In 2007, the director of national intelligence acknowledged the DHS's interest and designated the DHS as the executive agent and functional manager for what would become the National Applications Office (NAO).[121]

According to the NAO, it planned to begin operations in late 2007.[122] The NAO understood its existence as being within the context of previous US efforts—especially the CAC—to use imagery intelligence of domestic entities to assist non–intelligence community agencies. Its mission, as the NAO understood it, was to "facilitate the use of intelligence community technological assets for civil, homeland security, and law enforcement purposes within the United States."[123] The NAO's charter went into even greater detail, explaining that the office had eight primary functions, with the first being to facilitate access to intelligence community capabilities—a role that included prioritizing requests for intelligence community capabilities, submitting validated and approved requests to appropriate intelligence community entities for collection or response, and facilitating participants' requests for the processing, analysis, and dissemination of data and information. The charter also took into account how to promote the leveraging of technology through consideration of new and unique uses of intelligence community capabilities as well as promotion of unique analytical methodologies or technologies in solving civil, homeland security, or law enforcement problems.[124] Finally, consistent with the CAC study group's recommendation that non–intelligence community agencies become more integrally involved with the development of assets, the NAO would serve as an advocate for participants, in the intelligence community, for approving the acquisition of new intelligence systems and exploitation capabilities.[125]

However, almost as soon as the DHS developed plans to implement the NAO, the office encountered significant opposition from hyperventilating politicians and self-styled civil liberties advocates. Congress had initially been amenable to the establishment of the NAO and had provided funding to initiate operations.[126] However, on August 22, 2007, Congressman Bennie Thompson fired off a letter to Chertoff expressing concern about the DHS's "failure to vet [the NAO] with the Privacy and Civil Liberties Oversight Board" and referred to "the failure to consult the Board on a matter as controversial as using spy satellites for domestic homeland security law enforcement purposes" as "particularly worrisome."[127] On September 6, 2007, Thompson, along with Jane Harman and Christopher Carney, wrote to Charles Allen, the DHS's chief intelligence officer, advising that the signers were calling for a "moratorium" on the NAO until "constitutional, legal, and organizational questions" were answered.[128] As expected, groups such as the Center for National Security Studies and the American Civil Liberties Union hopped aboard the bandwagon of naysayers.

Neither Thompson nor Harman was in a position to credibly address issues of national security. Thompson, along with other members of the Congressional Black Caucus, had been feted by Fidel Castro at a dinner in the summer of 2000.[129] Thompson had taken the opportunity to complain to the communist leader, of a state sponsor of terrorism, that parts of Thompson's Mississippi Delta district had few medical personnel and facilities and had the second-highest infant mortality rate in the United States.[130] Castro seized on Thompson's disenfranchisement as justification to make a propagandistic offer of medical school scholarships, at Cuba's Latin American Medical School, for US students.[131]

Jane Harman has an equally troubling history when it comes to national security matters. Sometime in the middle of the first decade of the twenty-first century, the National Security Agency—the primary SIGINT agency of the United States—intercepted a telephone conversation between Harman and an Israeli agent who was the target of a US government investigation. Harman reportedly agreed to advocate, to the administration of George W. Bush, on behalf of two pro-Israel, American

Israel Public Affairs Committee (AIPAC)–affiliated lobbyists who were facing espionage charges for receiving and passing classified information to Israeli officials.[132] The Israeli intelligence operative had—according to published accounts—promised to pressure Nancy Pelosi, the House minority leader, into appointing Harman to the House Permanent Select Committee on Intelligence.[133] According to *New York Times* coverage of the story, the Israeli intelligence operative planned to pressure Pelosi by arranging for Haim Saban, a political donor, to withholds funds from Pelosi until Harman obtained the desired position on that committee.[134] The FBI opened a case on this matter in 2005, and the director of the central intelligence considered what had been obtained via the wiretap serious enough to warrant notifying congressional leaders about Harman's possible entanglement with Israeli influence activities.[135]

Geospatial Analysis

Despite their questionable activities, Harman and Thompson were successful in their crusade to disrupt the NAO's success. The office, after being delayed by controversy in 2007, finally became operational in 2008, but was soon disbanded, in 2009.[136] However, according to the DHS, dissolution of the NAO would "not affect the ability of the Department or its state, local and tribal partners to use satellite imaging as currently allowed under existing policy."[137]

Although the NAO was defunct, agencies continued to conduct analysis of geospatial data, even if no mechanism was in place to facilitate the collection of priority domestic information. As of 2005, the National Geospatial Intelligence Agency (NGA) had already established a liaison position within the DHS.[138] Specific DHS components that used geospatial intelligence (GEOINT) included IAIP's Infrastructure Coordination and Analysis Office and Customs and Border Protection's Office of Intelligence.[139]

The FBI also developed a geospatial intelligence capability. It has incorporated geospatial analysis into the concept of "domain awareness"— the "strategic understanding of threats vulnerabilities and gaps."[140] The Geospatial Intelligence Unit is one component of FBI headquarters' Directorate of Intelligence. This unit serves as the Bureau's "primary center of GEOINT analysis and product creation" and leverages internal and external datasets to create GEOINT products based on the FBI's threat priorities.[141] The FBI has drawn on a partnership with the NGA to develop an internet-based geospatial application known as iDomain, which provides an internet-based mapping capability.[142] According to the

FBI, its enterprise-wide mapping application is modeled after NGA's Palanterra X3 system.[143] The NGA has also provided the FBI assistance with procuring datasets. According to the Bureau's fiscal year 2009 budget justification, the NGA provided the FBI with more than 200 otherwise unavailable datasets.[144] Finally, the NGA has helped build the FBI's geospatial intelligence human capital. In partnership with the NGA, the Bureau's Directorate of Intelligence developed a one-week course that taught the basic applications of geographic information systems to the FBI's needs.[145]

Notes

1. Mark A. Randol, *The Department of Homeland Security Intelligence Enterprise: Operational Overview and Oversight Challenges for Congress* (Washington, DC: Congressional Research Service, 2009).
2. Ibid.
3. *Department of Homeland Security's Budget Submission for Fiscal Year 2005,* Before the Committee on Governmental Affairs, Senate, 108th Cong., S. Doc. 108-555 (2004).
4. Ibid.
5. Ibid.
6. Ibid.
7. Department of Homeland Security, *Progress in Developing the National Asset Database* (Washington, DC, 2006), https://www.oig.dhs.gov/sites/default/files/assets/Mgmt/OIG_06-40_Jun06.pdf.
8. *Departments of Commerce, Justice, and State, the Judiciary, and Related Agencies Appropriations for 1998,* Before a Subcommittee of the Committee on Appropriations, House of Representatives, 105th Cong. (1997).
9. Department of Homeland Security, *Progress in Developing the National Asset Database.*
10. Harold C. Relyea and Henry B. Hogue, *Department of Homeland Security Reorganization: The 2SR Initiative* (Washington, DC: Congressional Research Service, 2006).
11. Government Accountability Office, *DHS Intelligence Analysis: Additional Actions Needed to Address Analytic Priorities and Workforce Challenges* (Washington, DC, 2014).
12. Relyea and Hogue, *Department of Homeland Security Reorganization.*
13. Randol, *The Department of Homeland Security Intelligence Enterprise.*
14. Ibid.; Government Accountability Office, *DHS Intelligence Analysis.*
15. Randol, *The Department of Homeland Security Intelligence Enterprise.*
16. Ibid.
17. Department of Homeland Security, "Office of Intelligence and Analysis Organization Chart, 2016," https://www.dhs.gov/sites/default/files/publications/Current%20I%26A%20Organizational%20Chart.pdf
18. *Homeland Security Department's Budget Submission for Fiscal Year 2010,* Before the Committee on Homeland Security and Governmental Affairs, Senate, 111th Cong., S. Doc. 111-980 (2009).
19. Government Accountability Office, *DHS Intelligence Analysis.*
20. Randol, *The Department of Homeland Security Intelligence Enterprise.*
21. Government Accountability Office, *DHS Intelligence Analysis.*
22. *Reviewing the Department of Homeland Security's Intelligence Enterprise,* House Homeland Security Committee Majority Staff Report (2016).
23. Ibid.
24. Randol, *The Department of Homeland Security Intelligence Enterprise.*

25. *The DHS Intelligence Enterprise: Past, Present, and Future,* Before the Subcommittee on Counterterrorism and Intelligence of the Committee on Homeland Security, House of Representatives, 112th Cong. (2011).

26. Ibid.

27. *Department of Homeland Security Appropriations for 2016,* Before a Subcommittee of the Committee on Appropriations, House of Representatives, 114th Cong., pt. 1A (2015).

28. "Operations Support Assistant Commissioners' Offices: Office of Intelligence," https://www.cbp.gov/about/leadership-organization/executive-assistant-commissioners-offices/operations-support-assistant-commissioners-offices.

29. Randol, *The Department of Homeland Security Intelligence Enterprise.*

30. Ibid.; *Department of Homeland Security Appropriations for 2007,* Before a Subcommittee of the Committee on Appropriations, House of Representatives, 109th Cong., pt. 1A (2006).

31. Randol, *The Department of Homeland Security Intelligence Enterprise.*

32. *Department of Homeland Security Appropriations for 2005,* Before a Subcommittee of the Committee on Appropriations, House of Representatives, 108th Cong., pt. 1 (2004).

33. *Ten Years After 9/11: 2001,* Before the Committee on Homeland Security and Governmental Affairs, Senate, 112th Cong. (2012); *Department of Homeland Security Appropriations for 2007,* pt. 1A.

34. *Ten Years After 9/11: 2001.*

35. Ibid.; *Department of Homeland Security Appropriations for 2016,* pt. 1A.

36. *Department of Homeland Security Appropriations for 2007,* pt. 1A.

37. Randol, *The Department of Homeland Security Intelligence Enterprise.*

38. Customs and Border Protection, "Air and Marine Operations Center: Fact Sheet," https://www.cbp.gov/sites/default/files/assets/documents/2017-Feb/FS_2017_AMOC_FINAL.pdf.

39. *The DHS Intelligence Enterprise: Past, Present, and Future.*

40. Randol, *The Department of Homeland Security Intelligence Enterprise.*

41. Government Accountability Office, *Critical Infrastructure Protection: DHS Risk Assessments Inform Owner and Operator Protection Efforts and Departmental Strategic Planning* (Washington, DC, 2017).

42. *Joint Inquiry into Intelligence Community Activities Before and After the Terrorist Attacks of September 11, 2001,* Before the Select Committee on Intelligence, Senate, and the Permanent Select Committee on Intelligence, House of Representatives, S. Doc. 107-1086, vol. 2 (2002); *Department of Homeland Security Appropriations for 2007,* pt. 1A.

43. *Department of Homeland Security Appropriations for 2005,* pt. 1.

44. *Department of Homeland Security Oversight: Terrorism and Other Topics,* Committee on the Judiciary, Senate (2004).

45. *Department of Homeland Security Appropriations for 2007,* pt. 1A.

46. Randol, *The Department of Homeland Security Intelligence Enterprise*; *Department of Homeland Security Appropriations for 2013,* Before a Subcommittee of the Committee on Appropriations, House of Representatives, 112th Cong., pt. 2 (2012).

47. *Department of Homeland Security Appropriations for 2013,* pt. 2.

48. Randol, *The Department of Homeland Security Intelligence Enterprise.*

49. Ibid.

50. Jerome P. Bjelopera, *Homeland Security Investigations: A Directorate Within U.S. Immigration and Customs Enforcement—In Brief* (Washington, DC: Congressional Research Service, 2015).

51. Randol, *The Department of Homeland Security Intelligence Enterprise.*

52. Ibid.

53. Ibid.

54. See website of the Office of Intelligence, https://www.ice.gov/intelligence; Randol, *The Department of Homeland Security Intelligence Enterprise.*

55. Randol, *The Department of Homeland Security Intelligence Enterprise.*

56. *The DHS Intelligence Enterprise: Past, Present, and Future.*

57. *Department of Homeland Security Appropriations for 2007,* pt. 1A; see website of the National Security Integration Center, https://www.ice.gov/national-security-integration-center.

58. *Department of Homeland Security Oversight: Terrorism and Other Topics.*

59. *Department of Homeland Security Appropriations for 2007,* pt. 1A.

60. Randol, *The Department of Homeland Security Intelligence Enterprise.*

61. Ibid.

62. Ibid.

63. Ibid.

64. *Department of Homeland Security Appropriations for 2007,* pt. 1A; *Joint Inquiry into Intelligence Community Activities Before and After the Terrorist Attacks of September 11, 2001,* vol. 2.

65. Randol, *The Department of Homeland Security Intelligence Enterprise.*

66. *Reviewing the Department of Homeland Security's Intelligence Enterprise.*

67. Inspectors General of the Intelligence Community, Department of Homeland Security, and Department of Justice, *Review of Domestic Sharing of Counterterrorism Information* (Washington, DC, 2017).

68. Betsy Woodruff, "Trump's Border Agents Look to Team Up with U.S. Spies," *Daily Beast,* February 13, 2018, https://www.thedailybeast.com/trumps-border-agents -look-to-team-up-with-us-spies.

69. *Reviewing the Department of Homeland Security's Intelligence Enterprise.*

70. Ibid.; Government Accountability Office, *Critical Infrastructure Protection.*

71. *Reviewing the Department of Homeland Security's Intelligence Enterprise.*

72. Ibid.

73. Business Executives for National Security, *Domestic Security: Confronting a Changing Threat to Ensure Public Safety and Civil Liberties* (Washington, DC, 2015).

74. *The DHS Intelligence Enterprise: Past, Present, and Future.*

75. *Department of Homeland Security: Second Stage Review,* Before the Committee on Homeland Security and Governmental Affairs, Senate, 109th Cong., S. Doc. 109-359 (2005).

76. *The DHS Intelligence Enterprise: Past, Present, and Future.*

77. *The Progress of the DHS Chief Intelligence Officer,* Before the Subcommittee on Intelligence, Information Sharing, and Terrorism Risk Assessment of the Committee on Homeland Security, House of Representatives, 109th Cong. (2006).

78. *The DHS Intelligence Enterprise: Past, Present, and Future.*

79. *The Progress of the DHS Chief Intelligence Officer.*

80. Ibid.

81. *The DHS Intelligence Enterprise: Past, Present, and Future.*

82. Government Accountability Office, *DHS Intelligence Analysis.*

83. Randol, *The Department of Homeland Security Intelligence Enterprise.*

84. *Homeland Security Department's Budget Submission for Fiscal Year 2012,* Before the Committee on Homeland Security and Governmental Affairs, Senate, 112th Cong., S. Doc. 112-196 (2011).

85. *The DHS Intelligence Enterprise: Past, Present, and Future.*

86. Inspectors General, *Review of Domestic Sharing of Counterterrorism Information.*

87. Randol, *The Department of Homeland Security Intelligence Enterprise;* Government Accountability Office, *Critical Infrastructure Protection: DHS List of Priority Assets Needs to Be Validated and Reported to Congress* (Washington, DC, 2013).

88. Randol, *The Department of Homeland Security Intelligence Enterprise.*

89. *Is the Office of Intelligence and Analysis Adequately Connected to the Broader Homeland Communities?* Before the Subcommittee on Intelligence, Information Sharing, and Terrorism Risk Assessment of the Committee on Homeland Security, House of Representatives, 111th Cong. (2010).

90. Government Accountability Office, *Critical Infrastructure Protection: Department of Homeland Security Faces Challenges in Fulfilling Cybersecurity Responsibilities* (Washington, DC, 2005).

91. Ibid.

92. *A DHS Intelligence Enterprise: Still Just a Vision or Reality?* Before the Subcommittee on Intelligence, Information Sharing, and Terrorism Risk Assessment of the Committee on Homeland Security, House of Representatives, 111th Cong. (2010).

93. Randol, *The Department of Homeland Security Intelligence Enterprise.*

94. *How Is America Safer? A Progress Report on the Department of Homeland Security,* Before Select Committee on Homeland Security, House of Representatives, 108th Cong. (2003).

95. *A Report Card on Homeland Security Information Sharing,* Before the Subcommittee on Intelligence Information Sharing, and Terrorism Risk Assessment of the Committee on Homeland Security, House of Representatives, 110th Cong. (2008).

96. *A DHS Intelligence Enterprise: Still Just a Vision or Reality?*

97. *The DHS Intelligence Enterprise: Past, Present, and Future.*

98. *The DHS Intelligence Enterprise: Past, Present, and Future.*

99. "March 1973 Memorandum for the Director of Central Intelligence Re: 'Use of the Reconnaissance Satellite Photography by the Civilian Sector and Non-USIB Agencies,'" https://nsarchive2.gwu.edu/NSAEBB/NSAEBB229/index.htm.

100. Ibid.

101. Ibid.

102. Central Intelligence Agency, "Classification of TALENT and KEYHOLE Information," January 16, 1964, https://www.cia.gov/library/readingroom/docs/CIA-RDP79B 01202A000100050004-8.pdf; Director of National Intelligence Special Security Center, "Authorized Classification and Control Markings Register," May 12, 2008, https://www.dni .gov/files/documents/FOIA/Authorized%20Classification%20and%20Control%20Markings %20Register%20V1.2.pdf.

103. "March 1973 Memorandum."

104. "March 20, 1968, Letter to Special Assistant to the President for Science and Technology—Regarding Project ARGO Briefing," https://nsarchive2.gwu.edu/NSAEBB /NSAEBB229/index.htm.

105. *Report to the President by the Commission on CIA Activities Within the United States* (1975), p. 230.

106. Richard A. Best Jr. and Jennifer K. Elsea, *Satellite Surveillance: Domestic Issues* (Washington, DC: Congressional Research Service, 2008).

107. "White House, October 3, 1975, Re: 'Establishment of the Committee for Civil Applications of Classified Overhead Photography of the United States'" (authors are Henry A. Kissinger, William E. Colby, and James T. Lynn), https://nsarchive2.gwu.edu /NSAEBB/NSAEBB229/index.htm.

108. Ibid.

109. "National Reconnaissance Office, 14 October 1975, 'Committee for Civil Applications of Classified Photography of the United States,'" https://nsarchive2.gwu.edu /NSAEBB/NSAEBB229/index.htm.

110. "White House, October 3, 1975."

111. Ibid.

112. Ibid.

113. Jeffrey T. Richelson, "The Office That Never Was: The Failed Creation of the National Applications Office," *International Journal of Intelligence and CounterIntelligence* 24, no. 1 (2011): 65–118.

114. Government Applications Task Force, "Pilot Project Summary—October 1996," https://nsarchive2.gwu.edu/NSAEBB/NSAEBB229/index.htm.

115. Civil Applications Committee (CAC) Blue Ribbon Study, *Independent Study Group Final Report,* 2005, https://nsarchive2.gwu.edu/NSAEBB/NSAEBB229/index.htm.

116. Ibid.

117. Best and Elsea, *Satellite Surveillance.*

118. Civil Applications Committee (CAC) Blue Ribbon Study, *Independent Study Group Final Report.*

119. Best and Elsea, *Satellite Surveillance.*

120. "From Michael Chertoff [DHS secretary] to DNI John Negroponte," March 14, 2006, https://nsarchive2.gwu.edu/NSAEBB/NSAEBB229/index.htm.

121. Best and Elsea, *Satellite Surveillance.*

122. "Fact Sheet: National Applications Office," https://nsarchive2.gwu.edu/NSAEBB /NSAEBB229/index.htm.

123. Ibid.

124. "Charter: National Applications Office," https://nsarchive2.gwu.edu/NSAEBB /NSAEBB229/index.htm.

125. Ibid.

126. "Fact Sheet: National Applications Office."

127. Bennie G. Thompson to Michael Chertoff. August 22, 2007 https://fas.org/irp /congress/2007_cr/thompson082207.pdf

128. Bennie G. Trhompson, Jane Harman, and Christopher P. Carney to Michael Chertoff and Charles Allen. September 6, 2007. https://www.democraticleader.gov/news room/homeland-security-chairs-call-for-moratorium-on-spy-satellite-program.

129. Cindy Loose, "The Cuban Solution," *Washington Post,* July 23, 2006.

130. "Castro Sees Less Support for Embargo Black U.S. Lawmakers in Cuba for Meeting," *Associated Press,* June 5, 2000.

131. Ibid.; Jonathan Keyser and Wayne Smith, *Disaster Relief Management in Cuba: Why Cuba's Disaster Relief Model Is Worth Careful Study* (Washington, DC: Center for International Policy, 2009).

132. Tim Rutten, "The Real Story Behind a Faux Scandal," *Los Angeles Times,* April 22, 2009.

133. Mark Mazzetti and Neil A. Lewis, "Wiretap Said to Be Viewed As Serious in Late 2005," *New York Times,* April 24, 2009; Rutten, "The Real Story Behind a Faux Scandal."

134. Greg Miller, "Harmon [*sic*] Denies Lobbying Justice," *Los Angeles Times,* April 21, 2009.

135. Mazzetti and Lewis, "Wiretap Said to Be Viewed As Serious"; Dan Eggen, "Probe of Harman's AIPAC Ties Confirmed," *Washington Post,* October 25, 2006.

136. Department of Homeland Security, "Secretary Napolitano Announces Decision to End National Applications Office Program," June 23, 2009, https://www.dhs.gov/news/2009 /06/23/secretary-napolitano-announces-decision-end-national-applications-office-program.

137. Ibid.

138. Civil Applications Committee (CAC) Blue Ribbon Study, *Independent Study Group Final Report.*

139. *Department of Homeland Security Appropriations for Fiscal Year 2007,* pt. 2; see website of the Operations Support Assistant Commissioners' Offices, https://www.cbp .gov/about/leadership-organization/executive-assistant-commissioners-offices/operations -support-assistant-commissioners-offices.

140. *Commerce, Justice, Science, and Related Agencies Appropriations for 2011,* Before a Subcommittee of the Committee on Appropriations, House of Representatives, 111th Cong., pt. 1A (2010).

141. "Directorate of Intelligence, Geospatial Intelligence Unit: What We Do," https:// www.aclu.org/foia-document/racial-mapping-foia-all-affiliates-aclurm000132.

142. "FY 2009 FBI Congressional Budget Justification," https://fas.org/irp/agency /doj/fbi/2009just.pdf.

143. "Directorate of Intelligence, Geospatial Intelligence Unit: What We Do."

144. "FY 2009 FBI Congressional Budget Justification."

145. *Oversight of the Federal Bureau of Investigation,* Before the Committee on the Judiciary, Senate, 110th Cong., S. Doc. 110-881 (2007).

9

The Role of
Other Agencies

The FBI and the DHS are the two primary federal intelligence agencies within the domestic setting. However, several other federal entities from both the formal intelligence community and the broader national security enterprise have influenced the development of—and continue to play roles within—the domestically oriented intelligence enterprise.

The Central Intelligence Agency

Although the CIA is prohibited, by the National Security Act of 1947, from having "police, subpoena, law-enforcement powers, or internal-security functions," the Agency does have a long-established domestic presence. In 1951, the Domestic Contact Division joined the CIA's Directorate of Plans and, in 1952, it moved to the Agency's Intelligence Directorate.[1] In 1965, the CIA renamed the Domestic Contact Division the Domestic Contact Service, but left the service within the Intelligence Directorate.[2] In 1973, the Agency moved the Domestic Contact Service to the Agency's Directorate of Operations and renamed it the Domestic Collection Division. This transfer allowed the Domestic Collection Division to provide support to the CIA's Foreign Resources Division (the Agency's operational arm within the United States).[3] According to intelligence historian Jeffrey Richelson, the Domestic Collection Division became the National Collection Division in 1982.[4] That division became the National Collection Branch of the CIA's National Resources Division.[5] The Agency created the National Resources Division in 1991 (see Table 9.1).[6]

The infrastructure of quasi-overt collection—pursued through these divisions—expanded, in the United States, through successive decades.

143

Table 9.1 CIA Overt Collection Timeline

1951	Domestic Contract Division created
1965	DCD becomes the Domestic Contact Service
1973	DCS becomes the Domestic Division (D.Coll.D)
1982	D.Coll.D becomes the National Collection Division
1991	NCD becomes the National Collection Branch
	of the National Resources Division

Source: Author.

As of 1953, the Domestic Contact Division had established a network of offices in fifteen major cities, as well as several smaller residencies.[7] By 1970, the Domestic Contact Service had established seventeen field offices.[8] In 1975 the Domestic Collection Division was operating thirty-six offices in US cities and by 1976 this number had risen to thirty-eight offices, which it even listed in local telephone directories, consistent with the Domestic Collection Division's overt nature.[9] According to congressional testimony, in 1978 the CIA had officers in approximately forty cities across the United States. Based on the description of these offices as existing to "request our fellow citizens to share with their government information they may have about foreign matters," it is likely that they were part of the Domestic Collection Division.[10] Former National Resources Division chief Henry Crumpton, who held this position between 2003 and 2005, described that division as operating mostly under commercial cover (i.e., putative businesses), with offices in approximately thirty US cities.[11]

Overt activities of this succession of CIA components have been relatively consistent. The Domestic Contact Service established discreet, albeit overt, relationships with American private citizens; commercial, academic, and other organizations; and resident aliens for collecting information, which these entities provided on a voluntary basis.[12] Individuals in contact with the Domestic Contact Service tended to be businesspeople who, in the course of their work and travel abroad, had access to information that was not readily available via other means.[13] For instance, according to former director of central intelligence Richard Helms, an example of how the Domestic Contact Service operated might involve the president of a New York steel company who traveled to the Soviet Union, where he observed certain metallurgical plants that would be of interest to the US government. Individuals from the Domestic Contact Service would visit the steel company president and interview him about the details. According to Helms, there would be no pressure involved or money changing hands. Rather, the CIA was simply "giving [people] an opportunity as patriotic Americans to say what they know."[14]

The Domestic Collection Division conducted similar functions. Representatives of this division contacted residents—numbering in the tens of thousands—of the United States who voluntarily shared information with the US government.[15] These individuals received assurances that their relationship with the US government would remain confidential and that proprietary interests would be protected. The program focused exclusively on the collection of information about foreign areas and developments.[16] Information obtained by the Domestic Collection Division tended to be of an economic and technological nature.[17] The division also provided a conduit for US government agencies, that lacked channels for providing information to the US intelligence community, to furnish information pertaining to national intelligence objectives listed in the National HUMINT Collection plan.[18]

Although the CIA tended to rely on the voluntary provision of information in the context of division operations, it did on occasion apparently provide compensation in various forms. For instance, in 1971, the Domestic Contact Service's entertainment expenses for expenditures on contacts and sources, in furtherance of the service's mission, had to be included, for the first time, in the service's records control schedule, since the Domestic Contact Service had developed a significant volume of such records and wanted to provide for their systematic destruction.[19] Subsequent to this, Loch Johnson, who has extensive experience working in academia as well as for congressional intelligence oversight committees, indicated that National Collection Division did provide payment to certain individuals.[20]

CIA Clandestine Collection on US Soil

The CIA also has a lengthy history of clandestine collection within the domestic setting. In 1963, the Agency established its Domestic Operations Division.[21] The creation of this division did not represent a new venture for the CIA but rather a consolidation of the CIA's existing domestic activities.[22] E. Howard Hunt, a member of the Domestic Operations Division prior to his infamous association with Watergate, described how the division inherited multiple projects that had been run for a period of time by the CIA's commercial staff and by multiple geo-graphic divisions.[23] The division was responsible for directing, support-ing, and coordinating "clandestine operational activities," against for-eign targets, within the United States.[24] The division's setup paralleled foreign field stations. However, Director of Central Intelligence John McCone assured that these activities were directed "against foreign tar-gets" and that the instructions should "not be construed to vest in [the division] responsibility for the conduct of clandestine internal security or counterintelligence operations in the United States."[25]

The Domestic Operations Division's responsibilities included the management of CIA proprietaries (i.e., entities controlled by, but not ostensibly affiliated with, the CIA).[26] This function transferred to another CIA component in 1971.[27] In 1972, the CIA changed the name of the Domestic Operations Division to the Foreign Resources Division, located under the Directorate of Operations.[28] Like the CIA's overt collection entities, the Foreign Resources Division maintained offices in multiple US cities.[29] According to then–director of central intelligence William Colby, this name change was an effort to correct the misperception that the Domestic Operations Division was engaged in domestic operations.[30] The Foreign Resources Division became the Foreign Resources Branch of the National Resources Division.[31]

Although its origins were in maintaining CIA operational capabilities, the Domestic Operations Division/Foreign Resources Division evolved into an entity responsible for developing sources. Its principal mission was to establish relationships with foreigners in the United States who might be of assistance in the collection of intelligence once they returned to their home countries.[32] Officers of the Foreign Resources Division focused on spotting and assessing targets, whom CIA stations would then task once the foreign nationals returned to their home countries.[33]

To execute its mission, the Foreign Resources Division required assistance from US entities. The division maintained contacts with a large number of witting Americans who were willing to cooperate with the division's operations.[34] For instance, the Foreign Resources Division was responsible for confidential contacts at US academic institutions who could provide assistance with the recruitment of foreign intelligence sources.[35] These confidential contacts did not attempt to engage in recruitment of students but instead assisted the Foreign Resources Divi-sion by providing background information and, on occasion, brokering introductions.[36] In the early 1980s the Agency secured permission for the wide use of US venues, including athletic, entertainment, and cultural entities, to maintain cover and develop sources.[37] While many Foreign Resources Division contacts were aware that they were cooperating with the US government, the final report of the Select Committee to Study Governmental Operations with Respect to Intelligence Activities, of the US Senate (the Church Committee), noted that there were a number of Americans who were unaware that they were dealing with the CIA.[38]

The Foreign Resources Division also had to cooperate with other US government agencies. Its domestic, operational nature necessitated close coordination with the FBI.[39] The Bureau's responsibility for identifying and countering foreign intelligence officers operating within the United States meant that it might be looking at the same individuals who were of interest to the Foreign Resources Division, due to the foreign officials' access to sensitive information. This overlap was apparent in the case of Aldrich Ames, the CIA turncoat who worked for the Foreign Resources Division between 1975 and 1981.[40] Ames admitted that he had an opportunity to attract Soviet interest while ostensibly working, on behalf of the division, to establish a relationship with a Soviet embassy official.[41] The CIA also had to account for US State Department interests, since spying had the potential for creating diplomatic kerfuffles. One CIA clandestine operations officer described an early 1977 meeting between top CIA officials, including the chief of the Foreign Resources Division, with the US ambassador to the United Nations, for discussions of what the CIA could and could not do.[42]

Although the CIA components such as Domestic Collection Division primarily handled quasi-overt collection, they also had functions complementary to the Foreign Resources Division. The Domestic Contact Service's relationships with individuals from a wide array of backgrounds meant that it had a unique capability for facilitating the entry of individuals into clandestine relationships with the CIA.[43] Former CIA official Richard Ober acknowledged that if an individual indicated to the Domestic Collection Division that the individual was willing to assist the CIA abroad, the Domestic Collection Division would provide this information to the Agency's deputy director for plans.[44] Furthermore, according to the final report of the Church Committee, the Domestic Collection Division could produce leads regarding foreign nationals who might prove useful abroad.[45]

In addition to targeting foreign officials, the CIA, during the 1960s, contemplated the potential for using the American "New Left" as a means to develop sources' credibility with foreign, militant regimes. In 1968, the CIA considered one potential operation, Project 1, which was jointly developed by the Office of Security and a division in the Plans Directorate. The original version of this project would have agents penetrate various prominent domestic dissident groups and report on the communications, contacts, travels, and plans of participants that had a connection to a specific foreign region. The Agency scotched the domestic penetration of these groups and instead focused its efforts overseas. According to the Rockefeller Commission the deputy director for plans approved the modified proposal, but there is no indication that it was implemented.[46]

A similarly inventively named operation—"Project 2"—looked at the operational possibilities present in the domestic unrest of the late 1960s (the project was initiated in 1969). A specific area division initiated the project with the intention of penetrating foreign intelligence targets.[47] The CIA would recruit agents who lacked dissident affiliations and task them to develop ideological and personal affiliations with the New Left. After this indoctrination and insinuation, a process that one CIA officer referred to as "sheep dipping," an agent would be sent abroad on a specific intelligence mission.[48] Most of these individuals developed their leftist bona fides by enrolling in US universities, where they participated in the radical subculture.[49] Between 1970 and 1974, the CIA recruited twenty-three agents for Project 2, with eleven of these successfully completing the US-based development process.[50]

Overt and Clandestine Merger: The National Resources Division

The CIA merged the National Collection Division and the Foreign Resources Division into a new National Resources Division. The Foreign Resources Division became the National Resources Division's Foreign Resources Branch. Similarly the National Collection Division became the National Resources Division's National Collection Branch.[51] The marriage of overt and clandestine operations has created difficulties. According to intelligence scholar Gregory F. Treverton, the National Resources Division is handicapped since, as part of the Directorate of Operations, "it does not exactly advertise its presence."[52] This is problematic for a component that relies on volunteers who must know how to find the US government customers. Furthermore, a lingering distrust of the CIA—which seems to be reinvigorated by periodic scandals (real or perceived)—means that even if Americans are willing, in theory, to help the US government, they may be reticent about working with the Agency.

(Certainly, the American discourse about intelligence—at the time of writing this—with references to the nefarious "deep state," does not inspire confidence among the American population.)

The CIA's domestic operations call into question whether the Agency is shirking its responsibilities for intelligence collection abroad. Even during the Cold War, it was the Domestic Collection Division's gathering of information from émigré populations that provided some of the most useful information about developments within the Soviet Union.[53] More recent accounts suggests that the CIA has continued to place inordinate reliance on the National Resources Division, pursuing low-hanging foreign intelligence fruit in the domestic environment at the expense of its intelligence operations abroad. According to journalist Jeff Stein, as of 2010, insider estimates suggested that "most of the CIA's recruitment of foreign spies now takes place in the United States."[54]

If the CIA is going to rely, to a significant extent, on its domestic work force, overseers must ask if that work force is up to the challenge of meeting policymakers' requirements for information. A 1976 inspection of the Domestic Collection Division found that the division operated effectively and that its officers had a good understanding of their roles and the bounds within which they worked.[55] However, Crumpton, a former National Resources Division chief, acknowledged that National Resources Division was considered a "stepchild of the Clandestine Service" that operated with less-seasoned officers. Furthermore, Crumpton conceded the "subpar" nature of some National Resources Division officers who were in the division because they had failed to qualify for overseas work. Additionally, Henry Crumpton suggested that the division "seemed weakest . . . in field leadership," with several station chiefs who needed to be replaced.[56]

CIA Influence on Intelligence Activities Within the Domestic Setting After 9/11

As the CIA's domestic components moved into the twenty-first century, they continued to scour the US landscape for opportunities to develop foreign intelligence information and access to opportunities for collection abroad. In 2002, the *Los Angeles Times* cited sources who claimed that CIA stations on the West Coast focused on China and Pacific Rim countries; in Detroit, the Agency focused on the Middle Eastern population; and in New York, in addition to looking at foreign diplomats, the CIA was also interested in the prominent Russian population as well as the local communities, who represented more than 170 cultures.[57] In Los Angeles, the CIA had made a concerted effort to develop relationships with members of California's Iranian population, with a particular interest in developing "access agents" who might not have direct knowledge of developments in Iran but could gain information through various connections. As one former CIA officer described the Los Angeles activities, the goal was to make contacts with individuals who had family members who still resided in Iran.[58]

In the years following September 11, the CIA's influence on other US government agencies—particularly the FBI—was apparent. CIA analysts played an early role in the FBI's attempts to reform its intelligence program by serving among the staff of the Counterterrorism Division's Office of Intelligence.[59] Substantively, twenty-five CIA detailees assisted the Bureau with masses of information developed by the 9/11 investigations.[60] (One of these detailees was bitingly candid about what they had observed at the FBI, claiming that information went into a "black hole" when it entered the Bureau.[61]) In addition to the headquarters presence, the CIA established a presence in the field. As of 2002, the Agency had placed personnel with the majority of the FBI's Joint Terrorism Task Forces.[62]

In addition to these formal opportunities for influence, the CIA arguably had an additional impact as the result of former Agency officials joining the FBI. In 2003, Mueller noted that the FBI employed more than fifty former CIA analysts and officers.[63] In 2005, the FBI established its National Security Branch. Phil Mudd, a former Agency analyst, served as the branch's first deputy director.[64]

Working with the FBI, the CIA has engaged in collection activities within the United States. A 2004 report indicated that the CIA had brought some of its sources to the United States to work with the FBI in furtherance of penetrating radical Islamic groups.[65] (This is an interesting reversal of the 1960s, when the CIA borrowed domestically based assets to penetrate activities abroad.) More recently, the 9/11 Review Commission report, published in 2015, assessed that the FBI and the CIA's National Resources Division were jointly producing "great intelligence" and that the two agencies had developed excellent procedures for handing off sources.[66]

The FBI and CIA have had to navigate overlaps in the domestic aspects of their respective missions. In 2005, the two agencies reached what was the latest in a series of agreements about coordination of activities.[67] This agreement included what the 9/11 Review Commission described as "a useful framework for the interaction of [special agents in charge] in the [FBI's] 56 field offices with the CIA's [National Resources] Division Station and Base Chiefs across the United States."[68] The agreement included an understanding that the CIA's domestic division would furnish the Bureau with expanded information about the division's operations and debriefings.[69]

However, this agreement came in the midst of tensions between the two agencies. Top Bureau officials believed that they had a legal duty to monitor the CIA's activities in the United States and coordinate with Agency operations.[70] Furthermore, Mueller wanted to put the FBI in charge of disseminating all intelligence reports—regardless of whether the information came from foreigners or US citizens—who resided in the United states.[71] CIA personnel, on the other hand, viewed the FBI as attempting to infringe on CIA domestic tasks, including the recruitment of foreign travelers and US persons who visited countries of interest to the intelligence community.[72]

These dynamics may have provided context for the creation of the FBI's Foreign Intelligence Collection Program. The FBI and CIA reached their agreement in 2005 and, in the following year, the Office of the Director of National Intelligence tasked the FBI to use its collection authorities in furtherance of developing information responsive to the National Intelligence Priorities Framework.[73]

The tensions between the FBI and CIA could boil over into obstructionism. In 2012, Henry Crumpton, a former chief of the CIA's National Resources Division, described how the FBI had "repeatedly demanded the identities of NR sources" and how Crumpton "had explained that this was not possible, certainly not with U.S. citizens who refused to meet with the FBI even if [the CIA] asked them." Crumpton also characterized the Bureau as having "little interest and even less capability" in areas of foreign intelligence.[74]

In addition to the FBI, the CIA has also had an influence on the DHS, specifically the component that evolved into the Office of Intelligence and Analysis. According to then–DHS secretary Tom Ridge, in 2003 the CIA had deployed an analytical component to work with the department.[75] Then, in 2005, Charlie Allen, the former CIA assistant director of intelligence for collection, became the DHS's assistant secretary for information and analysis as well as its chief intelligence officer.[76] Even more recently, the CIA, as of 2010, had assigned Dawn Scalise to the DHS. As the DHS's principal deputy undersecretary for intelligence and analysis, Scalise had brought with her "a considerable amount of expertise as it relate[d] to analytical capabilities" and was in the process of implementing multiple programs to train DHS analysts.[77]

The Drug Enforcement Administration

Following 9/11, multiple US government agencies refocused their respective missions to emphasize counterterrorism. The Drug Enforcement Administration was a high-profile example of how an agency that had only a tenuous stake in counterterrorism refocused its resources toward the cause du jour. As the DEA changed its priorities, it shifted resources away from traditional counternarcotics work. This is problematic, since the FBI withdrew agents from counternarcotics, with the expectation that the DEA would step up its efforts in this area. Instead, both agencies have created a vacuum, which Immigration and Customs Enforcement, which is primed for mission creep, has sought to fill, in an uncoordinated fashion.

The DEA, in 2002, implemented policies that prioritized counternarcotics cases that had links to terrorism.[78] Resources followed suit. In December 2001, the DEA established the Special Coordination Unit, within the preexisting Special Operations Division, to coordinate all DEA investigations and intelligence with nexuses to terrorism. This new mission became even more pronounced in 2007, when the DEA redesignated the Special Coordination Unit as the Counter-Narcoterrorism Operations Center.[79] Additionally, in 2003, DEA headquarters directed DEA agents to question, on at least a quarterly basis, the organization's worldwide network of confidential informants, to determine whether these informants possessed information related to terrorist organizations or plots.[80] As of 2006, the DEA—through the Special Operations Division and the Office of Special Intelligence—had completed more than 20,000 counterterrorism products since September 11, 2001.[81]

Heightened concerns about terrorism in the decade following September 11 also provided the context for the DEA's participation within the intelligence community. The DEA had been a member of the intelligence community until 1981. Despite its formal departure, the DEA remained linked with intelligence community agencies and missions. Although no longer a member of the formal intelligence community, the DEA, in 1983, established a Special Intelligence Unit, which was responsible for coordinating intelligence community information.[82] As of 1990, the DEA's Office of Intelligence had started addressing aspects of terrorism, via its Organized Crime/Terrorism Division.[83] In 2006, the DEA, via its Office of National Security Intelligence—which is part of the Office of Special Intelligence—rejoined the intelligence community and had established liaison positions within other intelligence community agencies, including the CIA.[84]

The DEA's expanded counterterrorism mission has implications for how the agency works with federal and subfederal actors. In 2003, the DEA instituted procedures requiring its agents to share terrorism-related information with partners, including the FBI and the Bureau's Joint Terrorism Task Forces.[85] However, this apparently did not stop DEA informant David Headley from helping to plan the 2008 Mumbai, India, terrorist attacks, after receiving training from Pakistan's Inter-Service Intelligence agency.[86]

In the decade following 9/11, the DEA worked with the National Security Agency on SIGINT-related issues. The interaction with the NSA is not a new phenomenon. As of 1982, the DEA had conferred with the NSA and was attempting to resolve legal issues related to NSA material.[87] It was, perhaps, inevitable that the DEA's Special Operations Division—which focused on SIGINT-related information and which took on a counterterrorism aspect after 9/11—would become involved with the NSA. According to a 2013 *Reuters* exclusive story, the Special Operations Division received data from the NSA.[88] The division added the intercepts to a larger database of information from wiretaps, informants, and telephone records.[89] Although the SOD used this information as the basis for criminal investigations, it did so in a disguised manner, through parallel construction, in order to obfuscate their classified NSA origin.[90]

Contemporaneously with its increased role in counterterrorism, the DEA has decreased its resource commitments to traditional counternarcotics missions. For instance, the Special Operations Division, which has taken on an increased responsibility in the counterterrorism field, had historically focused on Organized Crime Drug Enforcement Task Force (OCDETF) investigations.[91] Furthermore, as of 2009, the DEA did not participate in each High-Intensity Drug Trafficking Area (HIDTA) task force.[92] Additionally, in 2007, the DEA suspended its Mobile Enforcement Team program—which focused resources on drug-related violent crime—due to budgetary constraints.[93]

During the decade following 9/11, the DEA attempted to move some of its counternarcotics responsibilities to subfederal actors, further underscoring the new emphasis on counterterrorism, at the expense of the agency's traditional mission. According to a 2009 Government Accountability Office study, the DEA had supplied state and local law enforcement with counternarcotics training and attempted to leverage these subfederal agencies' manpower and intelligence resources.[94] Subfederal actors on permanent task forces assist the DEA with developing cases against significant local drug-trafficking organizations that have links to regional and international groups.[95]

The DEA's prioritization of counterterrorism has created a vacuum in coverage of national security concerns. After 9/11, the FBI reassigned hundreds of agents from counternarcotics to counterterrorism and assumed that the DEA would pick up the slack.[96] However, the DEA has proven itself to be focused on counterterrorism, a development that has opened up space for the DHS's Immigration and Customs Enforcement to become involved with counternarcotics work. As of 2009, the Government Accountability Office assessed that Immigration and Customs Enforcement agents were not submitting all drug-related intelligence necessary to ensure that counternarcotics cases did not overlap.[97] Such rivalries are not new. Relationships between the Bureau of Narcotics and Dangerous Drugs—a predecessor to the DEA—and US Customs were so poor that the agencies attempted to sabotage each other's investigations, with operatives of the agencies spying on each other (as opposed to criminal targets), arresting each other's informants, and even kidnapping the other side's witnesses.[98]

The National Security Agency and Domestic Collectors

The National Security Agency—although it focuses on intelligence collection abroad—occasionally develops information of value to agencies working to thwart threats in the domestic setting. MINARET, a Cold War–era NSA program, is a clear example of how this process can work. Under MINARET, the NSA did not target US persons but instead reviewed legitimate coverage for any entities in which other federal entities had an interest. Collection, authorized by Section 702 of the FISA Amendments Act of 2008, can provide similar value for incisive intelligence activity within the domestic setting.

MINARET was simply a new name for an existing practice. US signals intelligence had provided information to law enforcement since the 1930s.[99] In 1962, the NSA developed a "watchlist" in response to a White House request for information about the identities of Americans who were traveling to Cuba. Then, in 1965, the Secret Service requested that the NSA provide information about individuals who might pose a threat to the president.[100] The FBI was the "prime source of names" for the watchlist, and its interests tended toward "domestic terrorist and foreign radical suspects."[101] In October 1967, the US Army also asked the NSA for assistance, specifically the provision of any available information about foreign influence over, or control of, civil disturbances within the United States.[102] (The Joint Chiefs of Staff, in 1963, had designated the Army Chief of Staff as the executive agent for civil disturbance issues.) Topics of interest to the Army included: "indications that foreign governments or individuals or organizations acting as agents of foreign governments are controlling or attempting to control or influence the activities of U.S. 'peace' groups and 'Black Power' organizations"; "identities of foreign agents exerting control or influence on U.S. organizations"; "identities of individuals and organizations in U.S. in contact with agents of foreign governments"; and "instructions or advice being given to U.S. groups by agents of foreign governments."[103] Watchlists from the CIA included requirements for information about international travel, foreign influence, and support of US extremists and terrorists. The Defense Intelligence Agency's contributions to the NSA's watchlist were premised on its requirements for information about a foreign nexus to the US antiwar movement, with names of individuals traveling to Vietnam. There were approximately twenty US persons among the DIA's terms.[104] The watchlist continued to expand in topics for collection.

In the late 1960s, narcotics trafficking became a prominent concern. According to an internal NSA history, "at one point most of the names on the list were individuals suspected of narcotics-related activity."[105] (Between 1970 and 1973, the NSA assisted the Bureau of Narcotics and Dangerous Drugs by monitoring communications between the United States and South America, to collect information about narcotics trafficking.[106])

This watchlisting process became known as MINARET in 1969.[107] According to the Church Committee, "the program applied not only to alleged foreign influences on domestic dissent, but also to American groups and individuals whose activities 'may result in civil disturbances or otherwise subvert the national security of the U.S.'" However, the committee's staff reports also stated that MINARET "established more stringent controls over the information collected on American citizens and groups involved in civil disturbances."[108] Reports were designed to look like they resulted from HUMINT collection, as opposed to being

SIGINT-derived, and the reports listed no originating agency. Establishment of MINARET did not equate to the NSA turning its resources on US persons. Rather, "information produced by the watchlist activity was . . . entirely a byproduct of [the NSA's] foreign intelligence mission. All collection was conducted against international communications with at least one terminal in a foreign country."[109]

The NSA ended the MINARET program in 1973. The director of the NSA, in September of that year, requested that the attorney general authorize retention of all names of the list. The attorney general directed the NSA to stop the project until he had reviewed it. Specifically, the attorney general requested a pause to collection concerning US citizens whose names the FBI and Secret Service had provided, although he noted that "relevant information acquired by [the NSA] in the routine pursuit of the collection of foreign intelligence may continue to be furnished to appropriate government agencies."[110] MINARET never resumed operation.[111]

Although MINARET ended in the 1970s, the type of activity that it represented has continued. The President's Surveillance Program—the NSA's warrantless post-9/11 collection known as STELLAR WIND—provided leads, or "tippers," to FBI field offices. Tippers usually consisted of domestic telephone numbers and internet communications addresses that the NSA had determined were connected to al-Qaeda.[112] In early 2003, the FBI assigned a team of personnel—known as Team 10—to work full-time at the NSA, managing the Bureau's participation in the President's Surveillance Program.[113]

The NSA, following the passage of Section 702 of the Foreign Intelligence Surveillance Amendment Act of 2008, has continued to provide assistance to the FBI. Although the NSA is the lead agency for Section 702 activities, the FBI acquires a part of the information obtained under the auspices of Section 702 PRISM collection.[114] The FBI only receives information associated with "full investigations."[115] According to the FBI's Domestic Investigations and Operations Guide, a full investigation "may be opened to detect, obtain information about, or prevent or protect against federal crimes or threats to the national security or to collect foreign intelligence."[116] The Bureau is also permitted to search 702 data—known colloquially as a "back door search"—for US persons' communications that can be used in criminal proceedings that do not have a foreign intelligence dimension.[117] However, this, in reality, is a very rare occurrence. According to the US intelligence community's 2016 transparency report, there was exactly one instance in which "FBI personnel received and reviewed Section 702–acquired information that FBI identified as concerning a U.S. person in response to a query that was designed to return evidence of a crime unrelated to foreign intelligence."[118]

Alcohol, Tobacco, Firearms, and Explosives

Following the attacks of September 11, the ATF continued to work in the field of counterterrorism. This was certainly not a new mission area for the ATF, which, as of the early 1980s, had established special agent "extremist coordinators" who were responsible for counterterrorist and counterextremist matters on a national scale.[119] The ATF remained part of the Department of the Treasury until 2002, when the Homeland Security Act transferred the ATF to the Department of Justice and formally added "explosives" to its name.[120] The ATF received explicit direction to investigate acts of "domestic terrorism" as part of its move to the Department of Justice.[121] In addition to its explosives and firearms expertise, the ATF brought its authority for tobacco-related crimes to bear in disrupting terrorists' use of bootlegged cigarette–derived financing.[122] According to ATF officials, Hezbollah, Hamas, and al-Qaeda have all used cigarette-related activities.[123]

Competition

Because its mandate overlaps with other agencies' missions, the ATF has repeatedly found itself at odds with other federal law enforcement elements. Historically, this tension has been most apparent in ATF-FBI relations. After 9/11, as multiple agencies found new relevance in counterterrorism work, the ATF-FBI conflict flared. The FBI took umbrage at the ATF's push to become the DoJ's primary responder to all US explosive incidents and coordinate the on-scene investigations of these events. In 2002, an FBI memo denigrated ATF agents as being poorly trained and lacking strategic vision.[124] The two agencies also engaged in a highly publicized disagreement about their competing repositories of bomb data.[125] This tension worsened as the ATF tried to demonstrate the value it brought to the US government's counterterrorism efforts. According to a former ATF supervisor, no one at interagency meetings wanted to hear about the ATF unless the bureau had something related to national security.[126]

Part of the problem is that the two agencies pull threads, from different directions, that unravel the same threats. This is especially clear in the area of counterterrorism, where ATF agents have uncovered foreign terrorists and their supports bootlegging cigarettes to finance their operations.[127] Coordination between the ATF and FBI was so dismal that on one occasion the ATF inadvertently purchased counterfeit cigarettes from the FBI because both agencies were running parallel investigations of tobacco smuggling.[128] The ATF also runs up against the DEA—another agency that focuses on the implements of crime, rather than the threat entities who use these implements in their illicit activities. As part of its defined role in the firearm aspects of counternarcotics investigations, the ATF either invites the DEA to participate in the investigations or turns the case over to the DEA.[129] ATF's responsibilities also overlap with Department of Homeland Security components, which has also led to friction. For instance, Immigration and Customs Enforcement accused the ATF of taking information that Immigration and Customs Enforcement had shared and using it in furtherance of the ATF's own investigations.[130]

Search for a New Mission

The ATF has—after 9/11 and its marginalization, by the FBI, in the counterterrorism space—tried to find an appropriate role. Since 2003, the ATF has focused its efforts on effecting a decrease in violent crime through an emphasis on combating illegal firearms trafficking, explosives, and arson.[131] In its continued search for a mission space, the ATF has wandered into several high-profile scandals that have left overseers—not to mention the public—scratching their collective heads.

Two major initiatives—Operation Wide Receiver, which began in 2006, and Operation Fast and Furious, which began in 2009—allowed for the trafficking of firearms into Mexico. These operations were similar in their ostensible purpose of identifying and ultimately prosecuting organizations engaged in illicit firearms trafficking activities. Unfortunately, the ATF was ill-prepared to run an operation of this scope. The ATF's Tucson, Arizona, office, which was responsible for Operation Wide Receiver, lacked the resources necessary for a case of this scope and at times was unable to conduct or maintain surveillance.[132] This was particularly problematic in the context of an operation that was premised on the physical movement of contraband. Not only was the Tucson office unable to conduct surveillance but also, due to a deficit of Spanish-speaking agents, it was at a disadvantage when monitoring the conversations of the investigation's subjects.[133]

Things, inevitably, got badly out of hand in both of these operations. Wide Receiver resulted in no arrests and the seizure of fewer than a quarter of the more than 400 firearms that the ATF had allowed criminals to obtain.[134] The uncontrolled trafficking in weapons had very real consequences. Following the 2010 murder of a Customs and Border Patrol agent, authorities determined that subjects of Operation Fast and Furious had been the purchasers of weapons subsequently found at the crime scene.[135] Furthermore, a .50 caliber rifle, found at a residence that Joaquín "Chapo" Guzmán had used, was associated with Operation Fast and Furious.[136]

The ATF has also encountered significant difficulties with its post-9/11 undercover operations. One type of operation known as a "storefront" involves law enforcement operation of a fake business or establishment where illicit merchandise is exchanged or services are rendered.[137] In 2014, according to the ATF director at that time, these storefronts are "designed to attract a certain criminal element so that [the ATF] can gather intelligence."[138] Often, these storefronts are wired for video and audio collection. Although the ATF's storefront operations were opportunities to remove guns from the streets, the then–ATF director advised Congress that they were "primarily an information, intelligence gathering technique."[139] However, according to a report by the DoJ's Office of the Inspector General, ATF storefront operations were characterized by "poor management, insufficient training and guidance to agents in the field, and a lax organizational culture that failed to place sufficient emphasis on risk management."[140] As in Operations Wide Receiver and Fast and Furious, the ATF failed to account for what would happen once an illicit transaction had occurred. Agents had no specific strategy about what to do if someone left the storefront with a weapon that the ATF did want the individual to possess. Furthermore, there was no plan to deal with the unintended impact, specifically the creation of market incentives for storefront customers to steal firearms for sale to the ATF's storefront purchasers, which the operation might create.[141]

The ATF also stumbled into a financially questionable venture when, in the mid-2000s, it became a partner in the tobacco business. In 2006, the ATF convinced a small-time tobacco distributor to open a warehouse in Bristol, Virginia; become an informant; and allow the ATF to operate in conjunction with him. It was apparently difficult to distinguish the provenance of profits in this operation, and when the origin of money was unclear, these profits went into a private account that the informant controlled. This fund—outside the reach of congressional scrutiny—became known as a "management account" and underwrote multiple ATF operations.[142] ATF officials would send agents to obtain everything from credit cards to luxury automobiles through this fund, in order to avoid red-tape. (According to a participant in the operation, it acquired so many automobiles that it established a company simply to conduct leasing.[143]) This questionable venture became the national warehouse for all of the ATF's smuggling investigations.[144] However, according to the authorization the ATF received to conduct undercover operations such as this one, proceeds of the operation were supposed to "offset necessary and reasonable expenses incurred in that operation."[145] This was very different from the ATF's use of the tobacco distribution operation as a slush-fund generator for the bureau.

State and Local Agencies After 9/11

Nonfederal agencies have played a significant role in the post-9/11 domestically oriented intelligence architecture. Although often discussed in terms of fusion centers, the value that state and local entities contribute to the identification of information and the disruption of threats is indigenous to these agencies and leveraged by federal partners. It is this paradigm—rather than an imposition of new missions—that makes subfederal entities important partners, and it is these strengths that the federal government should seek to bolster through targeted enhancement of these agencies' capabilities.

The concept of subfederal intelligence predates 9/11 by decades. However, the Office of the Director of National Intelligence has, more recently, drawn attention to their potential for contributing to the collection of intelligence within the domestic setting. According to a 2016 ODNI report on domestic approaches to national intelligence, criminal intelligence units are the principal collectors of this type of intelligence at the state and local law enforcement levels.[146] Individual federal agencies have acknowledged their reliance on subfederal authorities. Then–FBI director James Comey noted, in 2015, that "much of the Bureau's criminal intelligence is derived from state, local and tribal law enforcement partners, who know their communities inside and out."[147] Comey's predecessor, Mueller, as of 2003, stated, in regard to the gang problem, that "on the very basic level, the state police and then most particularly the local police know the individuals. . . . [T]he people to really know the individuals who are participants in these gangs are the local police officers."[148] Similarly, the DEA acknowledged, in 2015, that state and local officers provided expertise—regarding geographical familiarity, businesses and persons involved with trafficking activities, and hierarchical and transactional aspects of local and regional drug trafficking organizations—that was unmatchable at the federal level.[149]

Individual departments, concerned with local manifestations of national-level threats, have taken measures—with varying degrees of success—to counter these threats. As of 2012, the New York Police Department (NYPD) had expanded its existing focus on the core element of al-Qaeda to also include its affiliates, and the homegrown al-Qaeda-inspired threat. The NYPD also looked at the threat from Iran, and from Iran's terrorist proxy Hezbollah.[150] The NYPD has not been alone in developing local solutions to national problems. The Los Angeles Police Department (LAPD), for instance, elevated Iran and its proxies, including Hezbollah, to a tier-one threat.[151]

Prior to 9/11, subfederal entities organically developed early fusion center networks to address issues that crossed jurisdictional lines. Following 9/11, similar expansion occurred. As of 2005, municipal chiefs of police were discussing the formation of a nationwide counterterrorism network that would supplement the flow of information emanating from the FBI and DHS.[152] More recently, the New York Police Department's Strategic Intelligence Unit met—in furtherance of establishing working relationships and facilitating information sharing—with law enforcement counterparts from Buffalo and Albany, New York; Portland and Lewiston, Maine; and Boston, Massachusetts.[153] Networks such as these will continue to emerge if subfederal authorities do not get what they need from the federal government.

The Department of Justice has historically bolstered—and continues to bolster—subfederal agencies' capabilities. This has been especially apparent—sometimes controversially so—in assistance with technical collection, exploitation, and analysis. For instance, the FBI, as of 2014, had trained more than 5,000 state and local police investigators in the analysis of cell-site data.[154] Subfederal agencies have also, in conjunction with the federal government, become participants in the countering of threats operating in the cyber environment. According to a *Wall Street Journal* account, the FBI offered subfederal authorities clearances and training on how to identify hackers in foreign locations.[155] The FBI has encouraged state and local agency-level participation in cyber task forces, and as of January 2015 more than eighty state and local agencies had representation on these task forces.[156]

Furthermore, the US government has provided subfederal agencies with assistance in understanding political dynamics that might lead to local disturbances and acts of terrorism. This predates 9/11 by multiple decades. As of 1973, the US Department of Justice, via its Law Enforcement Assistance Administration and the National Institute of Law Enforcement and Criminal Justice, had provided guidelines for chiefs of police on the prevention and control of collective violence and emphasized the importance of intelligence operations to identify potential urban problems in advance of any actual violence.[157] More recently, the US Department of Justice has provided state and local law enforcement agencies with knowledge of political extremist movements.[158]

However, state and local efforts to identify the potential for disturbances in their areas of responsibility are fraught with political peril. For instance, the NYPD closed down its Zone Assessment Unit and Demographics Unit following discovery that these units had engaged in extensive intelligence-gathering efforts that included the infiltration of Muslim student groups on college campuses as well as gathering information about communities and locations where individuals wearing traditional Islamic garb ate and conversed.[159] Prior to the media's 2014 publicization of the NYPD program, the Los Angeles Police Department had considered instituting a similar initiative. In 2007, the LAPD developed a plan to map the Los Angeles's Muslim population. The department—which had hoped to identify potential hotbeds of extremism—scrapped the plan following a week of protests.[160]

The increasing competency of subfederal agencies to address sophisticated threats suggests an opportunity to reconsider the lines of jurisdictional demarcation—in order to alleviate strains on federal resources—and give subfederal agencies decisive leadership on specific issues. For this approach to be viable there need to be robust and reliable mechanisms for information sharing. At present, information sharing is predominantly oriented toward the counterterrorism mission, primarily through the national network of fusion centers. This approach is too limited in scope, as it addresses only one aspect of how US elements of national power are corroded by threats, and certainly does not facilitate the collection and dissemination of foreign intelligence information present within subfederal agencies' bailiwicks. To formalize the transmission of information, agencies need to work from a common set of intelligence requirements. However, as of 2016, there was no uniform process in place by which federal agencies could share priorities and information requirements with their subfederal counterparts. Furthermore, even if these shared requirements did exist, there is no simple way for subfederal agencies to provide information addressing the requirements to the intelligence community.[161]

The National Security Agency: From SHAMROCK to 702

The presence of infrastructure within the United States that transmits international communications traffic provides an opportunity to collect foreign intelligence that—by a quirk of geography—happens to be accessible on US soil. Although traitorous millennials like Edward Snowden may be shocked to find that the National Security Agency collects intelligence, the reality is that this activity is neither new nor nefarious.

One type of collection activity is epitomized by a program known as SHAMROCK, for which the NSA was responsible until the program's 1975 conclusion. SHAMROCK involved the collection of telegrams, via three international telegraph companies (RCA Global, ITT World Communications, and Western Union International), sent to, from, or through the United States. The program originated, in 1945, with the Army Security Agency; continued under the Armed Forces Security Agency; and ultimately became the responsibility of these agencies' successor, the National Security Agency, in 1952.[162]

Starting in 1939, the NSA's army predecessor began acquiring enciphered Soviet telegrams.[163] According to a declassified NSA in-house history, "since New York was the terminal for the transatlantic cable, Soviet diplomatic traffic was routed through that city. The army arranged with the cable companies to get copies of most of the cables that the Soviets were sending both to and from Washington and, more important, to and from Amtorg [the Soviet government-run trading company]."[164] These telegrams, ciphered with one-time-pads, originated from the Soviet government's commercial presence (Amtorg and the Soviet Government Purchasing Commission), Soviet diplomats, and officers of the Soviet intelligence agencies (KGB, GRU, and Naval GRU). The diplomats (and intelligence officers masquerading as diplomats) operated from the Soviet Union's embassy and consulates. Additionally, Soviet intelligence used the commercial offices located in Washington, DC, New York, and San Francisco.[165] The collection of telegrams continued after the conclusion of World War II and evolved into SHAMROCK. This program was so closely held that no president after Truman knew of its existence until the mid-1970s.[166] The NSA finally ended SHAMROCK when the director of the NSA decided that it had too much flap potential.[167]

A declassified internal history of the NSA discusses a variation of SHAMROCK known as New SHAMROCK. Congressional staffers discovered this program during the US government's scrutiny of its intelligence agencies during the mid-1970s. The NSA history provides limited information, noting that "it had become easier to use wiretaps than to get traffic from cable companies, and NSA was using this technique with increasing frequency."[168] New SHAMROCK began in the 1950s, using means not specifically identified by the NSA history. J. Edgar Hoover, the FBI's director, expressed periodic resistance to activities associated with New SHAMROCK.[169] Ultimately, the new guidelines, imposed by the attorney general in 1974, became impediments to New SHAMROCK, by increasing the length of time necessary for approval and broadening the exposure of these operations to a wider audience across the intelligence community.[170]

Subsequent to the end of SHAMROCK, the NSA was responsible for a program to collect information that passed through internet junctions within the United States. This program, code-named BLARNEY (supposedly in homage to SHAMROCK's Irish appellation), existed prior to 2001 and operated near significant fiber optic landing points in the United States to collect communications traffic with a foreign nexus.[171] Although it exploited more sophisticated technology—fiber optically transmitted communications rather than telegrams—BLARNEY was not conceptually different from SHAMROCK.

After 9/11, the NSA initiated a program, at the request of President George W. Bush, known as STELLAR WIND. Under STELLAR WIND—a highly classified and strictly compartmented program of electronic surveillance within the United States—the NSA attempted to detect communications that would disclose terrorist operatives, terrorist plans, or other information that would enable the disruption of attacks.[172]

STELLAR WIND was not a court-authorized program. Foreign Intelligence Surveillance Act legislation did not catch up with the country's needs until the FISA Amendments Act of 2008, which included a new provision under Section 702.[173] Under Section 702, the government is allowed to conduct "upstream collection," which involves scanning the communications moving across the internet backbone coming into and going out of the United States.[174] The NSA acquires the information from the flow of communications moving between communication service providers.[175] Collection is tied to specific "selectors" associated with designated foreign entities.[176] Additionally, the NSA may use upstream collection to obtain communications that reference email accounts, or other Section 702–targeted identifiers, that are not sent or received by the targets of Section 702.[177]

Implementing Section 702—although the measure can only be used to justify collecting the communications of non-US persons who are "reasonably believed" to be outside the United States—requires the participation of domestic entities. Upstream collection, once authorized by the Foreign Intelligence Surveillance Court (FISC), gathers information with the assistance of the telecommunications providers that control the internet backbone.[178] A second form of collection authorized by Section 702 is known as PRISM. This facet of collection compels assistance, once approved by the FISC, from electronic communications service providers (e.g., an internet service provider), to the NSA. Once the FISC has PRISM collection, the NSA—via the FBI—furnishes the selectors to the provider. The provider must give the government communications sent to or from the selector but is not required to turn over communications that are only about the selector.[179]

According to the ODNI, Section 702 collection has provided a wide variety of foreign intelligence insights. For instance, collection has acquired information about the highest decisionmaking of a Middle Eastern government, which directly informed US engagement with that country.[180] Furthermore, the NSA has used Section 702–authorized collection to develop a body of knowledge about the proliferation of military communications equipment and sanctions evasion activity by a specific country.[181]

The conceptual continuity of collection, from SHAMROCK to 702, illustrates that intelligence collection within the United States is not about spying on Americans but instead is pragmatic exploitation of a home-field advantage to provide US decisionmakers with an informational edge.

Notes

1. *Foreign and Military Intelligence,* book 1, *Final Report of the Select Committee to Study Governmental Operations with Respect to Intelligence Activities,* Senate, S. Doc. 94-755 (1976).

2. Ibid.; *Notification to Victims of Improper Intelligence Agency Activities,* Before a Subcommittee of the Committee on Government Operations, House of Representatives, 94th Cong., 2nd sess. on H.R. 12039, H.R. 13192, and H.R. 169 to amend the Privacy Act of 1974 (1978).

3. *Foreign and Military Intelligence,* book 1.

4. Jeffrey T. Richelson, *The U.S. Intelligence Community,* 7th ed. (New York: Avalon, 2015), p. 22; Mark Riebling, *Wedge: From Pearl Harbor to 9/11—How the Secret War Between the FBI and CIA Has Endangered National Security* (New York: Simon and Schuster, 2010), p. 419; "National Collection Division Inspection Report," https://www.cia.gov/library/readingroom/docs/CIA-RDP88-00428R000200090014-8.pdf.

5. Jeffrey T. Richelson, *The U.S. Intelligence Community,* 6th ed. (Boulder: Westview, 2011), p. 22.

6. Matt Apuzzo and Adam Goldman, *Enemies Within: Inside the NYPD's Secret Spying Unit and Bin Laden's Final Plot Against America* (New York: Simon and Schuster, 2013), p. 30.

7. *Foreign and Military Intelligence,* book 1.

8. "DCS Field Chiefs' Annual Meeting, Central Intelligence Agency, 10 September 1970," https://www.cia.gov/library/readingroom/docs/CIA-RDP78B05703A000300110003-8.pdf.

9. *Foreign and Military Intelligence,* book 1.

10. *National Intelligence Reorganization and Reform Act of 1978,* Before the Select Committee on Intelligence, Senate, 95th Cong. (1978).

11. Henry A. Crumpton, *The Art of Intelligence: Lessons from a Life in the CIA's Clandestine Service* (New York: Penguin, 2012), p. 289; Richelson, *The U.S. Intelligence Community,* 6th ed., p. 21; "Henry A. Crumpton, U.S. Department of State," http://2001-2009.state.gov/outofdate/bios/c/50493.htm.

12. *Notification to Victims of Improper Intelligence Agency Activities.*

13. Richard Helms, *A Look over My Shoulder: A Life in the Central Intelligence Agency* (New York: Random, 2003), p. 288.

14. *Nomination of Richard Helms to Be Ambassador to Iran and CIA International and Domestic Activities,* Before the Committee on Foreign Relations, Senate, 93rd Cong. (1973).

15. *Foreign and Military Intelligence,* book 1.

16. *Department of Defense Appropriations,* Before a Subcommittee of the Committee on Appropriations, House of Representatives, 94th Cong. (1975).

17. *Foreign and Military Intelligence,* book 1.

18. Central Intelligence Agency, *National HUMINT Collection Plan,* June 4, 1982, https://www.cia.gov/library/readingroom/docs/CIA-RDP85-00024R000400310022-9.pdf.

19. Central Intelligence Agency, *Records Control Schedule for the [Redacted]/Retention Schedule for Entertainment Expense Records of the Domestic Contact Service,* July 2, 1971, https://www.cia.gov/library/readingroom/docs/CIA-RDP78-00487A000400020001-7.pdf.

20. Loch Johnson, *America's Secret Power: The CIA in a Democratic Society* (New York: Oxford University Press, 1991), p. 163.

21. *Freedom of Information Reform Act,* Before a Subcommittee of the Committee on Government Operations, House of Representatives, 98th Cong. (1984).

22. *Surveillance Technology: Policy and Implications—An Analysis and Compendium of Materials,* Staff Report of the Subcommittee on Constitutional Rights of the Committee on the Judiciary, Senate, 94th Cong. (1976).

23. Testimony of E. Howard Hunt Accompanied by Randall Coleman.

24. *Surveillance,* Before the Subcommittee on Courts, Civil Liberties, and the Administration of Justice of the Committee on the Judiciary, House of Representatives, 94th Cong., pt. 1 (1975).

25. Riebling, *Wedge,* p. 264.

26. John Prados, *Safe for Democracy: The Secret Wars of the CIA* (Chicago: Ivan R. Dee. 2006), p. 295.

27. *US Intelligence Agencies and Activities: Intelligence Costs and Fiscal Procedures,* Before the Select Committee on Intelligence, House of Representatives, 94th Cong., pt. 1 (1975).

28. *Department of Defense Appropriations,* Before a Subcommittee of the Committee on Appropriations, House of Representatives, 94th Cong. (1975); *National Intelli-*

gence Reorganization and Reform Act, Before the Select Committee on Intelligence, Senate, 95th Cong. (1978).

29. *Department of Defense Appropriations.*

30. *Central Intelligence Agency Exemption in the Privacy Act of 1974,* Before a Subcommittee of the Committee on Government Operations, House of Representatives, 94th Cong. (1975).

31. Richelson, *The U.S. Intelligence Community,* 6th ed., p. 21.

32. *Department of Defense Appropriations.*

33. Apuzzo and Goldman, *Enemies Within,* p. 34.

34. *Foreign and Military Intelligence,* book 1.

35. *National Intelligence Reorganization and Reform Act of 1978,* Before the Select Committee on Intelligence, Senate, 95th Cong. (1978).

36. Richelson. *The U.S. Intelligence Community,* 7th ed., p. 22.

37. Riebling, *Wedge,* p. 348.

38. *Foreign and Military Intelligence,* book 1.

39. *Department of Defense Appropriations.*

40. *Report of Investigation: The Aldrich Ames Espionage Case,* House Permanent Select Committee on Intelligence (1994).

41. *An Assessment of the Aldrich H. Ames Espionage Case and Its Implications for U.S. Intelligence,* Report Prepared by the Staff of the Senate Select Committee on Intelligence, 103rd Cong., S. Doc. 103-90 (1994).

42. *Freedom of Information Act—Appendix,* Before the Subcommittee on the Constitution of the Committee on the Judiciary, Senate, 97th Cong., vol. 2 (1981).

43. *Foreign and Military Intelligence,* book 1.

44. President's Commission on CIA Activities, Deposition of Richard Ober, March 28, 1975.

45. *Foreign and Military Intelligence,* book 1.

46. *Report to the President by the Commission on C.I.A. Activities Within the United States, 1975,* https://www.fordlibrarymuseum.gov/library/document/0005/1561495.pdf.

47. *Supplementary Detailed Staff Reports on Intelligence Activities and the Rights of Americans,* Final Report of the Select Committee to Study Governmental Operations with Respect to Intelligence Activities, 94th Cong., S. Doc. 94-755, book 3 (1976).

48. *Report to the President by the Commission on C.I.A. Activities Within the United States.*

49. *Supplementary Detailed Staff Reports on Intelligence Activities and the Rights of Americans,* book 3.

50. *Report to the President by the Commission on C.I.A. Activities Within the United States.*

51. Richelson, *The U.S. Intelligence Community,* 6th ed., p. 22.

52. Gregory F. Treverton. *Reshaping National Intelligence for Age of Information* (New York: Cambridge University Press, 2003), p. 166.

53. Vernon Loeb, "Gathering Intelligence Nuggets One by One," *Washington Post,* April 19, 1999.

54. Jeff Stein, "CIA Domestic Ops Go Far Beyond Shahzad Probe," *Washington Post,* May 19, 2010, http://voices.washingtonpost.com/spy-talk/2010/05/cia_domestic_ops_go_far_beyond.html.

55. "Survey of the Domestic Collection Division," April 15, 1976, https://www.cia.gov/library/readingroom/docs/CIA-RDP79M00467A000300050015-8.pdf.

56. Crumpton, *The Art of Intelligence.*

57. Greg Miller, "CIA Looks to Los Angeles for Would-Be Iranian Spies, Informants," *Los Angeles Times,* January 15, 2002.

58. Ibid.

59. *Departments of Commerce, Justice, and State, the Judiciary, and Related Agencies Appropriations for 2005,* Before a Committee of the Committee on Appropriations, House of Representatives, 108th Cong., pt. 10 (2004).

60. Statement of Robert S. Mueller III, Director, Federal Bureau of Investigation, to the National Commission on Terrorist Attacks upon the United States, April 14, 2004.

61. *Department of Homeland Security's Budget Submission for Fiscal Year 2005,* Before the Committee on Governmental Affairs, Senate, 108th Cong., S. Doc. 108-555 (2004).

62. Dana Priest, "CIA Is Expanding Domestic Operations: More Offices, More Agents with FBI," *Washington Post,* October 23, 2002.

63. *Departments of Commerce, Justice, and State, the Judiciary, and Related Agencies Appropriations for 2004,* Before a Subcommittee of the Committee on Appropriations, House of Representatives, 108th Cong., pt. 6 (2003).

64. Federal Bureau of Investigation, "FBI Director Mueller Announces Leadership of National Security Branch," August 12, 2005, https://archives.fbi.gov/archives/news/pressrel/press-releases/fbi-announces-leadership-of-national-security-branch.

65. Elsa Walsh, "Learning to Spy," *The New Yorker,* November 8, 2004.

66. 9/11 Review Commission, *The FBI: Protecting the Homeland in the 21st Century* (Washington, DC, 2015), p. 86.

67. Dana Priest, "CIA Plans to Shift Work to Denver," *Washington Post,* May 6, 2005.

68. 9/11 Review Commission, *The FBI,* p. 86.

69. Priest, "CIA Plans to Shift Work to Denver."

70. Richard B. Schmitt and Greg Miller, "FBI in Talks to Extend Reach," *Los Angeles Times,* January 28, 2005.

71. Dana Priest, "FBI Pushes to Expand Domain into CIA's Intelligence Gathering; Common Ground Not Yet Reached on Agency Roles in U.S.," *Washington Post,* February 6, 2005.

72. Schmitt and Miller, "FBI in Talks to Extend Reach."

73. *Commerce, Justice, Science, and Related Agencies Appropriations for 2009,* Before a Subcommittee of the Committee on Appropriations, House of Representatives, 103rd Cong., pt. 1 (2009).

74. Crumpton, *The Art of Intelligence,* p. 295.

75. *How Is America Safer? A Progress Report on the Department of Homeland Security,* Before the Select Committee on Homeland Security, House of Representatives, 108th Cong. (2003).

76. On Charles Allen see https://www.chertoffgroup.com/about-us/our-team/209-charles-allen.

77. *A DHS Intelligence Enterprise: Still Just a Vision or Reality?* Before the Subcommittee on Intelligence, Information Sharing, and Terrorism Risk Assessment of the Committee on Homeland Security, House of Representatives, 111th Cong. (2010) (testimony of Bart Johnson).

78. Government Accountability Office, *Drug Control: Better Coordination with the Department of Homeland Security and an Updated Accountability Framework Can Further Enhance DEA's Efforts to Meet Post 9/11 Responsibilities* (Washington, DC, 2009).

79. *Commerce, Justice, Science, and Related Agencies Appropriations for 2010,* Before a Subcommittee of the Committee on Appropriations, House of Representatives, 111th Cong, pt. 1 (2009).

80. Government Accountability Office, *Drug Control.*

81. *Science, the Departments of State, Justice, and Commerce, and Related Agencies Appropriations for 2007,* Before a Subcommittee of the Committee on Appropriations, House of Representatives, 109th Cong., pt. 2 (2006).

82. *DEA Oversight and Budget Authorization,* Before the Subcommittee on Security and Terrorism of the Committee on the Judiciary, Senate, 98th Cong., S. Doc. 98-794 (1984).

83. *Drug Enforcement Administration's Alleged Connection to the Pan Am Flight 103 Disaster,* Before the Government Information, Justice, and Agriculture Subcommittee of the Committee on Government Operations, House of Representatives, 101st Cong. (1990).

84. Government Accountability Office, *Drug Control.*

85. Ibid.

86. Ginger Thompson, "Mumbai Plotter Says Work for U.S. Drug Agency Provided Cover," *New York Times,* May 26, 2011.

87. *DEA Oversight and Budget Authorization,* Before the Subcommittee on Security and Terrorism of the Committee on the Judiciary, Senate, 97th Cong. (1982).

88. John Shiffman and Kristina Cooke, "Exclusive: U.S. Directors Agents to Cover Up Program Used to Investigate Americans," *Reuters,* August 5, 2013.

89. Brian Fung, "The NSA Is Giving Your Phone Records to the DEA, and DEA Is Covering It Up," *Washington Post,* August 6, 2013.

90. Shiffman and Cooke, "Exclusive: U.S. Directors Agents to Cover Up Program"; Fung, "The NSA Is Giving Your Phone Records."

91. *Science, the Departments of State, Justice, and Commerce, and Related Agencies Appropriations for 2007,* pt. 2.

92. Government Accountability Office, *Drug Control.*

93. Government Accountability Office, *Combating Gangs: Better Coordination and Performance Measurement Would Help Clarify Roles of Federal Agencies and Strengthen Assessment of Efforts* (Washington, DC, 2009).

94. Government Accountability Office, *Drug Control.*

95. Ibid.

96. *Departments of Commerce, Justice, and State, the Judiciary, and Related Agencies Appropriations for 2004,* Before a Subcommittee of the Committee on Appropriations, House of Representatives, 108th Cong., pt. 10 (2003); *Departments of Commerce, Justice, and State, the Judiciary, and Related Agencies Appropriations for 2005,* Before a Subcommittee of the Committee on Appropriations, House of Representatives, 108th Cong., pt. 6 (2004).

97. Government Accountability Office, *Drug Control.*

98. *Reorganization Plan no. 2 of 1973,* Before the Subcommittee on Reorganization, Research, and International Organizations of the Committee on Government Operations, Senate, 93rd Cong., pt. 1 (1973) (statement of Senator Ribicoff).

99. National Security Agency, *American Cryptology During the Cold War,* book 3, *Retrenchment and Reform, 1972–1980* (Washington, DC, 1998), p. 84.

100. Ibid.

101. Ibid., p. 85.

102. *Intelligence Activities: Senate Resolution 21,* Before the Select Committee to Study Governmental Operations with Respect to Intelligence Activities, Senate, 94th Cong., vol. 5 (1976).

103. *Supplementary Detailed Staff Reports on Intelligence Activities and the Rights of Americans,* book 3.

104. *Intelligence Activities: Senate Resolution 21,* vol. 5.

105. National Security Agency, *American Cryptology During the Cold War,* book 3, p. 85.

106. *Intelligence Activities and the Rights of Americans,* Final Report of the Select Committee to Study Governmental Operations with Respect to Intelligence Activities, Senate, 94th Cong., S. Doc. 94-755, book 2 (1976).

107. Center for Cryptologic History, *American Cryptology During the Cold War, 1945–1989* (Washington, DC, 1995).

108. *Intelligence Activities and the Rights of Americans,* book 3.

109. *Intelligence Activities: Senate Resolution 21,* vol. 5.

110. Ibid.

111. Center for Cryptologic History, *American Cryptology During the Cold War.*

112. Inspectors General of the Department of Defense, Department of Justice, Central Intelligence Agency, National Security Agency, and the Office of the Director of National Intelligence, *Report on the President's Surveillance Program,* vol. 1 (2009).

113. Ibid.

114. Privacy and Civil Liberties Oversight Board, *Report on the Surveillance Program Operated Pursuant to Section 702 of the Foreign Intelligence Surveillance Act* (2014).

115. Asha Rangappa, "Don't Fall for the Hype: How the FBI's Use of Section 702 Surveillance Data Really Works," *Just Security,* November 29, 2017, https://www.justsecurity.org/47428/dont-fall-hype-702-fbi-works.

116. Federal Bureau of Investigation, *Domestic Investigations and Operations Guide* (2013).

117. *Section 702 of the Foreign Intelligence Surveillance Act,* Before the Committee on the Judiciary, House of Representatives, 115th Cong. (2017).

118. Office of the Director of National Intelligence, *Statistical Transparency Report Regarding Use of National Security Authorities for Calendar Year 2016.*

119. *Dismantling of the Bureau of Alcohol, Tobacco, and Firearms,* Before the Subcommittee on Crime of the Committee on the Judiciary, House of Representatives, 97th Cong. (1981).

120. Chelsea Parson and Arkadi Gerney, *The Bureau and the Bureau: A Review of the Bureau of Alcohol, Tobacco, Firearms, and Explosives and a Proposal to Merge It with the Federal Bureau of Investigation* (Washington, DC: Center for American Progress, 2015).

121. Jerry Markon, "FBI, ATF Battle for Control of Cases," *Washington Post,* May 10, 2008.

122. William J. Krouse, *The Bureau of Alcohol, Tobacco, Firearms, and Explosives (ATF): Budget and Operations* (Washington, DC: Congressional Research Service, 2008).

123. General Accounting Office, *Terrorist Financing: U.S. Agencies Should Systematically Assess Terrorists' Use of Alternative Financing Mechanisms* (Washington, DC, 2003).

124. Markon, "FBI, ATF Battle for Control of Cases."

125. Department of Justice *Explosives Investigation Coordination Between the Federal Bureau of Investigation and the Bureau of Alcohol, Tobacco, Firearms, and Explosives* (Washington, DC, 2009).

126. Parson and Gerney, *The Bureau and the Bureau.*

127. Krouse, *The Bureau of Alcohol, Tobacco, Firearms and Explosives.*

128. Markon, "FBI, ATF Battle for Control of Cases."

129. Government Accountability Office, *Drug Control.*

130. Government Accountability Office, *Firearms Trafficking: U.S. Efforts to Combat Arms Trafficking to Mexico Face Planning and Coordination Challenges* (Washington, DC, 2009).

131. Government Accountability Office, *Bureau of Alcohol, Tobacco, Firearms, and Explosive: Enhancing Data Collection Could Improve Management of Investigations* (Washington, DC, 2014).

132. Department of Justice, *A Review of ATF's Operation Fast and Furious* (Washington, DC, 2012).

133. Ibid.

134. Ibid.

135. Ibid.

136. Matt Zapotosky, "Rifle at 'El Chapo' Hideout Tied to Flawed ATF Operation 'Fast and Furious,'" *Washington Post,* March 16, 2016.

137. Department of Justice, *A Review of ATF's Undercover Storefront Operations* (Washington, DC, 2016).

138. *Undercover Storefront Operations: Continued Oversight of ATF's Reckless Investigative Techniques,* Before the Committee on Oversight and Government Reform, House of Representatives, 113th Cong. (2014).

139. Ibid.

140. Department of Justice, *A Review of ATF's Undercover Storefront Operations.*

141. Ibid.

142. Matt Apuzzo, "'I Smell Cash': How the A.T.F. Spent Millions Unchecked," *New York Times,* September 8, 2017.

143. Ibid.

144. Ibid.

145. Department of Justice, *Audit of the Bureau of Alcohol, Tobacco, Firearms, and Explosives' Use of Income-Generating, Undercover Operations* (Washington, DC, 2013).

146. Office of the Director of National Intelligence, *Domestic Approach to National Intelligence* (Washington, DC, 2016).

147. Statement of James B. Comey, Director, Federal Bureau of Investigation, Before the House Committee on the Judiciary, House of Representatives, at a Hearing Entitled "Oversight of the Federal Bureau of Investigation," October 22, 2015.

148. *Departments of Commerce, Justice, and State, the Judiciary, and Related Agencies Appropriations for 2004*, pt. 6 (2003).

149. *Commerce, Justice, Science, and Related Agencies Appropriations for 2016*, Before a Subcommittee of the Committee on Appropriations, House of Representatives, 114th Cong., pt. 2B (2015).

150. *Department of Homeland Security: An Assessment of the Department and a Roadmap for Its Future*, Before the Committee on Homeland Security, House of Representatives, 112th Cong. (2012).

151. Ibid.

152. *Federal Bureau of Investigation Oversight*, Before the Committee on the Judiciary, Senate, 109th Cong., S. Doc. 109-763 (2005).

153. Brian Michael Jenkins, *Stray Dogs and Virtual Armies: Radicalization and Recruitment to Jihadist Terrorism in the United States Since 9/11* (Santa Monica: Rand, 2011).

154. Tom Jackman, "Cellphone Evidence Called Into Question," *Washington Post*, June 28, 2014.

155. Danny Yadron, "Grappling with Cybercrime—Police Struggle to Keep Up As Online Cases Grow; FBI Lends a Hand in Utah," *Wall Street Journal*, April 21, 2014.

156. Department of Justice, *Audit of the Federal Bureau of Investigation's Implementation of Its Next Generation Cyber Initiative* (Washington, DC, 2015).

157. *Nationwide Drive Against Law Enforcement Intelligence Operations*, Before the Subcommittee to Investigate the Administration of the Internal Security Act and Other Internal Security Laws of the Committee on the Judiciary, Senate, 94th Cong., pt. 2 (1975).

158. Shawn Reese, *Selected Federal Homeland Security Assistance Programs: A Summary* (Washington, DC: Congressional Research Service, 2008).

159. Matt Apuzzo and Joseph Goldstein, "New York Drops Unit That Spied Among Muslims," *New York Times*, April 16, 2014.

160. Duke Helfand. "A Bridge Between Muslims and the LAPD," *Los Angeles Times*, June 29, 2009; Richard Winton, Teresa Watanabe, and Greg Kirkorian, "Outcry over Muslim Mapping," *Los Angeles Times*, November 10, 2007.

161. Intelligence and National Security Alliance, *Protecting the Homeland: Intelligence Integration 15 Years After 9/11* (Washington, DC, 2016).

162. *Intelligence Activities: Senate Resolution 21*, vol. 5; *Supplementary Detailed Staff Reports on Intelligence Activities and the Rights of Americans*, book 3.

163. John Earl Haynes and Harvey Klehr, *Venona: Decoding Soviet Espionage in America* (New Haven: Yale University Press, 1999), p. 31.

164. Center for Cryptologic History, *American Cryptology During the Cold War*.

165. Haynes and Klehr, *Venona*, p. 32.

166. *Intelligence Activities: Senate Resolution 21*, vol. 5.

167. National Security Agency, *American Cryptology During the Cold War, 1945–1989*, book 3, *Retrenchment and Reform, 1972–1980* (Ft. Meade, MD: 1995).

168. Ibid.

169. Ibid.

170. Ibid.

171. Siobhan Gorman and Jenifer Valentino-DeVries, "NSA Reaches Deep into U.S. to Spy on Net—Fresh Details Show Programs Cover 75 % of Nation's Traffic; Can Share Emails," *Wall Street Journal*, August 21, 2013.

172. "Memorandum for the Attorney General Re: Review of the Legality of the STEL-LAR WIND Program," May 6, 2004 (declassified).

173. Office of the Director of National Intelligence, "The FISA Amendments Act: Q&A," https://www.dni.gov/files/icotr/FISA%20Amendments%20Act%20QA%20for%20Publication.pdf.

174. *Section 702 of the Foreign Intelligence Surveillance Act,* Before the Committee on the Judiciary, House of Representatives, 115th Cong. (2017).

175. Privacy and Civil Liberties Oversight Board, *Report on the Surveillance Program Operated Pursuant to Section 702 of the Foreign Intelligence Surveillance Act* (2014).

176. *Section 702 of the Foreign Intelligence Surveillance Act.*

177. Department of Justice, *A Review of the Federal Bureau of Investigation's Activities Under Section 702 of the Foreign Intelligence Surveillance Act Amendments Act of 2008* (Washington, DC, 2012) (re-release).

178. Privacy and Civil Liberties Oversight Board, *Report on the Surveillance Program Operated Pursuant to Section 702 of the Foreign Intelligence Surveillance Act.*

179. Ibid.

180. Office of the Director of National Intelligence, "The FISA Amendments Act: Q&A."

181. Ibid.

10

Federally Driven Fusion

Following 9/11, the federal government, in response to significant criticism, placed newfound emphasis on information sharing. The Intelligence Reform and Terrorism Prevention Act of 2004 enshrined the concept in statute by creating the National Counterterrorism Center as well as a National Counterproliferation Center (NCPC). Additionally, the IRTPA moved the existing National Counterintelligence Executive (now known as the National Counterintelligence and Security Center) under the purview of the director of national intelligence. Finally, the legislation provided an open door to the creation of future centers, similar in concept to the NCTC, to address other intelligence priorities.[1] Exercising this option, the ODNI created one new entity—the Cyber Threat Intelligence Integration Center—in 2015.[2]

Fusion, however, has been counterterrorism-heavy. The NCTC, for instance is composed of no fewer than eleven directorates and offices and was, as of 2011, staffed by more than 500 personnel from more than sixteen departments and agencies.[3] In comparison, intelligence scholar Gregory Treverton has pointed out that the NCPC was "structured very differently from NCTC" in that it "will be small and focused on assessing collection and analysis. Planning and operations will be left to wider interagency groupings."[4] Similarly, by its own description, the Cyber Threat Intelligence Integration Center is "a small, multiagency center."[5]

The Terrorism Threat Integration Center and National Counterterrorism Center

The basis for the National Counterterrorism Center, known as the Terrorist Threat Integration Center, predates the IRTPA. In his 2003 State of the

Union address, President George W. Bush announced that he would instruct the heads of the FBI, CIA, and DHS, and the Department of Defense, to develop the TTIC as a mechanism to merge and analyze all threat information in a single location. The TTIC had the primary responsibility for terrorism analysis, with the exception of purely domestic terrorism.[6] In May 2003, the DHS, FBI, CIA, DoD, and State Department officially established the TTIC to assess terrorism-related intelligence collected both domestically and abroad.[7] The TTIC's significant interagency partners included the FBI's Counterterrorism Division and the CIA's Counterterrorism Center—both of which the TTIC was envisioned as eventually encompassing—as well as the DHS's Information Analysis and Infrastructure Protection Directorate and the Defense Intelligence Agency's Joint Intelligence Task Force–Counterterrorism.[8] The TTIC did not have any operational authority but did have the authority to task collection and analysis from intelligence community member agencies.[9]

The creation of the TTIC kicked the original mission of the IAIP out from under the DHS. The TTIC paralleled and arguably usurped the IAIP's intended role. Not only did its creation throw the purpose of the DHS into question, but its creation also dissuaded other agencies from cooperating with the DHS. Agencies that had committed to providing the DHS with resources reversed course in an effort to preserve those resources.[10] Instead of serving as the hub for interagency counterterrorism analysis, the IAIP detailed personnel, from its Information Analysis Unit, to the TTIC to participate in the processing and analysis of terrorist threat–related information and ensuring that TTIC products reached appropriate DHS headquarter elements as well as the appropriate state, local, and private-sector entities.[11] These IAIP analysts also served as the conduits through which DHS information contributed to the TTIC's work.[12]

The IRTPA created the National Counterterrorism Center, the successor to the TTIC, in 2004 (see Figure 10.1). The NCTC's foundation is in the strategic work of integrating foreign and domestic intelligence for the US government as a whole. It conducts strategic planning—which transcends individual agencies' parochial perspectives—and translates policy direction into coordinated counterterrorism activities.[13]

In addition to these strategic functions, the NCTC conducts more tactically oriented analysis, through its Pursuit Group. The NCTC established the Pursuit Group in January 2010 to develop leads and focus exclusively on information that could lead to the discovery of threats against the domestic environment or US interests abroad. The pursuit

Figure 10.1 Organization of the National Counterterrorism Center

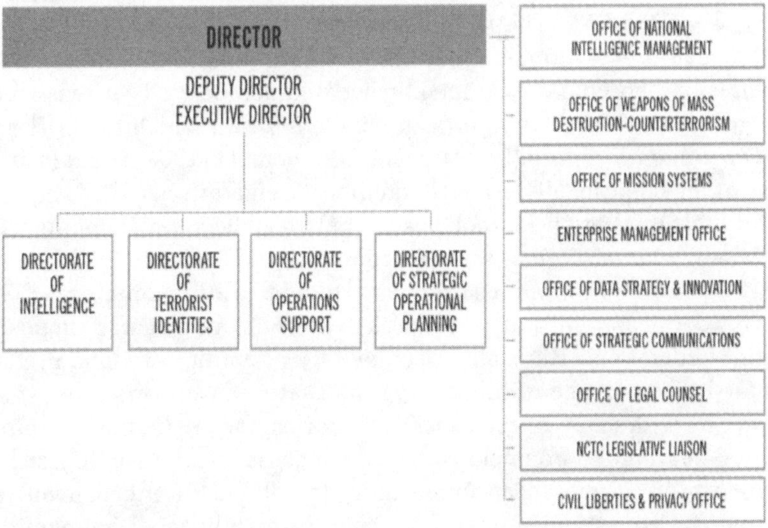

Source: National Counterterrorism Center, *Today's NCTC* (McLean, VA, 2017).

concept originated with then–NCTC director Michael Leiter's realization that, incredibly, after the breakdowns in information sharing that the 9/11 Commission had identified, there was still no single entity within the US intelligence community that had the sole responsibility for detecting and piecing together disparate threat information. The NCTC established pursuit teams to map terrorist networks and track threats in a way that bridges intelligence agencies.[14]

The Pursuit Group consists of co-located analysts from across the intelligence community who possess access to a wide variety of data and who examine nonobvious and unresolved connections between terrorism cases. The group's work impacts the domestic setting in the form of investigative leads, collection requirements, and potential source candidates that it provides to agencies including the FBI and DHS.[15]

Director of National Intelligence–Driven Fusion Efforts

The Intelligence Reform and Terrorism Prevention Act of 2004 created a director of national intelligence (DNI). Leadership of the intelligence community had previously been the bailiwick of the director of central intelligence (DCI), who served as the head of both the intelligence community and the CIA. The DNI concept was not a new one when it was included as a provision of the IRTPA. Instead, it dated to at least 1980, when the proposed National Intelligence Act incorporated a provision to create this position.[16] A significant challenge with which the DNI has had to contend, especially in terms of the homeland, is the extensiveness of the domestically oriented intelligence enterprise, specifically the reality that this enterprise includes not only members of the intelligence community but also other federal and nonfederal agencies.

Several DNI initiatives are meant to address this deficiency. The IRTPA defined an information-sharing environment that was supposed to link federal entities; state, local, and tribal entities; and the private sector in furtherance of facilitating the sharing of terrorism information.[17] As with many of the post-9/11 reforms, the creation of an information-sharing environment reflected concerns about a single issue—terrorism—and missed an opportunity to establish a mechanism for developing and maintaining a comprehensive intelligence picture of the threats and opportunities present within the domestic environment. In June 2005, the White House made the program manager for the information-sharing environment part of the ODNI.[18] Furthermore, the DNI established a national intelligence manager for the Western Hemisphere and the homeland. National intelligence managers—which the ODNI established as part of a 2010 reorganization—serve as "the principal substantive advisors on all or specified aspects of intelligence related to designated countries, regions, topics, or functional areas."[19] Additionally, the ODNI Partner Engagement office reaches beyond to formal intelligence community, in order to facilitate integration between the intelligence community and other federal, state, local, and tribal partners.[20] Finally, the ODNI's National Intelligence Coordination Center, established in 2007, is a mechanism for strategic management of collection across defense, foreign, and domestic realms.[21] The center provides another venue for the incorporation of the domestic environment into an overarching intelligence picture.

The ODNI has also implemented several policies that incorporate the homeland into the broader intelligence picture. For instance, the Unifying Intelligence Strategy for the Western Hemisphere integrates the intelligence community's efforts, including those in the US domestic setting, and provides "opportunities and priorities for intelligence integration in support of [intelligence community] and [federal, state, local, tribal, and territorial] partners" where foreign intelligence has a nexus to these partners' activities.[22] Furthermore, as of 2016, the ODNI had established a Homeland Threat Framework, which provided a basis by which intelligence community agencies could identify and prioritize threats, relevant collection requirements, and analytic functions.[23]

DNI Domestic Representative Program

Unlike the DCI, who also controlled the CIA's resources, the DNI—which is not an operational entity—has had to work through intelligence community members to advance operational objectives. This has, on occasion, sparked controversy. In May 2009, then-DNI Dennis Blair issued a directive that—contrary to tradition—allowed the DNI to select someone other than a CIA official to serve as the DNI's representative to a foreign government or international organization.[24] The DNI has also attempted to establish similar representatives within the domestic setting. As of 2009, the DNI had launched a pilot program by which the heads of four FBI field offices would serve as DNI representatives.[25] With the memorandum of agreement between the DNI and the director of the FBI titled "Domestic Director of National Intelligence Representative Program," as well as Intelligence Community Directive 402, issued in 2012, which established intelligence community representatives, the Domestic Director of National Intelligence Representative Program (DDNIR) expanded to twelve Bureau field offices.[26] The inspectors general of the intelligence community, the DHS, and the DoJ subsequently suggested that the overly broad geographic regions had hindered the program's development.[27]

However, there is not unanimous belief that the FBI should have sole responsibility for enacting the DDNIR program. As noted by Intelligence Community Directive 402, "representatives shall take care to distinguish their responsibilities as DNI representatives from their responsibilities in their parent organization."[28] The heads of FBI divisions, which serve as the DNI domestic representatives, are, by definition, in charge of Bureau resources and consequently, despite their best intents, may conflate their responsibilities to the intelligence community and the FBI. A 2015 report from the industry group Business Executives for National Security suggested that the DNI domestic representatives "should be selected from the agency most appropriate to the threat matrix in the Domestic Representative's area of responsibility."[29]

This approach would open the door for other members of the intelligence community—including the Department of Homeland Security[30] and the Drug Enforcement Administration—to take the lead domestic coordination of intelligence community entities.

The DDNIR program, regardless of its leadership, focuses on the coordination of formal intelligence community members' activities within the domestic setting. Specifically, the DDNIR is responsible for ensuring that intelligence community elements are acting in an integrated community, unified behind a common purpose, and pursuing shared objectives.[31] Through quarterly meetings, the DDNIR program focuses on a specific threat or issue of interest to the region. However, according to the intelligence community, the DHS, and DoJ inspectors general, the program lacks in-depth guidance and a well-defined strategy for implementation.[32] This makes it incumbent on the Bureau to flesh out the program. In 2009, Congress indicated concern that FBI field offices might not be sufficiently familiar with national intelligence priorities.[33] Since then, the Bureau has adopted the Threat Review and Prioritization process, rather than the NIPF, as its rubric for allocating resources, which makes Congress's question even more relevant in 2018 than when it was originally asked. Congress also indicated skepticism that the Bureau's officials were "acquainted sufficiently with the capabilities and missions of the [intelligence community] elements in their area to ensure that it is an integrated community."[34] Other participating intelligence community members are not well-positioned to pick up the slack and provide a structure in lieu of strong leadership, since, according to the intelligence community, the DHS, and FBI inspectors general, the DDNIR program objectives have not been clearly communicated to representatives of intelligence community members.[35]

Whether the FBI can conceptualize and manage overarching intelligence issues—of which a reactive law enforcement/threat-oriented approach is a subset—to effectively implement the DDNIR program has yet to be demonstrated. The Bureau has justified its leadership of the DNI domestic representative program with an approach to intelligence that emphasizes reactive functions. According to the FBI, in 2009 each of the four original offices—Los Angeles, New York, Chicago, and Washington, D.C.—selected for participation in the DDNIR program had "a large and strong Joint Terrorism Task Force . . . and a Counterintelligence Working Group."[36] The Bureau continued to emphasize this limited interpretation of intelligence work by stating that all assistant directors in charge (the heads of the FBI's largest field offices) and special agents in charge (who lead the rest of the FBI's offices) were "ultimately responsible for the myriad counterterrorism, counterintelligence, cyber, and weapons of mass destruction operations in their areas of responsibility."[37] This conceptualization of intelligence does not account for systematic, proactive exploitation of opportunities to obtain information that will provide policymakers with a decision advantage. Instead, the FBI's explanation remains strictly focused on the warning aspects of intelligence and the facilitation of tactical disruptions against threats, whether state (e.g., spies) or nonstate (e.g., terrorists and other criminals).

The DDNIR program does not resolve problems of stovepiping and disjointedness. As the FBI described, in 2015, "FBI senior-level field executives in 12 geographic locations are serving as DNI representatives throughout the United States."[38] The subdivision of the United States along these geographically arbitrary lines has already proven problematic for the Bureau's ability to operate as a coherent corporate entity, and introducing this shortcoming into the DNI's effort to establish an integrated intelligence enterprises simply creates additional potential points of failure, rather than improving seamless continuity. Another point of disjunction that the DDNIR program exacerbates is the one between the formal intelligence community and the non–intelligence community contributors to the domestically oriented intelligence enterprise. Absent from the 2011 memorandum establishing the DDNIR program is guidance on the inclusion of non–intelligence community members and local entities into the initiative.[39] This leaves the three intelligence community members with a significant domestic presence—the FBI, DHS, and DEA—to serve as the hinges that join the intelligence community with the broader domestically oriented intelligence enterprise.

NCTC Domestic Representative Program

Although it is global in coverage, the National Counterterrorism Center has also established a domestic representative program. This initiative, which exists as a memorandum of understanding with the FBI, has put representatives at eleven locations throughout the United States.[40] The program is further linked to the Bureau by the fact that representatives typically sit in FBI spaces. Additionally, NCTC representatives attend FBI-run DDNIR meetings. These individuals serve as issue-specific liaisons for the director of the NCTC with regional intelligence community agencies as well as other federal, state, and local-level counterterrorism officials. NCTC domestic representatives' primary responsibilities include the provision of counterterrorism-related intelligence support to regional customers. This support entails the facilitation of collaboration that contributes to targeting, collection, processing, and reporting of targets. However, according to the inspector generals of the intelligence community, DHS, and DoJ, NCTC representatives have struggled to provide sufficient coverage of their regions.[41]

ODNI and the Interagency Threat Assessment and Coordination Group

The counterterrorism focus of reforms in the decade following the September 11 attacks had a significant impact on the development of integration efforts. In 2007, the DHS's OI&A, in conjunction with the FBI, established the Interagency Threat Assessment and Coordination Group (ITACG), as part of the National Counterterrorism Center.[42] The program manager for the information-sharing environment in 2006 recommended the creation of the ITACG.[43] The 9/11 Commission Act statutorily mandated the creation of this body and designated it as the federal agency responsible for facilitating the flow of finished intelligence products to state and local homeland security entities.[44] The ITACG consists of two components: the ITACG Advisory Council, which sets policy and develops processes for the integration, analysis, and dissemination of federally coordinated information; and the ITACG Detail, which comprises state, local, and tribal officers and intelligence analysts who work alongside federal personnel at the NCTC. The ITACG Detail is managed by a senior DHS intelligence officer.[45]

Facilitating a flow of information between federal and subfederal collectors and analysts is the ITACG's primary function. Through the ITACG, National Counterterrorism Center analysts gain knowledge of the information that state, local, tribal, and private-sector entities need. By reviewing hundreds of highly classified intelligence reports on a daily basis, ITACG personnel determine what should be enhanced or sanitized to assist subfederal agencies.[46] The ITACG then assists those analysts in preparing products at the lowest possible level of classification, in order to disseminate them to relevant customers.[47] However, the ITACG has not been met with unanimous praise. According to one senior police official, the ITACG "is limited to editing intelligence and returning those products to originating agencies where the information may or may not reach state and local law enforcement personnel."[48]

The information flow tends to be one-way. While subfederal entities gain access to intelligence community products, the federal government does not get access, through the ITACG, to state and local information. Instead, according to a 2016 report by the Intelligence and National Security Alliance (INSA), there is no uniform process for federal agencies to provide subfederal agencies with guidance about national priorities and information requirements.[49] This is not for a lack of trying. As early as 2005, the FBI, in conjunction with the Global Intelligence Working Group Requirements Subcommittee, attempted to develop a standing set of intelligence requirements—covering national security and criminal topics—for collectors including state, local, and tribal law enforcement agencies.[50] However, even if a standardized requirements formulation and distribution process existed, the INSA noted that, as of 2016, no simple mechanism—by which subfederal entities could provide information in response to requirements—existed.[51] The federal/subfederal intelligence cycle, therefore, remains incomplete.

The Joint Counterterrorism Assessment Team (JCAT) fills several of the functions previously conducted by the ITACG. For instance, JCAT fellows are state, local, tribal, and territorial first responders and public safety professionals who work with NCTC, DHS, and FBI intelligence analysts.[52] JCAT enhances information sharing between federal and subfederal agencies through a variety of specialized, downgraded products that can be shared with a wide audience.[53] In addition to simply facilitating the release of information, JCAT produces relevant, federally coordinated threat information on significant international terrorism issues that have the potential to impact US public safety at the local or regional levels.[54]

In the absence of an ITACG/JCAT feedback loop to drive collection by subfederal entities, there are several routes, through the FBI and DHS, that could facilitate the process of eliciting, as well as providing, information. According to Department of Justice guidance for state, local, and tribal law enforcement agencies, "intelligence information needs" are "questions expressed by customers of the FBI and other intelligence producers, the answers to which support law enforcement functions."[55] Bureau participation in the national requirements process provides a channel for these subfederal needs to inform national-level requirements, since the FBI, as a member of the intelligence community, has a responsibility to "represent customer priorities in the DNI's NIPF process."[56] Therefore, the FBI could bridge the gap between the subfederal entities that have an intelligence component, and the formulation of requirements against which intelligence community entities and other collectors could develop information. Similarly, the DHS has assisted fusion centers in developing a national set of state and local fusion center priority information needs that articulate requirements.[57] The DHS has used the priority information needs to expand analytic exchanges between fusion centers and to drive OI&A production planning.[58] The concept integrates the needs of subfederal entities into the federal intelligence enterprise.

FBI Engagement of Federal and Subfederal Entities

The FBI has a long history of working with federal and subfederal partners. After 9/11 it added a new entity—the Office of Law Enforcement Coordination (OLEC)—to facilitate coordination. OLEC—located within the Criminal, Cyber Response, and Services Branch—entered existence in April 2002 and was intended to ensure that relevant intelligence reached appropriate state and local law enforcement authorities.[59] The functions of this office would end up overlapping with the fusion center network for which the DHS eventually assumed responsibility. A new FBI Office of Partner Engagement, within the Bureau's Intelligence Branch, assumed OLEC's resources and responsibilities and also handled programs to engage a wider variety of entities, ranging from the US intelligence community (via the DDNIR program) to public and private partners, as well as law enforcement (through fusion centers), with the purpose of enhancing "the FBI's capabilities in the domestic architecture for national intelligence."[60]

Issue-Specific FBI Initiatives

While the FBI facilitates overall engagement through the Office of Partner Engagement, it also has a significant level of participation and leadership in multiple issue-oriented bodies. These include the Terrorist Screening Center as well as the National Gang Intelligence Center.

National Joint Terrorism Task Force

The FBI began establishing field-based Joint Terrorism Task Forces in 1980. However, it was only in 2002 that the FBI created the National

Joint Terrorism Task Force (NJTTF), which consists of more than forty government agencies and critical-industry representatives, located at the National Counterterrorism Center.[61] The NJTTF differs from the operational, field-based JTTFs in that its function is to provide "administrative, logistical and training support to the JTTFs"; coordinate "special information and intelligence gathering initiatives assigned from FBI headquarters"; and produce intelligence analysis.[62]

Although field-based JTTFs became highly visible parts of the domestically oriented intelligence enterprise in the post-9/11 years, their origin predates 9/11 by two decades. In 1980, the FBI's New York field office established the first JTTF, modeled on a bank robbery task force that the field office and the New York Police Department had created in 1979.[63] The New York's JTTF became the model—including the deputizing of nonfederal authorities so that they could pursue leads that would otherwise be beyond their jurisdiction—for future JTTFs.[64] The FBI established JTTFs on a piecemeal basis, in response to specific terrorism issues within offices' areas of responsibility. For instance, the New York JTTF focused on investigating the October 1981 Brinks armored truck robbery in Nanuet, New York.[65] The Chicago Terrorism Task Force was occupied with the criminal activity of the Armed Forces of National Liberation (FALN), a terrorist group trying to bomb its way toward Puerto Rican independence.[66] However, the FBI only expanded the JTTF concept to all fifty-six field offices after 9/11. The FBI extended the reach of the JTTF concept by establishing JTTF annexes at selected resident agency (satellite) offices.[67] By 2015, there were FBI JTTFs in 104 cities nationwide.[68]

JTTFs are an essential link between the domestic and foreign intelligence pictures. Affirming the two domains' inextricable relationship, the CIA had four managers, twenty-five analysts, and thirty full-time and six part-time officers assigned to JTTFs nationally as of 2003.[69] By 2011, the original New York JTTF included representatives from forty-four different agencies including federal components (CIA, NSA, ATF, DHS, DIA, the State Department's Diplomatic Security Service, the US Park Police, and the US Marshals Service) as well as state and local components.[70] In addition to providing a venue for the FBI to draw on federal, state, and local partners' resources, JTTFs also provide participant entities, including local police services, access to information from the intelligence community. For instance, the NYPD, through its membership on the JTTF, gained access to CIA and NSA information, which the NYPD did not have, prior to 9/11.[71]

However, the JTTF concept is problematic—and offers a false assurance of fusion—in the context of intelligence reform. JTTFs have become a significant mechanism for information sharing but—consistent with other post 9/11 developments—they are premised on the single issue of terrorism. This is not a viable, long-term concept on which to build an intelligence architecture that must address a multitude of state and nonstate actor issues. JTTFs will be less effective venues for interagency collaboration on nonterrorism threats or on opportunities for positive intelligence collection. Therefore, although JTTFs are useful implements in the context of counterterrorism, the United States should not rely on them to serve as points of connectivity for the domestically oriented intelligence enterprise.

Furthermore, JTTFs, as they exist, may not be sufficient for their current purpose. The DoJ's Office of the Inspector General determined that the Bureau lacked signed memorandums of understanding that "define the roles, responsibilities, information sharing protocols, and length of commitment" with all agencies on the JTTFs, as well as participants in other FBI-run interagency projects.[72] Furthermore, JTTFs have experienced frequent turnovers in leadership.[73] Churning leadership can create a lack of continuity and can corrode the consistency of JTTF operations. Additionally, according to the DoJ inspector general, the JTTFs, despite their eponymous purpose, have lacked counterterrorism expertise.[74] These entrenched issues are problematic not only for the JTTFs and their missions but also for the broader domestically oriented intelligence enterprise, since the JTTFs are looked to as models for other information-sharing efforts such as the Bureau's Cyber Task Forces.[75] By using the wrong template to inform future efforts, the FBI will perpetuate existing errors.

Terrorist Screening Center

In December 2003, the FBI, in conjunction with the DHS, the State Department, and members of the US intelligence community, established the Terrorist Screening Center (TSC).[76] The TSC did not arise *sui generis* from the FBI but instead was established under the Bureau's auspices in response to Homeland Security Presidential Directive 6. The TSC assumed responsibility for preexisting initiatives—the no-fly and selectee lists—that the Federal Aviation Administration, and subsequently the Transportation Security Administration, had maintained.[77] An interagency memorandum of understanding stipulated that the TSC director would report to the attorney general, via the FBI—which was designated as the TSC's lead agency—and that the TSC principal deputy would be a DHS employee.[78] Although the DHS is a significant participant in the TSC, the center's creation, like that of the TTIC before it, further stunted the DHS's development as an agency. For instance, a report by the US House of Representatives Committee on Appropriations assessed that the "IAIP has seen the scope of its national intelligence mission reduced."[79]

The TSC's primary function is to maintain the Terrorist Screening Database. Commonly known as the "Terrorist Watchlist," according to the 2014 congressional testimony of a TSC director the purpose of the Terrorist Screening Database was to rectify the existence of twelve separate watchlists that had developed based on individual agencies' missions, as well as their legal, cultural, and information technology.[80] Once in the Terrorist Screening Database, watchlist information—tailored to agencies' specific missions—is sent "downstream" to populate six major US government systems: the Department of State's Consular Lookout and Support System for passport and visa screening; the Department of Homeland Security's TECS system for border and port-of-entry screening; the DHS Secure Flight System for air passenger screening by the Transportation Security Administration; the DHS Transportation Vetting System for credentialing transportation and critical infrastructure workers; the Department of Defense, for base access and screening; and the FBI's National Crime and Information Center's Known or Suspected Terrorist File (formerly known as the Violent Gang/Terrorist Organization File) for domestic law enforcement screening. The TSC also notifies fusion centers when encounters with watchlisted individuals occur within a fusion center's area of responsibility, or when encounters occur with cases that originated from a fusion center's area of responsibility.

When an agency identifies a name that appears to be a match against Terrorist Screening Database information, it calls the TSC twenty-four-hour call center for assistance in confirming the subject's identity. If the subject is positively identified as a watchlist hit or the match is inconclusive, the TSC forwards the call to the FBI's Terrorist Screening Operations Unit—the FBI's twenty-four-hour global command center for terrorism prevention operations. The TSC passes the information on matches to the FBI's Counterterrorism Watch, which coordinates the operational response through the local Joint Terrorism Task Force. Each record within the consolidated watchlist database is designed to contain information about the law enforcement action to be taken when encountering an individual on the watchlist.

The Terrorist Screening Database supports not only federal agencies but also subfederal entities. As of 2008, the TSC had conducted outreach to state and local fusion centers to provide those institutions with an aggregate picture of positive TSC hits with a nexus to those fusion centers' areas of responsibility.[81] More recently, in 2014, the director of the TSC explained to Congress that the Terrorist Screening Database did not include substantive derogatory information or classified national security information, in order to facilitate information sharing with state and local law enforcement officers.[82]

Interestingly, reflecting the reality that national security and counterterrorism are not synonymous, the TSC has recently taken on a new intelligence task. As of 2016, the FBI was developing a consolidated "Transnational Organized Crime Watchlist" within the TSC. This new initiative resulted from a 2014 National Security Council direction for the TSC to conduct a pilot project demonstrating the value associated with watchlisting and screening these criminal actors. The TSC subsequently determined that it would transition to a broader national security screening mission for a whole-of-government approach.[83]

The TSC's experience with the need for diversification of its mission is not isolated. Many fusion centers, for which the DHS is the primary federal point of contact, have evolved from a counterterrorism-centric post-9/11 identity to addressing a wider variety of threats. Limited resources, coupled with an expansive array of national security threats and opportunities, make a counterterrorism-centric architecture untenable in the long term.

National Gang Intelligence Center

Gangs are a significant threat to national security in their degradation of an area's economic livelihood, their drain on security resources, and the image of lawlessness they create that damages the image of the United States abroad. The FBI has had a National Gang Strategy since the 1990s.[84] However, it was not until after 9/11—when "fusion" and "information sharing" were the decade's national security buzzwords (and when the FBI was looking to leverage its partners' capabilities to keep pace with an overly broad set of missions)—that the Bureau became the leader of a new National Gang Intelligence Center (NGIC).

The NGIC took form in 2006 with the mission of collection, analysis, and dissemination of information—from multiple federal, state, and local law enforcement, prosecutorial, and corrections agencies—about gang activities.[85] It focuses on gangs that operate on regional and national levels and that demonstrate criminal connectivity.[86] As of 2010, the FBI had introduced a transnational element, by co-locating its MS-13 National Gang Task Force with the NGIC.[87]

Although the NGIC is FBI-led, it is an interagency entity, drawing its work force of intelligence analysts from federal, state, and local law enforcement.[88] The NGIC's "director" position is filled by an FBI special agent who reports to the Bureau's Gang and Criminal Enterprise Section. There are two "deputy director" positions, one of which is filled by an FBI employee and the other, on a rotational basis, by a participant agency.[89]

Despite its ostensibly interagency nature, the NGIC has drawn criticism for its perceived parochialism. Law enforcement personnel have suggested that it is FBI-centric in the analysis it provides and the products it develops. This failure to serve non-FBI customers is suggested by the NGIC's limited customer base. As of 2009, despite having been in existence for three years, it had received only 213 requests for assistance from law enforcement agencies (an average of six requests per month). Furthermore, agencies that regularly deal with gang issues, such as the Bureau of Alcohol, Tobacco, Firearms, and Explosives and the US Marshals Service, "rarely used NGIC for gang-related intelligence products and services," according to the DoJ's inspector general.[90]

Although the NGIC emphasized the FBI's own needs, the Bureau, in its 2013 budget, proposed eliminating the NGIC, which was at that point staffed by one special agent and thirteen intelligence analysts.[91] Mueller's solution to eliminating the NGIC would be to have the FBI's Directorate of Intelligence develop the National Gang Threat Assessment by combining information from Bureau field offices and to reach out to other agencies in order to incorporate additional intelligence information.[92] This was consistent with Mueller's philosophy of intelligence—which amounted to the aggregation of information churned up, in a one-off manner, during the course of investigations—rather than a continuous, requirements-driven approach, which an entity such as the NGIC could facilitate.

The case of the NGIC is a good example of an institution that could benefit from different management. Other agencies, including the ATF and the US Marshals Service, demonstrated an interest in the NGIC's potential, and the ATF would be a logical federal facilitator for NGIC functions. A subfederally driven approach would be another option for managing the NGIC. Pre-9/11 fusion centers were state and local affairs—albeit ones that received federal assistance—that focused on issues that cut across their respective areas of responsibility. The state, tribal, and correctional law enforcement customers of the NGIC's online platform could constitute an information-sharing network capable of assuming responsibility for coordinating the distribution of gang-related information both laterally and vertically. Finally, a hybrid federal/sub-federal approach would follow the path of other fusion centers and become part of the national network for which the DHS currently serves as the point of federal connectivity.

National Cyber Investigative Joint Task Force

The FBI established the National Cyber Investigative Joint Task Force in 2007. A predecessor to the NCIJTF, the Cyber Investigative Joint Task Force, began operating in 2005 as a partnership between the FBI and the Department of Defense's Cyber Crime Center. This limited task force focused on cyber intrusions with national security implications. By presidential directive, issued in early 2008, the Bureau serves as the lead agency for the NCIJTF, and the NCIJTF serves as the focal point for all government agency coordination, integration, and information sharing related to domestic cyber threat investigations. In an early formation, the NCJITF consisted of two complementary components: the Information Operations Group, which provided centralized coordination for operational initiatives and facilitated deconfliction and collaboration on investigations; and the Analytical Group, which was supposed to synthesize a common operating picture of hostile intrusion-related activity and to review all-source data.[93]

The Bureau has sought to strengthen and solidify the NCIJTF as the center for coordinating cyber threat investigation and disruption options. In 2012, the FBI began a process of formally separating the NCIJTF from the Bureau's Cyber Division.[94] Furthermore, the FBI has incorporated representatives from other agencies into senior NCIJTF leadership positions.[95] As of 2015, the NCIJTF was the venue for deconfliction on cyber investigations among approximately twenty federal agencies. Participants include the National Security Agency, Central Intelligence Agency, Department of Homeland Security (including the Secret Service), and US Cyber Command.[96] The NCIJTF uses threat focus cells—teams of personnel working on a specific set of cyber intrusions that share a common actor, method, or target—to better analyze intrusions and attacks against US infrastructure. (NCIJTF members who were interviewed for a Department of Justice inspector general report indicated that the majority of NCIJTF information sharing occurs during meetings of threat focus cells.)

Multiple US government agencies have a piece of the cybersecurity mission. For instance, the mission of the Department of Homeland Security's National Cybersecurity and Communications Integration Center is to reduce the likelihood and severity of incidents that may significantly compromise the security and resilience of the nation's critical information technology and communications networks. The NCIJTF, rather than focusing on the defensive functions of securing vulnerabilities, contributes to internet security by pursuing the terrorists, spies, and criminals who use the cyber setting to facilitate threat activities.

However, this division of labor, in which one agency has purview over the chessboard while a separate agency is responsible for the pieces on the board, is inefficient, and in a fast-moving field, elimination of inefficiency is essential. At the end of the day, the DHS sees the battlefield, whereas the FBI sees the muzzle flashes. These two centers should be brought under the same roof, perhaps with an impartial third party, such as the Department of Commerce's National Institute of Standards and Technology (NIST), overseeing the effort. NIST—which developed the National Cybersecurity Framework—would facilitate the rapid translation of NCIJTF and NCCIC findings into US cybersecurity policy.[97]

Hybrid Threat Center

The FBI established an entity to support Department of Commerce objectives. Then-director Comey, in 2015, advised Congress that the FBI had "directed the development, deployment, and operation" of a Hybrid Threat Center that would support the Department of Commerce's "Entity List" investigations.[98] According to Comey, the Bureau brought together "a lot of elements of the intelligence community and other parts of the U.S. government" to think about the threat that corporations, which allowed themselves to be co-opted and act as agents of foreign powers, as well as foreign powers attempting to penetrate the supply chain, posed to the United States.[99] According to Comey, the Hybrid Threat Center had been "well-received" by the intelligence community.[100]

Notes

1. *Intelligence Reform and Terrorism Prevention Act of 2004*, S. 2845, 108th Cong (2004).
2. "Cyber Threat Intelligence Integration Center," https://www.dni.gov/files/CTIIC /documents/CTIIC-Overview_for-unclass.pdf.

3. "Today's NCTC," https://www.dni.gov/files/NCTC/documents/features_documents/NCTC-Primer_FINAL.pdf; Richard A. Best, *The National Counterterrorism Center (NCTC)—Responsibilities and Potential Congressional Concerns* (Washington, DC: Congressional Research Service, 2011).

4. Gregory F. Treverton, *The Next Steps in Reshaping Intelligence* (Santa Monica: Rand, 2005), p. 12.

5. "Cyber Threat Intelligence Integration Center," https://www.dni.gov/files/CTIIC/documents/CTIIC-Overview_for-unclass.pdf.

6. Harold C. Relyea and Henry B. Hogue, *Department of Homeland Security Reorganization: The 2SR Initiative* (Washington, DC: Congressional Research Service, 2006).

7. *Departments of Commerce, Justice, and State, the Judiciary, and Related Agencies Appropriations for 2005,* Before a Subcommittee of the Committee on Appropriations, House of Representatives, 108th Cong., pt. 10 (2004).

8. *Department of Homeland Security's Budget Submission for Fiscal Year 2005,* Before the Committee on Governmental Affairs, Senate, 108th Cong., S. Doc. 108-555 (2004); "Homeland Security: Intelligence Support," https://fas.org/irp/crs/RS21283.html.

9. *Department of Homeland Security's Budget Submission for Fiscal Year 2005,* Before the Committee on Governmental Affairs, Senate, 108th Cong., S. Doc. 108-555 (2004).

10. *FBI Oversight,* Before the Committee on the Judiciary, Senate, 109th Cong., S. Doc. 109-706 (2006).

11. *Department of Homeland Security's Budget Submission for Fiscal Year 2005; How Is America Safer? A Progress Report on the Department of Homeland Security,* Before the Select Committee on Homeland Security, House of Representatives, 108th Cong. (2003).

12. *Department of Homeland Security's Budget Submission for Fiscal Year 2005.*

13. *Ten Years After 9/11: 2001,* Before the Committee on Homeland Security and Governmental Affairs, Senate, 112th Cong. (2012).

14. Ibid.

15. Ibid.

16. *H.R. 6588: National Intelligence Act of 1980,* Before the Subcommittee on Legislation of the Permanent Select Committee on Intelligence, House of Representatives, 96th Cong., 2nd sess. (1980).

17. *Federal Bureau of Investigation Oversight,* Before the Committee on the Judiciary, Senate, 109th Cong., S. Doc. 109-76 (2005).

18. Ibid.

19. "Intelligence Integration—Who We Are," https://www.dni.gov/index.php/who-we-are/organizations/ddii/ddii-who-we-are; National Intelligence Program, *FY 2012: Congressional Budget Justification,* vol. 12, https://fas.org/irp/dni/cbjb-2012.pdf.

20. "Partner Engagement—Who We Are," https://www.dni.gov/index.php?option=com_content&view=article&id=402&Itemid=813.

21. "National Intelligence: A Consumer's Guide," 2009, https://www.dni.gov/files/documents/IC_Consumers_Guide_2009.pdf; *An Overview of the United States Intelligence Community for the 111th Congress,* 2009, https://fas.org/irp/eprint/overview.pdf.

22. Office of the Director of National Intelligence, *Domestic Approach to National Intelligence 2016* (Washington, DC, 2016); National Intelligence Program, *FY 2012: Congressional Budget Justification,* vol. 12, https://fas.org/irp/dni/cbjb-2012.pdf (accessed April 22, 2018).

23. Intelligence and National Security Alliance, *Protecting the Homeland: Intelligence Integration 15 Years After 9/11* (Washington, DC, 2016).

24. Walter Pincus, "Senate Committee Sides with DNI in Its Bureaucratic Turf War with CIA," *Washington Post,* July 23, 2009.

25. *Oversight of the Federal Bureau of Investigation,* Before the Committee on the Judiciary, Senate, 111th Cong., S. Doc. 111-441 (2009).

26. Intelligence and National Security Alliance, *Protecting the Homeland.* The assistant directors in charge of Los Angeles, New York, and Washington, D.C., and the special agents in charge of Atlanta, Boston, Chicago, Denver, Houston, Miami, Pittsburgh, San Francisco, and Seattle, serve as the DNI domestic representatives with each representative being responsible for covering a designated geographic region. Originally, the DNI considered designating the heads of all fifty-six field divisions as DNI domestic representatives, a decision that would have more closely resembled the DNIR program abroad, in which all CIA chiefs of station are considered DNIRs; Inspectors General of the Intelligence Community Department of Homeland Security, Department of Justice, *Review of Domestic Sharing of Counterterrorism Information* (Washington, DC, 2017).

27. Inspectors General, *Review of Domestic Sharing of Counterterrorism Information.*

28. *Intelligence Community Directive 402* (2012), https://www.dni.gov/files/documents/ICD/ICD402.pdf.

29. Business Executives for National Security, *Domestic Security: Confronting a Changing Threat to Ensure Public Safety and Civil Liberties* (Washington, DC, 2015).

30. The DHS realigned its Office of Intelligence and Analysis field operations, in 2014, to conform with the DDNIR program; its chief intelligence officer designated the OI&A regional directors to serve as the DHS senior field representatives to the DDNIR program in specified geographic regions. Inspectors General, *Review of Domestic Sharing of Counterterrorism Information.*

31. *Oversight of the Federal Bureau of Investigation,* S. Doc. 111-441.

32. Inspectors General, *Review of Domestic Sharing of Counterterrorism Information.*

33. *Oversight of the Federal Bureau of Investigation,* S. Doc. 111-441.

34. Ibid.

35. Inspectors General, *Review of Domestic Sharing of Counterterrorism Information.*

36. *Oversight of the Federal Bureau of Investigation,* S. Doc. 111-441.

37. Ibid.

38. *Commerce, Justice, Science, and Related Agencies Appropriations for Fiscal Year 2015,* Before a Subcommittee of the Committee on Appropriations, Senate, 113th Cong. (2014).

39. Inspectors General, *Review of Domestic Sharing of Counterterrorism Information.* Several DDNIR regions have informally included non–intelligence community members in quarterly meetings and working groups.

40. Inspectors General, *Review of Domestic Sharing of Counterterrorism Information.*

41. Ibid.

42. Government Accountability Office, *Homeland Security: Federal Efforts Are Helping to Address Some Challenges Faced by State and Local Fusion Centers* (Washington, DC, 2008).

43. House of Representatives, *The State of Homeland Security 2007: An Annual Report Card on the Department of Homeland Security* (Washington, DC, 2007).

44. Government Accountability Office, *Homeland Security.*; John Rollins, *Fusion Centers: Issues and Options for Congress* (Washington, DC: Congressional Research Service, 2008).

45. Mark A. Randol, *The Department of Homeland Security Intelligence Enterprise: Operational Overview and Oversight Challenges for Congress* (Washington, DC: Congressional Research Service, 2009).

46. *A Report Card on Homeland Security Information Sharing,* Before the Subcommittee on Intelligence Information Sharing, and Terrorism Risk Assessment of the Committee on Homeland Security, House of Representatives, 110th Cong., H. Rep. 110-141 (2008).

47. Randol, *The Department of Homeland Security Intelligence Enterprise,*

48. Ibid.

49. Intelligence and National Security Alliance, *Protecting the Homeland.*

50. *Federal Bureau of Investigation Oversight,* Before the Committee on the Judiciary, Senate, 109th Cong., S. Doc. 109-763 (2005).

51. Intelligence and National Security Alliance, *Protecting the Homeland.*

52. "Joint Counterterrorism Assessment Team," https://www.dni.gov/index.php/nctc-how-we-work/joint-ct-assessment-team.

53. *Worldwide Threats to the Homeland,* Before the Committee on Homeland Security, House of Representatives, 113th Cong. (2014) (testimony of Matt Olsen).

54. "Joint Counterterrorism Assessment Team."

55. Department of Justice, *Law Enforcement Intelligence: A Guide for State, Local, and Tribal Law Enforcement Agencies* (Washington, DC, 2004).

56. *Intelligence Community Directive Number 204.*

57. *A Report Card on Homeland Security Information Sharing.*

58. Ibid.

59. *Federal Bureau of Investigation Oversight,* Before the Committee on the Judiciary, Senate, 109th Cong., 1st sess. (2005); *Commerce, Justice, Science, and Related Agencies Appropriations for 2016,* Before a Subcommittee of the Committee on Appropriations, House of Representatives, 114th Cong., pt. 2B (2015).

60. *Commerce, Justice, Science, and Related Agencies Appropriations for 2016,* pt. 2B; *Commerce, Justice, Science, and Related Agencies Appropriations for 2017,* Before a Subcommittee of the Committee on Appropriations, House of Representatives, 114th Cong., pt. 2B (2016).

61. 9/11 Commission, "Reforming Law Enforcement, Counterterrorism, and Intelligence Collection in the United States," Staff Statement no. 12, undated, http://govinfo.library.unt.edu/911/staff_statements/staff_statement_12.pdf); Federal Bureau of Investigation, *FBI Information Sharing & Safeguarding Report 2012* (Washington, DC, 2012), http://www.fbi.gov/stats-services/publications/national-information-sharing-strategy-1/fbi-information-sharing-and-safeguarding-report-2012.

62. Department of Justice, *The Department of Justice's Terrorism Task Forces* (Washington, DC, 2005), https://oig.justice.gov/reports/plus/e0507/final.pdf; Government Accountability Office, *Combating Terrorism: Federal Agencies Face Continuing Challenges in Addressing Terrorist Financing and Money Laundering* (Washington, DC, 2004).

63. Garrett M. Graff, *The Threat Matrix: The FBI at War* (New York: Back Bay, 2011), p. 158; Department of Justice, *The Department of Justice's Terrorism Task Forces* (Washington, DC, 2005), p. 15.

64. Jerome P. Bjelopera and Kristin Finklea, *Domestic Federal Law Enforcement Coordination: Through the Lens of the Southwest Border* (Washington, DC: Congressional Research Service, 2014), https://fas.org/sgp/crs/homesec/R43583.pdf.

65. *FBI Oversight and Budget Authorization for Fiscal Year 1986,* Before the Subcommittee on Security and Terrorism of the Committee on the Judiciary, Senate, 99th Cong., S. Doc. 99-208 (1985).

66. Ibid.

67. Department of Justice, *The Department of Justice's Terrorism Task Forces.*

68. Anne Daugherty Miles, *Intelligence Authorization Legislation for FY2014 and FY2015: Provisions, Status, Intelligence Community Framework* (Washington, DC: Congressional Research Service, 2015).

69. Department of Justice, *The Federal Bureau of Investigation's Efforts to Improve the Sharing of Intelligence and Other Information* (Washington, DC, 2003).

70. Graff, *The Threat Matrix,* p. 158; Department of Justice, *The Department of Justice's Terrorism Task Forces,* p. 159.

71. Department of Justice, *The Department of Justice's Terrorism Task Forces.*

72. Ibid.

73. *Federal Bureau of Investigation Oversight,* Before the Committee on the Judiciary, Senate, 109th Cong., 1st sess., S. Doc. 109-763 (2005).

74. Ibid.

75. Statement of Joseph M. Demarest Jr., Assistant Director, Cyber Division, Federal Bureau of Investigation, Before the Committee on Judiciary, United States Senate, May 8, 2013, https://www.judiciary.senate.gov/imo/media/doc/5-8-13DemarestTestimony.pdf.

76. *Departments of Commerce, Justice, and State, the Judiciary, and Related Agencies Appropriations for 2005*, pt. 10.

77. Randol, *The Department of Homeland Security Intelligence Enterprise.*

78. Department of Justice, *Review of the Terrorist Screening Center* (Washington, DC, 2005).

79. Relyea and Hogue, *Department of Homeland Security Reorganization.*

80. Statement of Christopher M. Piehota, Director, Terrorist Screening Center, Federal Bureau of Investigation, Department of Justice, Before the Subcommittee on Transportation Security, Committee on Homeland Security United States House of Representatives, September 18, 2014.

81. *A Report Card on Homeland Security Information Sharing.*

82. Statement of Piehota.

83. *Commerce, Justice, Science, and Related Agencies Appropriations for 2017,* Before a Subcommittee of the Committee on Appropriations, House of Representatives, 114th Cong., pt. 2B (2016).

84. Ibid.

85. Department of Justice, *A Review of the Department's Anti-Gang Intelligence and Coordination Centers* (Washington, DC, 2009).

86. *Commerce, Justice, Science and Related Agencies Appropriations for 2011,* Before a Subcommittee of the Committee on Appropriations, House of Representatives, 111th Cong., pt. 6 (2010).

87. Ibid.

88. Department of Justice, *A Review of the Department's Anti-Gang Intelligence and Coordination Centers.*

89. As of 2009, the agencies contributing staff to the NGIC included the FBI, ATF, DEA, Federal Bureau of Prisons, National Drug Intelligence Center, US Marshals Service, DHS (including Immigration and Customs Enforcement and Customs and Border Patrol), DoD National Guard, and state and local law enforcement.

90. Department of Justice, *A Review of the Department's Anti-Gang Intelligence and Coordination Centers.*

91. *Commerce, Justice, Science, and Related Agencies Appropriations for 2014,* Before a Subcommittee of the Committee on Appropriations, House of Representatives, 113th Cong., pt. 2B (2013).

92. *Commerce, Justice, Science, and Related Agencies Appropriations for 2013,* Before a Subcommittee of the Committee on Appropriations, House of Representatives, 112th Cong., pt. 6 (2012).

93. *Commerce, Justice, Science, and Related Agencies Appropriations for 2009,* Before a Subcommittee of the Committee on Appropriations, House of Representatives, 103rd Cong., pt. 1 (2009).

94. Department of Justice, *Audit of the Federal Bureau of Investigation's Implementation of Its Next Generation Cyber Initiative* (Washington, DC, 2015).

95. Ibid.

96. Statement of Joseph M. Demarest Jr., Assistant Director, Cyber Division, Federal Bureau of Investigation, Before the Subcommittee on Crime and Terrorism, Committee on Judiciary, Senate, Entitled "Cyber Threat: Law Enforcement and Private Sector Responses," May 8, 2013; Statement of Gordon M. Snow, Assistant Director, Cyber Division, Federal Bureau of Investigation, Before the Committee on Judiciary, Senate, Crime and Terrorism Subcommittee, Entitled "Cybersecurity: Responding to the Threat of Cyber Crime and Terrorism," April 12, 2011.

97. National Institute of Standards and Technology, "Cybersecurity Framework," https://www.nist.gov/cyberframework.

98. Statement of James B. Comey, Director Federal Bureau of Investigation, Before the Committee on the Judiciary, Senate, December 9, 2015.

99. *Commerce, Justice, Science, and Related Agencies Appropriations for 2017,* pt. 6.

100. Statement of Comey, December 9, 2015.

11

Fusion and Confusion
at the Subfederal Level

The fusion center concept is not new, and neither is the concept of federal support for these state and local enterprises. However, following 9/11, with the newly realized concerns about terrorism as well as the new ethos of information sharing, state and local-dominated fusion centers—with a counterterrorism emphasis—began to proliferate throughout the United States. Throughout the first decade of the twenty-first century, several agencies attempted to incorporate these fusion centers into the domestically oriented intelligence enterprise. By the second decade of the century it became increasingly clear that state and local fusion centers were, in a number of instances, diverging from supporting federal objectives, as they focused on more localized concerns. The challenge, as the United States stares down the barrel of the third decade of the new century, is how to leverage fusion centers in addressing the wide range of challenges, beyond terrorism, that the United States faces.

Discussion of the role of fusion centers has at times been muddied by a lack of agreed definitions and parameters. For instance, as defined by the US Congress, a fusion center is a collaborative effort of two or more federal, state, local, or tribal government agencies that "combines resources, expertise, or information with the goal of maximizing the ability of such agencies to detect, prevent, investigate, apprehend, and respond to criminal or terrorist activity."[1] However, the DHS's first chief intelligence officer, Charles Allen, described fusion centers as "interagency facilities designed by the States to maximize State and local ability to detect, prevent, and respond to criminal and terrorist activity, and to recover from natural disasters."[2]

The imprecise definition of what a fusion center is or does has resulted in these entities varying widely in how they organize and

195

operate. The bespoke nature of fusion centers dates from the earliest days of the Regional Information-Sharing System (RISS), which allowed each fusion center to tailor its resources on the specific needs of its area of responsibility while also coordinating and sharing information that would contribute to addressing issues of national scope.[3] After 9/11, although fusion centers shifted their focus, malleability remained a feature of their organizational concept. According to a 2007 Congressional Research Service report, there is no single model for how a fusion center should be structured.[4] In 2008, a congressional report identified that, based on interviews with fusion center directors, fusion centers had anywhere from five to eighty personnel and their member agencies ranged from just a handful to twenty.[5] According to the DHS, this variation is by design, since these centers are supposed to meet their jurisdictions' "specific criminal and homeland security needs."[6]

Despite these differences, fusion centers have some shared points of reference. As of 2006, most states used the Global Fusion Center Guidelines, which subfederal entities, the private sector, the Department of Justice, and the DHS developed collaboratively.[7] The Congressional Research Service, in a 2007 report, identified several attributes that most fusion centers shared, including acting as intelligence/information relay centers; functioning as points of co-location for personnel from various agencies (who often had reachback to their agencies' databases); providing coordination on a variety of projects; and serving as analytic centers.[8]

Importantly, the ODNI has incorporated fusion centers into the wider intelligence enterprise. According to Allen, the director of national intelligence recognized fusion centers as a "center of gravity" and a "key to the effective exchange and assessment of information between the Federal government and state and local partners."[9] Fusion centers are a component of the information-sharing environment operating under the ODNI.[10]

Fusion centers interface with the intelligence community in multiple ways. First, they are directly connected to the ODNI's National Counterterrorism Center via the ITACG. Additionally, they work with and their development has been influenced by the FBI and DHS.

The FBI

Shortly after 9/11, the FBI became involved with establishing the groundwork for an interconnected group of fusion centers. The Regional

Information-Sharing System program, which began in 1974, with the support of a DoJ grant, was the foundation for the creation of fusion centers.[11] The USA PATRIOT Act expanded RISS to facilitate the sharing of information relating to "multi-jurisdictional terrorist conspiracies and activities."[12] This added a new dimension to the previously criminal investigative–oriented fusion centers. In mid-2002, the FBI became involved with RISS to identify ways in which the RISS Network (RISS-NET) and the Bureau's Law Enforcement Online (LEO) system could be integrated. LEO and RISSNET were joined—although not consolidated—with full encryption, in September 2002.[13]

The FBI, in the years after 9/11, provided a point of reference for fusion centers. One example involved California's establishment of its Terrorism Threat Assessment System—composed of five centers—which was responsible for regional and statewide information collection, analysis, and information-sharing activities.[14] The state established its five centers to mirror FBI areas of responsibility. Arguably, the FBI facilitated the early growth of the fusion center concept by providing space to house these entities. For instance, three of California's fusion centers were co-located with the Bureau and the other two had plans to be similarly situated.[15] By 2007, sixteen of the thirty-six fusion centers with which the FBI was involved, nationally, were co-located with the respective Bureau division's Field Intelligence Group.[16] However, this was not the optimal solution. The House Committee Homeland Security expressed its concern that "the FBI and the fusion center [were] so closely tied together that there may be suppression of the independent State and local perspective."[17] Given that the value of these fusion centers is to provide a local perspective that helps to develop a more nuanced national picture and hopefully identify threats before they can have a national impact, the shouldering aside of regional perspectives is indisputably counterproductive.

In addition to geographic alignment, the FBI also shaped fusion centers through the detailing of personnel to these entities. In 2006, the FBI's National Security Branch (which included the Directorate of Intelligence) directed each field office to assess their respective information-sharing environments and detail, as appropriate, a FIG special agent or intelligence analyst to the leading fusion center within the office's territory.[18] (Selection criteria for identifying fusion centers with which to engage included the facility's connectivity to local systems, the commitment of full-time personnel by multiple agencies, and the fusion center's coverage of a significant region or metropolitan area. If a fusion center met these criteria, FBI participation was mandatory.) As of 2007, the FBI had assigned approximately 200 agents and analysts to thirty-six fusion centers nationwide.[19] By 2009, thirty-nine field office FIGs had assigned personnel—including agents, analysts, and specialized support personnel with language and financial expertise—to regional fusion centers.[20] Bureau officials at fusion centers were supposed to establish connectivity between the FBI and sub-federal partners across all investigative programs; facilitate the effective two-way communication of information, through the intelligence cycle, between the FBI and fusion centers; participate as an investigative and analytic partner in responding to threats; and ensure the timely flow of terrorism-related threat information between the fusion center and the local JTTFs and FIGs.[21]

Throughout the first half of the twenty-first century's opening decade, the FBI formalized its institutional relationship with fusion centers. In 2005, Mueller launched the FBI's fusion center initiative and directed the heads of field divisions to ensure coordination between the Bureau and all statewide fusion centers as well as significant regional centers.[22] Then, in 2007, the FBI's Directorate of Intelligence established an Interagency Integration Unit, which provided headquarters oversight of field offices' relationships with fusion centers.[23] The Bureau's engagement with fusion centers is now the responsibility of the Intelligence Branch's Office of Partner Engagement, which according to the FBI "has program management responsibility for the FBI's engagement with State and local fusion centers. The OPE supports communication, coordination, and cooperative efforts between Federal, State, local, and Tribal law enforcement by providing varying levels of support to fusion centers throughout the United States."[24]

The DHS and Fusion Centers

Despite the FBI's early involvement, responsibility for federal coordination of fusion centers transferred to the DHS mid-decade. The DHS's undersecretary and first chief intelligence officer, Charles Allen, established a State and Local Fusion Center Pilot Project Team to enhance DHS support at six fusion centers in five states.[25] In mid-2006, the DHS tasked its Office of Intelligence and Analysis with the responsibility for managing the department's support for fusion centers; this resulted in OI&A's establishment of a State and Local Program Office as a focal point for this function.[26] (In 2010, DHS secretary Janet Napolitano created the Joint Fusion Center Program Management Office, which leveraged all of the DHS's resources—rather than simply those of OI&A—to support information sharing.[27]) With the Implementing Recommendations of the 9/11 Commission Act of 2007, the secretary of homeland security became responsible for establishing a state, local, and regional fusion center initiative within the Department of Homeland Security. Through this initiative, the DHS provides fusion centers with operational and intelligence advice and assistance.[28] The phrase "national network of fusion centers"—which simply refers to the "combined effort of fusion center and fusion center nodes across the nation"—entered popular usage circa 2010.[29] Although the DHS is the primary federal point of contact for this national network, the network is "self-organizing [and] self-governing."[30]

The 2007 legislation put the DHS in a unique position vis-à-vis fusion centers. As part of the new initiative, the DHS was tasked to review information collected by fusion centers and incorporate this into its own information. However, the DHS cannot use these entities to actively target and collect information. Officials can only review information that state and local agencies have collected on their own volition. Furthermore, while DHS officials can be present at interviews of subjects, they can only ask questions that are meant to clarify information that has already been solicited. Although these measures imposed constraints on the DHS, they also further incorporated subfederal authorities' role as intelligence collectors whose work ultimately informed US strategic decisionmaking.[31]

Like the FBI, the DHS has had an opportunity to influence fusion centers' development through the forward deployment of personnel to these entities. The State and Local Program Office is responsible for assigning DHS personnel with both operational and intelligence skills to fusion centers, in order to facilitate coordination and the flow of information between the center and the DHS; provide expertise with analysis and intelligence reporting functions; and provide the DHS with local situational awareness and access to unique fusion center information.[32] It provides a link between the intelligence community, subfederal entities, and private-sector partners.[33] In 2006, the State and Local Program Office deployed its first intelligence officer,[34] with its assignment of the officer to the Joint Regional Intelligence Center, in Los Angeles, California.[35] During 2008, the DHS deployed more than twenty-five intelligence officers to fusion centers.[36] According to the

DHS, these officers were the "lynchpins in the execution of the critical DHS information-sharing mission."[37] It was the DHS's intention, as of 2010, to deploy an intelligence officer to each center, and as of that year it had put fifty-five intelligence officers in the field.[38] As of mid-2014, the DHS's OI&A had deployed seventy-four intelligence officers, as well as nine regional directors, to fusion centers.[39] State and Local Program Office personnel were augmented, starting in 2008, by OI&A reports officers, who came from a separate OI&A element.[40] These personnel disseminated information, gleaned at the state and local levels, to the federal level, via homeland intelligence reports.[41] As of 2014, these reports officers collectively covered every fusion center in the national network.[42] Despite the (belated) assignment of reports officers, the DHS has experienced difficulty in deriving sufficient intelligence from these fusion centers. A Senate review of fusion centers, released in 2012, showed that much of the reporting came from only three states, while most other states' centers produced little or no reporting.[43] In 2015, the OI&A restructured the State and Local Program Office in order to consolidate all intelligence officers and reports officers under one organization.[44] Finally, the OI&A has deployed analysts, who provide assistance in accordance with OI&A's standards, to fusion centers. The OI&A has indicated it hopes these analysts will provide an avenue for improving the analytical skills of fusion center analysts.[45]

Other DHS Platforms for Information Sharing with Federal and Subfederal Partners

In addition to its role as the primary federal point of contact with the national network of fusion centers, the DHS, through its components, is responsible for information sharing with state and local partners through several other venues. The Bureau of Immigration and Customs Enforcement is responsible for providing support to state and local authorities through the Law Enforcement Support Center (LESC). This center's primary function is to assist law enforcement agencies with determining whether a person with whom the agencies have been in contact, or who has been taken into custody, is a criminal or fugitive alien.[46] The LESC is specifically linked to Immigration and Customs Enforcement databases, including data from legacy agencies such as the Immigration and Naturalization Service (INS) and Customs.[47] The existence of the LESC seems a pointless fragmentation of functions that could be consolidated under the FBI's Criminal Justice Information Services Division. The LESC has also engaged in the sharing of information through Customs and Border Protection's Operations Integration Center, located in Detroit, Michigan, which increases information sharing with partners, including state and local agencies, to combat the smuggling of narcotics, money, and contraband along the US-Canada border.[48] Customs and Border Protection had previously established a border interdiction support center at the DEA's El Paso Intelligence Center.[49]

Fusion, Confusion, and Contusion

The involvement of the two departments that dominate the domestically oriented intelligence enterprise has led to friction. According to one congressional report, various fusion center personnel expressed concerns about what seemed to be "constant battle" between DHS and FBI representatives.[50] Furthermore, a 2013 study, reflecting the fusion center landscape as it existed more than five years after the DHS became prominently involved with fusion centers, assessed that Bureau relationships with various centers had become strained and, in at least one instance, "toxic."[51] In another instance, the wretched relationship resulted in the FBI pulling its people out of a fusion center.[52]

FBI fusion center involvement appears to have declined as the DHS's role has become more pronounced. The FBI kept a foot jammed in the door after the DHS took primary responsibility for interaction with the national network of fusion centers. As of 2008, the federal government had established the National Fusion Center Coordination Group, which the DHS and the FBI cochaired, in conjunction with the DoJ, Global Justice Information Sharing Initiative, ODNI, and the information-sharing environment.[53] Among other items, the group was responsible for ensuring that designated fusion centers achieved a baseline level of capability.[54] In 2009, the DHS announced that, in conjunction with the FBI, it had designated seventy fusion centers.[55] However, several years later it was difficult not to get the impression that the Bureau was packing up its marbles and going home. As of 2014, it had only 94 personnel—down from approximately 200—assigned to fusion centers.[56] New FBI requirements for participation included the demand that FBI management participate in the governance structure of fusion centers.[57] By 2016, the Bureau reportedly had little permanent presence at fusion centers.[58]

The Changing Nature of Fusion Centers

Incidents of catastrophic terrorism have receded from the public memory. Recent episodes have instead been one-off instances of violent crime by deranged individuals who happen to have latched onto the rhetoric of Islamic extremism, whereas in previous decades they would have filled their mental void with anarchism, racial extremism, or any number of conspiracy theories as motivation. Other challenges in the domestic environment (e.g., gang activity that borders on insurgency, the opioid addiction epidemic) are increasingly vivid in the minds of the subfederal officials who must respond to these threats. This has shifted the focus of fusion centers but should not result in a divergence from national-level intelligence efforts. The current dominant threats can corrode elements of national power as significantly as acts of terrorism, and the federal government would be short-sighted to ignore them or the entities on the front lines against these threats.

Fusion centers, because of their perceptions of threats to their areas of responsibility, will gravitate toward addressing the greatest local concerns, rather than operate to support federally identified priorities. Each member of the national network of fusion centers is free to innovate and to develop its operations based on its "unique legal, political, geographical, and cultural operating environment."[59] This means that federal/subfederal alignment will persist only if there is a shared interest.

The origins of fusion centers are in combating crime, so it is not surprising that once the fear of an imminent terror attack subsided, fusion centers would revert to their original mission. As early as 2007, slightly more than 40 percent of fusion centers characterized themselves as being "all-crimes" in nature.[60] There is variation within this category, with some centers providing support to investigations of any criminal act, while others focused on large-scale, organized, and destabilizing crimes.[61] This definition does not exclude terrorism but counts it as one of many concerns within a fusion center's area of responsibility.

Fusion centers' evolution is driven by their evaluation of threats as well as by a need for bureaucratic survival. As a group of federal inspectors general noted, "fusion centers are focused on sustaining operations rather than enhancing capabilities due to unpredictable federal support."[62] A number of fusion center leaders have indicated that obtaining buy-in from local law enforcement agencies and other public-sector entities—the partners on which a fusion center must rely if federal support disappears—requires a broader mission than counterterrorism, since the terrorist threat seems distant to potential partners, especially in contrast with more urgent issues such as gangs and narcotics.[63]

This shift in focus may lead a shortsighted federal government to withdraw support and thereby hasten fusion centers' transformation as the centers attempt to fill the void. The inspectors general of the intelligence community, DoJ, and DHS assessed that the DHS might lose its oversight and influence over fusion centers as it decreased its support to these entities.[64] The FBI has also demonstrated an increasing lack of interest in fusion centers. New guidance that the Bureau developed in 2011 premised field office support to fusion centers on alignment of fusion centers with the FBI's counterterrorism mission and on fusion centers' immediate sharing of all emerging terrorism-related information with the FBI.[65]

Relations between fusion centers and the federal government are a chicken-and-egg dilemma. As the federal government withdraws support, fusion centers feel the need to change priorities in order to attract other partners. However, this new focus further speeds the decrease in federal interest, as the centers branch out from the counterterrorism mission. The federal government's continued fixation with terrorism blinds it to other threat issues. Fusion centers are well positioned to identify the concerns that are degrading their areas of responsibility. In aggregate this information highlights trends with national significance. Such trends are most efficiently addressed through federal, rather than subfederal, action.

The federal government has doubled down on counterterrorism at the state and local levels. In 2013, the House Committee on Homeland Security recommended the establishment of specialized analytic units within fusion centers to enhance the identification and analysis of information.[66] This recommendation evolved into the National Mission Cell concept. According to the ODNI's information-sharing environment, the National Mission Cell pilot project was designed to focus on terrorism, regardless of other events demanding attention from fusion center personnel.[67] The pilot program operated in four fusion centers between January 2014 and July 2015.[68] The National Mission Cell, in turn, evolved into the FBI's Enhanced Engagement Initiative.[69] This initiative, according to the National Fusion Center Association, is intended to "ensure the FBI continues to improve its sharing of relevant counterterrorism information with fusion centers, while also enhancing the contribution of information and analysis from fusion centers in a coordinated and efficient manner to address the growing terrorism threat."[70] The National Mission Cell/Enhanced Engagement Initiative approach put the United States at risk of missing the next strategic threat to US national security.

Cyber Threats and Fusion Centers

Historically, federal interaction with fusion centers has been characterized by federal entities bolstering state- and locally established capabilities. This has taken a distinctly twenty-first-century turn as the state and local entities have increasingly taken on the countering of cyber-based threats.

State and local entities have demonstrated their interest in developing cyber capabilities. In 2010, the Multi-State Information-Sharing and Analysis Center opened its Cyber Security Operations Center. This twenty-four-hour watch and warning facility enhances the situation awareness at the state and local levels and also facilitates the federal government's provision of critical cyber risk, vulnerability, and mitigation data to state and local governments.[71] Similarly, as of 2015, the state of New Jersey had established its own Cybersecurity and Communications Integration Cell.[72]

The federal government has started to facilitate the development of state and local expertise in the cybersecurity field. For instance, the FBI Cyber Investigator Certification program, which Carnegie Mellon University's Software Engineering Institute assisted with creating, provides customized training, knowledge assessments, and capstone cyber exercises to help subfederal agencies develop, maintain, and advance their analytical skills. The program's intent is to "constantly improve overall national analysis and response capabilities." The Bureau expected that more than 100,000 law enforcement first responders would take the course, virtually, in 2015.[73]

Federal/subfederal coordination on cyber issues indicates that fusion centers—even if they do not focus strictly on counterterrorism—can serve as a first line of defense against a multitude of threats. Helping these centers to strengthen their capabilities provides an opportunity for burden sharing in areas of importance to national security.

Notes

1. Mark A. Randol, *The Department of Homeland Security Intelligence Enterprise: Operational Overview and Oversight Challenges for Congress* (Washington, DC: Congressional Research Service, 2010).

2. *State and Local Fusion Centers and the Role of DHS,* Before the Subcommittee on Emergency, Preparedness, Science, and Technology of the Committee on Homeland Security, House of Representatives, 109th Cong. (2006) (testimony of Charles Allen).

3. Randol, *The Department of Homeland Security Intelligence Enterprise.*

4. Todd Masse, Siobhan O'Neil, and John Rollins, *Fusion Centers: Issues and Options for Congress* (Washington, DC: Congressional Research Service, 2007).

5. *Focus on Fusion Centers: A Progress Report,* Before the Ad Hoc Subcommittee on State, Local, and Private Sector Preparedness and Integration of the Committee on Homeland Security and Governmental Affairs, Senate, 110th Cong., S. Doc. 110-694 (2008).

6. *Homeland Security Department's Budget Submission for Fiscal Year 2011,* Before the Committee on Homeland Security and Governmental Affairs, Senate, 111th Cong., S. Doc. 111-1019 (2010); Government Accountability Office, *Information Sharing: Federal Agencies Are Helping Fusion Centers Build and Sustain Capabilities and Protect Privacy but Could Better Measure Results* (Washington, DC, 2010).

7. *State and Local Fusion Centers and the Role of DHS,* Before the Subcommittee on Emergency, Preparedness, Science, and Technology of the Committee on Homeland Security, House of Representatives, 109th Cong. (2006) (testimony of Charles Allen).

8. Masse, O'Neil, and Rollins, *Fusion Centers.*

9. *State and Local Fusion Centers and the Role of DHS* (testimony of Charles Allen).

10. Government Accountability Office, *Information Sharing.*

11. Harold C. Relya and Jeffrey W. Seifert, *Information Sharing for Homeland Security: A Brief Overview* (Washington, DC: Congressional Research Service, 2005), https://fas.org/sgp/crs/RL32597.pdf.

12. *Reforming the FBI in the 21st Century,* Before the Committee on the Judiciary. Senate, 107th Cong., S. Doc. 107-971 (2002).

13. Ibid.

14. *Focus on Fusion Centers.*

15. Ibid.

16. *The Way Forward with Fusion Centers: Challenges and Strategies for Change,* Before the Subcommittee on Intelligence, Information Sharing, and Terrorism Risk Assessment of the Committee on Homeland Security, House of Representatives, 110th Cong. (2007).

17. *The National Network of Fusion Centers,* House Homeland Security Committee, Majority Staff Report (Washington, DC, 2013).

18. Government Accountability Office, *Homeland Security: Federal Efforts Are Helping to Alleviate Some Challenges Encountered by State and Local Information Fusion Centers* (Washington, DC, 2007).

19. *The Way Forward with Fusion Centers.*

20. *Commerce, Justice, Science, and Related Agencies Appropriations for 2010,* Before a Subcommittee of the Committee on Appropriations, House of Representatives, 111th Cong, S. Doc. 110-694, pt. 1 (2009); *Focus on Fusion Centers.*

21. *The Way Forward with Fusion Centers.*

22. Ibid.

23. Government Accountability Office, *Homeland Security.*

24. Federal Bureau of Investigation, *FBI Information Sharing & Safeguarding Report 2012* (Washington, DC, 2012), http://www.fbi.gov/stats-services/publications/national-information-sharing-strategy-1/fbi-information-sharing-and-safeguarding-report-2012.

25. Randol, *The Department of Homeland Security Intelligence Enterprise.*

26. Government Accountability Office, *Information Sharing.*

27. *A DHS Intelligence Enterprise: Still Just a Vision or Reality?* Before the Subcommittee on Intelligence, Information Sharing, and Terrorism Risk Assessment of the Committee on Homeland Security, House of Representatives, 111th Cong. (2010).

28. Government Accountability Office, *Information Sharing.*

29. *The National Network of Fusion Centers,* Majority Staff Report; *2014–2017 National Strategy for the National Network of Fusion Centers,* https://www.dni.gov/files/ISE/documents/DocumentLibrary/National-Strategy-for-the-National-Network-of-Fusion-Centers-2014.pdf.

30. *The National Network of Fusion Centers,* Majority Staff Report; *2014–2017 National Strategy for the National Network of Fusion Centers.*

31. *Federal Support for an Involvement in State and Local Fusion Centers,* Senate Committee on Homeland Security and Governmental Affairs, Majority and Minority Staff Report (Washington, DC, 2012), https://fas.org/irp/congress/2012_rpt/fusion.pdf.

32. Government Accountability Office, *Homeland Security.*

33. Government Accountability Office, *Information Sharing.*

34. "Intelligence officer," in DHS parlance, is not an intelligence officer in the CIA or DIA sense but rather a law enforcement–to–law enforcement liaison.

35. *The National Network of Fusion Centers,* Majority Staff Report.

36. *Homeland Security Department's Budget Submission for Fiscal Year 2010,* Before the Committee on Homeland Security and Governmental Affairs, Senate, 111th Cong., S. Doc. 111-980 (2009).

37. *Homeland Security Department's Budget Submission for Fiscal Year 2011,* Before the Committee on Homeland Security and Governmental Affairs, Senate, 111th Cong., S. Doc. 111-1019 (2010).

38. Ibid.; *A DHS Intelligence Enterprise: Still Just a Vision or Reality?*

39. Government Accountability Office, *Information Sharing,*

40. *Federal Support for an Involvement in State and Local Fusion Centers,* Majority and Minority Staff Report.

41. Homeland intelligence reports are supposed to contain information that satisfies valid intelligence community collection requirements or DHS standing information needs. They are supposed to contain information that is not available via open sources or other intelligence community elements. Finally, they are supposed to contain information of interest to federal agencies other than the DHS. As Congress has identified, this has not always been the reality.

42. Government Accountability Office, *Information Sharing.*

43. *Federal Support for an Involvement in State and Local Fusion Centers,* Majority and Minority Staff Report.

44. *Reviewing the Department of Homeland Security's Intelligence Enterprise,* House Homeland Security Committee, Majority Staff Report (Washington, DC, 2016).

45. Government Accountability Office, *DHS Intelligence Analysis: Additional Actions Needed to Address Analytic Priorities and Workforce Challenges* (Washington, DC, 2014).

46. *Department of Homeland Security Transition: Bureau of Immigration and Customs Enforcement,* Before the Subcommittee on Immigration, Border Security, and Claims of the Committee on the Judiciary, House of Representatives, 108th Cong. (2003).

47. Ibid.; *Law Enforcement Efforts Within the Department of Homeland Security,* Before the Subcommittee on Crime, Terrorism, and Homeland Security of the Committee on the Judiciary, House of Representatives, 108th Cong. (2004).

48. *Department of Homeland Security,* Before the Committee on the Judiciary, House of Representatives, 112th Cong. (2012).

49. *Drugs and Security in a Post–September 11 World: Coordinating the Counternarcotics Mission at the Department of Homeland Security,* Before the Subcommittee on Criminal Justice, Drug Policy, and Human Resources of the Committee on Government Reform and the Subcommittee on Infrastructure and Border Security of the Committee on Homeland Security, House of Representatives, 108th Cong. (2004).

50. *The National Network of Fusion Centers,* Majority Staff Report.

51. *Federal Support for an Involvement in State and Local Fusion Centers,* Majority and Minority Staff Report.

52. *The National Network of Fusion Centers,* Majority Staff Report.

53. *The Future of Fusion Centers: Potential Promise and Dangers,* Before the Subcommittee on Intelligence, Information Sharing, and Terrorism Risk Assessment of the Committee on Homeland Security, House of Representatives, 111th Cong. (2009).

54. Government Accountability Office, *Homeland Security.*

55. *The Future of Fusion Centers.*

56. Government Accountability Office, *Information Sharing.*

57. Ibid.

58. Intelligence and National Security Alliance, *Protecting the Homeland: Intelligence Integration 15 Years After 9/11* (Washington, DC, 2016).

59. *The National Network of Fusion Centers,* Majority Staff Report.

60. Masse, O'Neil, and Rollins, *Fusion Centers.*

61. Ibid.

62. Inspectors General of the Intelligence Community Department of Homeland Security, Department of Justice, *Review of Domestic Sharing of Counterterrorism Information* (Washington, DC, 2017).

63. Masse, O'Neil, and Rollins, *Fusion Centers.*

64. Inspectors General, *Review of Domestic Sharing of Counterterrorism Information.*

65. Government Accountability Office, *Information Sharing.*

66. *Advancing the Homeland Security Information Sharing Environment: A Review of the National Network of Fusion Centers,* House Homeland Security Committee, Majority Staff Report (Washington, DC, 2017).

67. See www.ise.gov.

68. Inspectors General, *Review of Domestic Sharing of Counterterrorism Information.* The fusion centers that hosted the National Mission Cell pilot programs were the Iowa Intelligence Fusion Center, the Montana All-Threat Intelligence Center, the Georgia Information-Sharing Analysis Center, and the Northern California Regional Intelligence Center; see https://www.dni.gov/index.php/who-we-are/organizations/ic-cio/ic-cio-related -menus/ic-cio-related-links/ic-cio-contact-us/309-about/organization/information-sharing -environment/mission-stories/2125-national-mission-cell-pilot-program.

69. *Advancing the Homeland Security Information Sharing Environment,* Majority Staff Report.

70. Mike Sena, President, National Fusion Center Association, Before the House Committee on Homeland Security, September 8, 2016.

71. *Ten Years After 9/11: 2001.*

72. *Examining the Mission, Structure, and Reorganization Effort of the National Protection and Programs Directorate,* Before the Subcommittee on Cybersecurity, Infrastructure, Protection, and Security Technologies, Committee on Homeland Security, House of Representatives, 114th Cong. (2015).

73. *Commerce, Justice, Science, and Related Agencies Appropriations for 2016,* pt. 2B.

12

Lessons Observed (If Not Learned)

The domestically oriented intelligence enterprise is a product of reaction. It has grown—both within individual agencies and in totality—by aggregation rather than by design. Although this increasingly complex architecture is in need of renovation, reforms since 9/11 have not addressed systemic problems that emerged as the domestic mission space grew increasingly crowded with overlapping and sometimes competing federal and subfederal agencies. The current status quo has not served policymakers well. Rather than providing an understanding of the panoply of issues and opportunities on the horizon, the intelligence enterprise within the domestic setting has become anchored to the issue of terrorism.

Although the FBI is the primary domestically focused intelligence service—as much by de facto occurrence as by deliberate decision—it is a flawed foundation for the federal and subfederal architecture. The Bureau has never been able to—and if its track record in reform is any indication, will never be able to—transcend its reactive, law enforcement roots to become a coherent intelligence service.

The FBI's fundamentally reactive culture—a legacy from its earliest days—has created two significant and likely insurmountable obstacles to becoming a fully realized intelligence service. First, the "case closed" mentality of law enforcement makes it easy to justify moving resources from issue to issue as needed. This undermines the development of deep expertise, and this shallowness is apparent in the underdevelopment of the Bureau's analytical corps. Mueller's view of analysts, as indicated by the Strategic Execution Team initiative, was one of interchangeability. This commoditization of personnel disregards the role of expertise (and provides no incentive to develop human capital beyond automaton status). The second obstacle is the indifference of an investigative agency—even when it is supposed to function as an intelligence service—to external

209

constituents. Mueller made it clear that intelligence was the by-product of cases and that the Bureau answered intelligence requirements as a function ancillary to disruption threats. The introduction of the Threat Review and Prioritization Process institutionalized the self-licking ice cream cone mentality.

Looking beyond the Bureau, the domestically oriented intelligence enterprise exists on an unlevel foundation. Two taxonomies for understanding intelligence within the domestic setting emerged during the twentieth century. These two conceptual frameworks—actor-oriented and implement-oriented—have created confusion within, and conflict among, agencies.

During the 1970s, both the DEA and the ATF (both of which evolved from existing agencies) became part of the domestically oriented national security enterprise and were organized around implements rather than actors. As a result, both of these agencies have intersected—at times acrimoniously—with the FBI. The Bureau itself, after 9/11, developed its own components—the Cyber Division and the WMD Directorate—with structures oriented around implements. This approach broke from the established adversary-centric model around which the Bureau's Counterterrorism Division, Counterintelligence Division, and Criminal Investigative Division were organized.

Collection of foreign intelligence within the domestic setting remains a largely unmet challenge. The FBI, coming from a reactive legacy, has never been able to systematically exploit opportunities for collection of foreign intelligence information present in the domestic setting, even though the Bureau's long-standing counterterrorism, counterintelligence, and criminal investigative missions have brought it into contact with foreign intelligence information. Rather than establishing a systematic approach to assessing and exploiting opportunities to collect in furtherance of providing policymakers with an information advantage, the FBI—with a few notable exceptions (e.g., the SOLO operation, which provided indicators of the Sino-Soviet split)—has treated foreign intelligence information as not worth collecting in a dedicated manner but instead as a by-product that might be churned up by traditional threat-focused activity. The CIA, even though it does have a domestic component—the National Resources Division—is limited in what it can do within the United States by the National Security Act of 1947.

Another development in the evolution of the domestically oriented intelligence enterprise is the increasing integration of subfederal entities into the intelligence infrastructure. The FBI throughout much of the twentieth century played a significant role in connecting state and local agencies with national-level information. This function eventually took the form of the Bureau's Criminal Justice Information Services Division. Additionally, subfederal agencies began working in earnest during the 1970s to develop lateral integration in furtherance of combating criminal threats. These information-sharing initiatives were the predecessors to the modern fusion centers. The DHS has become the primary federal point of contact for the national network of fusion centers.

Lessons Observed (If Not Learned) from the Post-9/11 Reform Efforts

The United States cannot afford to allow its ersatz domestically oriented intelligence enterprise to simply lurch along from crisis to crisis. It is essential to consciously assess and eliminate the structural deficiencies that have developed during more than a century of evolution by aggregation. To return to the analogy of architecture, the intelligence infrastructure within the United States does not need a wrecking ball—but it does need a renovation.

The changes to intelligence in the domestic setting, responsive to 9/11, illustrate the perils of crisis-driven, reactive decisionmaking. First, reform can become anchored to a specific issue that has particular vividness but decreasing relative significance in the long term. Second, reform may respond to public and political demands rather than address realities. A third related concern is that the urgency of responding to pressure from the electorate may lead to the path of least resistance, allowing bureaucrats to dig in their heels to protect their turf and thereby redirect reform efforts toward easier targets.

In the wake of an intelligence failure, it becomes too easy to construct bureaucracies around—and to reorient existing organizations toward—a single issue. The creation of the Counterterrorism Center, a relatively large entity, is an example of a new bureaucracy that—as terrorism devolves into incidents of violent crime and becomes relatively less significant than other unforeseen issues—has the potential to become a white elephant. Existing agencies find reasons to refocus their efforts toward the issue du jour, as in the case of the DEA making narcoterrorism its primary mission after 9/11. Arguably this narrowing of perspective has made the United States less attuned to other threats (e.g., foreign interference in the US political process).

Additionally, decisions may be only tangentially responsive to reality and instead address public and political perceptions of the problem, no matter how distorted those perceptions might be. The creation of the DHS falls squarely into this category. Members of Congress—especially Joseph Lieberman—attempted to score political points against the White House (and placate the electorate) by calling for the creation of a Department of Homeland Security. The White House responded with its own proposal for a new department, which the Oval Office had previously believed should not exist. The DHS's composition, rather than including the necessary components, included only the politically feasible ones. Nearly two decades later, the DHS is still struggling to define itself.

Finally, the sense of urgency to demonstrate progress means that bureaucrats intent on preserving a fiefdom may be able to dig in their heels and ride out the storm, since it may simply be easier for elected officials to demonstrate success to their constituencies in some other way. Robert Mueller's intransigence is an example of this. In the face of demands to carve up the FBI, Mueller stood firm and insisted on keeping the agency intact. Unfortunately, leaving the Bureau intact resulted in redundancies across the government (e.g., the competing missions of the Bureau and the DHS's Immigration and Customs Enforcement). Realigning the FBI's functions—especially those that the Bureau admitted it lacked the resources to execute—would have contributed to a more effective whole-of-government approach to intelligence within the domestic environment.

The best time for a well-considered renovation of the domestically oriented intelligence architecture of the United States is during a period of calm rather than crisis. Unfortunately, the potential for reform in peacetime is significantly constrained by the reality that there is not a political will to create a new agency that can effectively collect intelligence within the domestic setting. In the months and years immediately following 9/11—when the public perceived the need for a dramatic solution to intelligence failures—the will did exist, especially when it came to the question of splitting the FBI. However, Mueller's insistence on keeping the Bureau unified (only to subsequently fail at fundamentally fixing the agency) thwarted this proposal.

Without a countervailing crisis, Cassandras and skeptics can too easily dominate the public discussion. Nearly two decades have passed since the trauma of September 11. The civil liberties lobby's histrionics would likely scuttle any proposal for a United Kingdom–like MI5, just as it killed the DHS's National Applications Office. Furthermore, the government's own previous missteps have created skepticism about the efficacy of reform. The inauspicious example of the DHS has become shorthand for federal ineptitude.

Realistic Reform

Even with the present parameters, reform is still possible. However, rather than creating new agencies, policymakers should focus on realigning missions and functions in order to create comparative advantages among those agencies responsible for the intelligence picture within the domestic setting. This approach would also force integration and information sharing by eliminating redundancies and engendering interagency reliance. Necessity, rather than nicety, will do more for integration than the ODNI's coaxing and cajoling.

Create a Common Point of Reference

Intelligence entities—whether part of the formal intelligence community or not—should share a common point of reference. The National Intelligence Priorities Framework is currently the vehicle for communicating the issues of concern to policymakers. However, the DHS's need to create a Homeland Security Intelligence Priorities Framework indicates that the NIPF may not be sufficiently inclusive of domestic topics. The NIPF should, consequently, be reviewed and revised, as necessary, to reflect intelligence needs of a foreign and domestic nature. Requirements, based on whatever framework results, must be effectively communicated to non–intelligence community and nonfederal collectors.

Furthermore, the agencies engaged in the collection of intelligence domestically should be speaking the same language, consistently. There are numerous examples of how nomenclature varies from one agency to the next. For instance, "sources" and "informants" are synonymous and this problem becomes even more complex when the term "agent"—which, depending on who is talking, can mean either a source or a federal gun-toter—enters the mix. Similarly, while the term "measures and signatures intelligence" means the collection and analysis of ephemera, the FBI refers to related functions as forensics. The list goes on: "wiretap"/"SIGINT," "indicator"/"evidence," "collector"/"investigator." Standardization of terminology will help to create a more unified culture—and facilitate information sharing—across agencies.

The problem of inconsistent terminology—and the competing cultures that it creates—can even create divisions within a single agency. A prime example of this is the FBI during the Mueller years. Although any FBI special agent who developed sources was engaged in human intelligence collection, Mueller's Bureau limited the term "HUMINT" to specific squads, which allowed the corporate FBI to avoid adopting this aspect of an intelligence identity. This was a microcosm of a larger problem within the Bureau under Mueller and Comey, both of whom propagated a bifurcated organizational identify of "intelligence" and "law enforcement." Personnel who opposed the institutionalization of intelligence could invoke their role in "law enforcement" as cover for not adopting an intelligence-oriented identity.

Finally, for an organization to develop a coherent corporate culture that its personnel will adopt, there needs to be a shared sense of history and mission. As the Strategic Execution Team initiative demonstrated, the FBI was unable to demonstrate the underlying continuity—although it existed—between its historical experience with intelligence and its attempt to institutionalize an intelligence-oriented culture. A larger problem is that agencies may simply become too large, or diversified, for their employees to share a meaningful common point of reference. This is currently the case with both the DHS and the FBI, and it is a conundrum that can be resolved only with judicious pruning.

Orient Intelligence Agencies Around Intelligence

Once the broader US national security community has found a common language, agencies should put this language to use and orient their architecture around intelligence. Amazingly, this has not been the case so far. Mueller gilded the FBI's underlying dysfunctions with intelligence jargon but failed to actually transform a reactive law enforcement agency into one that treated intelligence as a starting point for all of its work—whether that work entailed running anomalies to the ground in order to effect prosecutions or involved providing policymakers with an informational advantage. The DHS has experienced similar difficulties with organizing around a unified intelligence mission, thanks to its origins as a stew of injudiciously combined bureaucratic entities.

Federal Bureau of Investigation. Contrary to received wisdom the FBI should not be divided along "law enforcement" and "national security" lines. "National security" is an arbitrary term, since domestic criminal problems imperil national security by corroding elements of US national power—such as economic strength—from within the homeland.

Rather, the Bureau should think of intelligence as its common denominator—with collection across programs of concern to policymakers. This understanding should incorporate not only an understanding of threats but also an ongoing assessment of opportunities for collection of foreign intelligence information. By maintaining a dynamic understanding—rather than surging resources from one crisis to the next—of its area of responsibility, the Bureau would be well-positioned to protect and promote the country's interests.

Intelligence collection, by special agents and others, against NIPF topics, would provide a point of departure for strategic and tactical functions. Strategically, the Bureau would be able to continuously contribute to policymakers' informational advantage. Orienting the FBI toward a common intelligence picture would also provide it the starting point to conduct specific, tactical activities—premised on anomalies—to disrupt discrete threat actors. Therefore, the Bureau should be structured like a triptych: the central portion would be collection against requirements that correspond with US strategic interests; the left panel would be investigations to address anomalies identified throughout the course of requirements-premised collection; and the right panel would be the elevation of requirements-driven collection to policymakers.

Department of Homeland Security. The majority of the DHS's components are passive collectors of information entering and exiting the United States, whether physically (in the case of borders) or virtually (in the case of the cyber environment). It is not structured to conduct requirements-driven collection but instead to gather and analyze data and assess and reinforce the vulnerabilities of borders (ranging from national lines of demarcation to the security of individual industrial facilities' physical and intellectual property). Its analytic function should be exploiting the data that pass through the DHS's points of collection in order to identify trends that might, in their own right, pose a threat to the United States, or that contribute to a broader understanding of how larger threats (or opportunities) might develop.

Realign Missions and Individual Components to Bolster Comparative Advantages

Once agencies have a common point of reference and a distilled sense of their intelligence role, mission sets should be realigned to create comparative advantages across agencies. Form should follow function; when discussing the architecture of intelligence in the domestic setting, this means ensuring that the right agencies have competencies that align with their overarching cultural identity (e.g., the DHS is a passive collector and coordinator of information). The creation of comparative advantages will help individual agencies function more efficiently, by facilitating their cohesion around a shared vision and sense of identity.

Furthermore, the process will produce greater integration across the
domestic security community, since it will eliminate redundancies, forcing agencies to leverage counterparts' capabilities.

Orienting the FBI around a mission of proactive intelligence collection will serve as a point of departure for reforms. The Bureau should
absorb Homeland Security Investigations, which as an investigative
agency is an outlier in the primarily passive Department of Homeland
Security. Furthermore, the FBI should incorporate the Drug Enforcement Administration and the Bureau of Alcohol, Tobacco, Firearms, and
Explosives. Both of these agencies are repositories of expertise and
would complement the FBI's current approach of matrixing knowledge
of implements (i.e., cyber and WMD) to collection of specific types of
activity (i.e., intelligence, terrorism, and crime). Consolidating Homeland Security Investigations, the ATF, and the DEA within the Bureau
would eliminate current jurisdictional conflicts.

The Bureau should thoroughly integrate with the CIA's National
Resources Division in order to ensure that opportunities for the collection
of foreign intelligence within the domestic setting are fully exploited.
Several developments have already moved the FBI and CIA toward
greater integration. The CIA is already represented on the FBI's JTTFs
and is a member of the intelligence community, which the FBI's DNI
domestic representatives coordinate. There is clearly a vacuum within
the FBI when it comes to the identification and exploitation of opportunities for the collection of foreign intelligence information. Incorporating CIA's National Resources Division into the Bureau's structure while
allowing the Agency to retain control of its integrated resources—similar in concept but on a larger scale than the assignment of representatives to the JTTFs—would benefit both organizations.

However, the Bureau also needs to relinquish certain functions. Its
Criminal Justice Information Services Division is the product of the
FBI's legacy as a hub for information sharing with law enforcement
entities. This mission predates the formation of the DHS, which is now
the primary point of contact for subfederal fusion centers. Moving the
CJIS to the DHS would complement the DHS's current role in the information-sharing environment.

Relocating the CJIS from the FBI to the DHS would help to reduce
a potential point of failure in the sharing of information. The events
leading up to the Parkland school shooting illustrate the need for this
consolidation. The FBI's Public Access Line—part of the CJIS—which
fields tips, received both an email and a telephone warning of the

potential for violence by the individual who was ultimately responsible for the shooting.[1] Had the CJIS been more closely tied to the national network of fusion centers, this information may have been made more readily available to the state and local participants who constituted the relevant regional center.

Additionally, there is already redundancy between the FBI and the DHS in the area of information sharing with subfederal entities. The FBI's CJIS operates the National Crime Information Center, but the DHS's Bureau of Immigration and Customs Enforcement operates its own Law Enforcement Support Center, which fields inquiries from authorities who are trying to determine the status of individuals who authorities have encountered or detained.[2] For the sake of streamlining government, FBI and Immigration and Customs Enforcement information-sharing services should be consolidated under the DHS, in conjunction with the department's responsibility for the national network of fusion centers.

Furthermore, the DHS's Office of Intelligence and Analysis should assume responsibility for the DNI domestic representatives program. The OI&A—especially if the DHS can be streamlined around a mission of passive collection—is responsible for assessing a landscape, rather than engaging in operations. Therefore, unlike the FBI, which is dual-hatted as a coordinator and collector, the OI&A can serve as an honest broker, since the OI&A is an element of an agency that cannot claim credit for investigatory outcomes.

Identify Opportunities to Divest Functions That Can Be Handled at the Subfederal Level

Federal agencies are currently overstretched. Mueller acknowledged that there are functions that the FBI did not have the resources to address and therefore needed to enlist assistance from other agencies. This should have led policymakers to ask why the Bureau should continue to maintain responsibilities for those functions, rather than relinquishing them to other entities. One solution to this dilemma is to identify those missions that subfederal agencies are capable of carrying out, and recusing the Bureau from these responsibilities.

Several developments have made this a realistic option. Subfederal entities have become de facto components of the domestically oriented intelligence enterprise and are already addressing national-level concerns. Furthermore, with their greater knowledge and technical sophistication, federal agencies have provided assistance to subfederal entities, thereby enhancing subfederal agencies' capacities for addressing issues of greater complexity.

Consider the Roles of Nontraditional Participants

The evolving nature of challenges to US national security requires thinking about possible partners in new ways. For instance, the National Institute of Standards and Technology would be an ideal coordinator of functions of the National Cyber Investigative Joint Task Force and the National Cybersecurity and Communications Integration Center. These two bodies, currently under the FBI and the DHS respectively, handle the two aspects—neutralizing threats and assessing the landscape—of the cyber domain and the threats that exploit this domain. NIST, as the body responsible for the National Cybersecurity Framework, would benefit from the findings of the NCIJTF and the NCCIC to enhance US cybersecurity policy. Furthermore, NIST already engages with the US intelligence community. It is an observer on the Committee on National Security Systems, where it interacts with the National Security Agency on issues of cryptography.[3] NIST is therefore not a stranger to the world of intelligence.

Nothing Is Sacred

Individual and institutional pride are dangerous impediments to improving how the United States conducts intelligence work within the domestic setting. An ersatz infrastructure of agencies created ad hoc over more than a century has emerged and currently does not function efficiently or effectively. To ensure the security of the American people and to improve decisionmakers' decision advantage, the United States needs to rework its current domestically oriented intelligence enterprise around a common vision, into a coherent community capable of comprehensive collection.

Notes

1. "Oversight of the Parkland Shooting and Legislative Proposals to Improve School Safety," March 14, 2018, https://www.fbi.gov/news/testimony/oversight-of-the-parkland-shooting-and-legislative-proposals-to-improve-school-safety.

2. *Department of Homeland Security Transition: Bureau of Immigration and Customs Enforcement,* Before the Subcommittee on Immigration, Border Security, and Claims of the Committee on the Judiciary, House of Representatives, 108th Cong. (2003).

3. National Institute of Standards and Technology, *NIST Cryptographic Standards and Guidelines Development Process* (Gaithersburg, MD, 2016), https://nvlpubs.nist.gov/nistpubs/ir/2016/NIST.IR.7977.pdf.

Acronyms

AIPAC	American Israel Public Affairs Committee
AMOC	Air and Marine Operations Center (Customs and Border Protection)
ANSIR	Awareness of National Security Issues and Response (FBI)
ASI	America's Shield initiative
ATF	Bureau of Alcohol, Tobacco, Firearms, and Explosives
CAARS	Cargo Advanced Automated Radiography System (DNDO)
CAC	Civil Application Committee
CFATS	Chemical Facility Anti-Terrorism Standards
CIA	Central Intelligence Agency
CINRAD	Communist Infiltration of Radiation Laboratory (FBI)
CINT	chief intelligence officer (DHS)
CJIS	Criminal Justice Information Services Division (FBI)
CPC	Counterproliferation Center (FBI)
CPIP	Counter Proliferation Investigations Program (FBI)
CTT	Cyber Threat Team (FBI)
CyD	Cyber Division (FBI)
DCI	director of central intelligence (succeeded by the director of national intelligence)
DDINR	Domestic Director of National Intelligence Representative Program
DEA	Drug Enforcement Administration
DECA	Development of Espionage, Counterintelligence, and Counterterrorism Awareness (FBI)
DHCC	Domestic Human Intelligence Collection Course (FBI)
DHS	Department of Homeland Security
DIA	Defense Intelligence Agency

DNDO	Domestic Nuclear Detection Office (DHS)
DNI	director of national intelligence
DoD	Department of Defense
DoJ	Department of Justice
DOP	Desk Officer Program (FBI)
EPIC	El Paso Intelligence Center (DEA)
FAA	Federal Aviation Administration
FALN	Armed Forces of National Liberation (Puerto Rico)
FBI	Federal Bureau of Investigation
FDNS	Office of Fraud Detection and National Security (CIS)
FEMA	Federal Emergency Management Agency
FFRDC	Federally Funded Research and Development Center (FBI)
FICP	Foreign Intelligence Collection Program (FBI)
FIG	Field Intelligence Group (FBI)
FISA	Foreign Intelligence Surveillance Act
FISC	Foreign Intelligence Surveillance Court
FSB	Federal Security Service (Russia)
GAO	General Accounting Office (Government Accountability Office after 2007)
GATF	Government Applications Task Force
GEOINT	geospatial intelligence
GSA	General Services Administration
HIDTA	High-Intensity Drug Trafficking Area (DEA)
HITRAC	Homeland Infrastructure Threat and Risk Analysis Center (DHS)
HSIC	Homeland Security Intelligence Council (DHS)
HSIPF	Homeland Security Intelligence Requirements Framework (DHS)
HUMINT	human intelligence
IAIP	Information Analysis and Infrastructure Protection Directorate (DHS)
IASD	Information Analysis and Strategy Division (NPPD)
ICS-CERT	Industrial Control Systems–Cyber Emergency Response Team (DHS)
IIR	Intelligence Information Report (FBI)
IMINT	imagery intelligence
INS	Immigration and Naturalization Service
INSA	Intelligence and National Security Alliance
IPD	Investigative Programs Division (Homeland Security Investigations)

IRCMU	Intelligence Requirements and Collection Management Unit (FBI)
IRS	Internal Revenue Service
IRTPA	Intelligence Reform and Terrorism Prevention Act
ISD	Investigative Services Division (FBI)
ITACG	Interagency Threat Assessment and Coordination Group (National Counterterrorism Center)
JCAT	Joint Counterterrorism Assessment Team
JRIG	Joint Regional Intelligence Group (FBI)
JTTF	Joint Terrorism Task Force (FBI)
LAPD	Los Angeles Police Department
LEAA	Law Enforcement Assistance Administration (DoJ)
LEO	Law Enforcement Online (FBI)
LESC	Law Enforcement Support Center (Bureau of Immigration and Customs Enforcement)
MASINT	measures and signatures intelligence
NAO	National Applications Office
NAPA	National Academy of Public Administration
NASA	National Aeronautics and Space Administration
NCC	National Coordinating Center for Communications
NCCIC	National Cybersecurity and Communications Integration Center (DHS)
NCIJTF	National Cyber Investigative Joint Task Force (FBI)
NCPC	National Counterproliferation Center
NCSD	National Cyber Security Division (DHS)
NCTC	National Counterterrorism Center
NGA	National Geospatial Intelligence Agency
NGIC	National Gang Intelligence Center
NIPC	National Infrastructure Protection Center
NIPF	National Intelligence Priorities Framework
NIST	National Institute of Standards and Technology (Department of Commerce)
NJTTF	National Joint Terrorism Task Force (FBI)
NO&I	NCCIC Operations and Integration
NOAA	National Oceanic and Atmospheric Administration
NPPD	National Protection and Programs Directorate (DHS)
NSA	National Security Agency
NSB	National Security Branch (FBI)
NSID	National Security Investigations Division (Immigration and Customs Enforcement)

NTC	National Targeting Center (Customs and Border Protection)
NYPD	New York Police Department
ODNI	Office of the Director of National Intelligence
OHS	Office of Homeland Security
OI&A	Office of Intelligence and Analysis (DHS)
OIG	Office of the Inspector General (DoJ)
OIOC	Office of Intelligence and Operations Coordination (Customs and Border Protection)
OLEC	Office of Law Enforcement Coordination (FBI)
PFIAB	President's Foreign Intelligence Advisory Board
R&D	research and development
RISS	Regional Information-Sharing System
RISSNET	RISS Network
SET	Strategic Execution Team (FBI)
SIGINT	signals intelligence
SOD	Special Operations Division (DEA)
TECS	Treasury Enforcement Communication System
TRAC	Terrorist Research and Analytic Center (FBI)
TRP	Threat Review and Prioritization (FBI)
TSA	Transportation Security Administration
TSC	Terrorist Screening Center
TSIS	Transportation Security Intelligence Service (TSA)
TTIC	Terrorist Threat Integration Center
US-CERT	US Computer Emergency Readiness Team
USCIS	US Citizenship and Immigration Services (DHS)
USDS	US Digital Service
WMD	weapons of mass destruction
WMDD	Weapons of Mass Destruction Directorate (FBI)

Bibliography

Allen, Michael. *Blinking Red: Crisis and Compromise in American Intelligence After 9/11.* Washington, DC. Potomac. 2016.

American Civil Liberties Union. *Unleashed and Unaccountable: The FBI's Unchecked Abuse of Authority.* New York. American Civil Liberties Union. 2013.

Andrew, Christopher. *For the President's Eyes Only: Secret Intelligence and the American Presidency from Washington to Bush.* New York. Harper Perennial. 1996.

Apuzzo, Matt, and Adam Goldman. *Enemies Within: Inside the NYPD's Secret Spying Unit and Bin Laden's Final Plot Against America.* New York. Simon and Schuster. 2013.

Attorney General. *Guidelines for FBI Foreign Intelligence Collection and Foreign Counterintelligence Investigations.* Washington, DC. Department of Justice. 1983.

———. *Guidelines on FBI Undercover Operations.* Washington, DC. Department of Justice. 1982.

———. *Guidelines Regarding Disclosure to the Director of Central Intelligence and Homeland Security Officials of Foreign Intelligence Acquired in the Course of a Criminal Investigation.* Washington, DC. Department of Justice. 2002.

———. *Guidelines Regarding the Use of FBI Confidential Human Sources.* Washington, DC. Department of Justice. 2006.

———. *Intelligence Sharing Procedures for Foreign Intelligence and Counterintelligence Investigations Conducted by the FBI.* Washington, DC. Department of Justice. 2002.

———. *Report on Federal Law Enforcement and Criminal Justice Assistance Activities.* Washington, DC. Department of Justice. 1979.

Baginski, Maureen A., Executive Assistant Director for Intelligence, Federal Bureau of Investigation. Before the House Permanent Select Committee on Intelligence. Washington, DC. August 4, 2004.

———. Before the House Select Committee on Homeland Security. Washington, DC. August 19, 2004.

Bald, Gary M. Before the Senate Committee on the Judiciary. Washington, DC. September 21, 2005.

Barron, John. *Operation SOLO: The FBI's Man in the Kremlin.* Washington, DC. Regnery. 1996.

Bazan, Elizabeth B., and Jennifer K. Elsea. *Presidential Authority to Conduct Warrantless Electronic Surveillance to Gather Foreign Intelligence Information.* Washington, DC. Congressional Research Service. 2006.

Bell, Griffin B., and Lee Colwell. *Study of the FBI's Office of Professional Responsibility.* Washington, CD. Federal Bureau of Investigation. 2004.

Berkman Center for Internet & Society. *Don't Panic: Making Progress on the "Going Dark" Debate.* Cambridge. Harvard University Press. 2016.

Best, Richard A. *Homeland Security Intelligence Support.* Washington, DC. Congressional Research Service. 2004.

————. *The National Counterterrorism Center (NCTC)—Responsibilities and Potential Congressional Concerns.* Washington, DC. Congressional Research Service. 2011.

Best, Richard A., and Jennifer K. Elsea. *Satellite Surveillance: Domestic Issues.* Washington, DC. Congressional Research Service. 2008.

Bjelopera, Jerome P. *The Federal Bureau of Investigation and Terrorism Investigations.* Washington, DC. Congressional Research Service. 2013.

————. *Homeland Security Investigations: A Directorate Within U.S. Immigration and Customs Enforcement—In Brief.* Washington, DC. Congressional Research Service. 2015.

Boorestein, Michelle. "Muslim Activists Alarmed by the FBI's New Game-Like Counterterrorism Program for Kids." *Washington Post.* November 2, 2015.

Business Executives for National Security. *Task Force on Domestic Security Structures and Processes.* Washington, DC. 2014.

Center for Cryptologic History. *American Cryptology During the Cold War, 1945–1989.* Washington, DC. 1995.

Commission on the Intelligence Capabilities of the United States Regarding Weapons of Mass Destruction. *Report to the President of the United States.* Washington, DC. 2005.

Critical Incident Response Group. *Bureau Aviation Regulations Policy Directive and Policy Guide.* Washington, DC. Federal Bureau of Investigation. 2015.

Crumpton, Henry A. *The Art of Intelligence: Lessons from a Life in the CIA's Clandestine Service.* New York. Penguin. 2012.

Cumming, Alfred, and Todd Masse. *FBI Intelligence Reform Since September 11, 2001: Issues and Options for Congress.* Washington, DC. Congressional Research Service. 2004.

————. *Intelligence Reform Implementation at the Federal Bureau of Investigation: Issues and Options for Congress.* Washington, DC. Congressional Research Service. 2005.

Dowing, Michael P., and Matt Mayer. *The Domestic Counterterrorism Enterprise: Time to Streamline.* Washington, DC. Heritage Foundation. 2012.

Doyle, Charles. *The USA PATRIOT Act: A Legal Analysis.* Washington, DC. Congressional Research Service. 2002.

Electronic Frontier Foundation. *New FBI Documents Provide Details on Government's Surveillance Spyware.* San Francisco. 2011.

————. *Report on the Investigative Data Warehouse.* San Francisco. 2009.

Federal Bureau of Investigation. *CJIS Annual Report 2013.* Washington, DC. 2013.

————. *Confidential Funding Policy Implementation Guide.* Washington, DC. 2009.

————. *Confidential Human Source Policy Manual.* Washington, DC. 2007.

————. *Confidential Human Source Validation Standards Manual.* Washington, DC. 2010.

————. *Domestic Intelligence Division Inspection, 1/8–2/6/71.* Washington, DC. 1971.

————. *Domestic Intelligence Division Inspection, 2 April 1970.* Washington, DC. 1970.

————. *Domestic Intelligence Division Inspection, 8/17–9/9/71.* Washington, DC. 1971.

————. *Domestic Intelligence Division Inspection, 8/18–9/1/72.* Washington, DC. 1972.

————. *FBI Counterintelligence National Strategy: A Blueprint for Protecting U.S. Secrets.* Washington, DC. 2011.

————. *FBI Domestic Investigations and Operations Guide.* Washington, DC. 2008, 2011.

————. *FBI Information Sharing & Safeguarding Report 2012.* Washington, DC. 2012.

————. *FBI Intelligence Requires and Collection Management Handbook.* Washington, DC. Undated.

————. *FBI Laboratory 2007: Supporting FBI's Operations for 75 Years.* Washington, DC. 2007.

————. *Federal Bureau of Investigation Assumption of Federal Drug Enforcement: A Feasibility Study.* Washington, DC. 1977.

————. *FY 2008 Authorization and Budget Request to Congress.* Washington, DC. 2007.

————. *FY 2012 Authorization and Budget Request to Congress.* Washington, DC. 2011.

————. *FY 2013 Authorization and Budget Request to Congress.* Washington, DC. 2012.

————. *FY 2014 Authorization and Budget Request to Congress.* Washington, DC. 2013.

————. *FY 2015 Authorization and Budget Request to Congress.* Washington, DC. 2014.

————. *Inspection—Domestic Intelligence Division, May 26, 1969.* Washington, DC. 1969.

————. *Intelligence Division Inspection, 10/23/73.* Washington, DC. 1973.

————. *Intelligence Division Inspection, 3/11/75–4/4/75.* Washington, DC. 1975.

————. *Intelligence Information Report Policy Implementation Guide.* Washington, DC. 2010.

————. *National Foreign Intelligence Program Manual.* Washington, DC. 2010.

————. *The New Field Intelligence: March 2008–March 2009.* Version 1.5. Washington, DC. 2009.

————. *Regional Computer Forensics Laboratory Annual Report for Fiscal Year 2013.* Washington, DC. 2013.

————. *A Review of FBI Electronic Surveillance and Records Management Programs in Response to a Referral by the U.S. Office of Special Counsel.* Washington, DC. 2013.

————. *Revised National Foreign Intelligence Program Manual.* Washington, DC. 2006.

————. *Summary of PENTTBOM Investigation.* Washington, DC. 2004.

General Accounting Office. *Accomplishments of FBI Undercover Operations.* Washington, DC. 1984.

————. *ADP Procurement: FBI Addresses Risk to Its National Crime Information Center Acquisition.* Washington, DC. 1991.

————. "Comments of Comptroller General of the United States on Draft Guidelines for Curtailing the FBI's Domestic Intelligence Operation." Washington, DC. 1976.

————. *Costs of FBI Undercover Operations.* Washington, DC. 1983.

————. *Critical Infrastructure Protection: Department of Homeland Security Faces Challenges in Fulfilling Cybersecurity Responsibilities.* Washington, DC. 2005.

————. *Drug Control: DEA's Strategies and Operations in the 1990s.* Washington, DC. 1999.

————. *Drug Investigations: Organized Crime Drug Enforcement Task Force Program: A Coordinating Mechanism.* Washington, DC. 1986.

————. *FBI Advanced Communications Technologies Pose Wiretapping Challenges.* Washington, DC. 1992.

————. *FBI Continues to Make Progress in Its Efforts to Transform and Address Priorities.* Washington, DC. 2004.

————. *FBI Domestic Intelligence Operations: An Uncertain Future.* Washington, DC. 1977.

————. *FBI Domestic Intelligence Operations: Their Purpose and Scope—Issues That Need to Be Resolved.* Washington, DC. 1976.

————. *FBI Intelligence Investigations: Coordination Within Justice on Counterintelligence Criminal Matters Is Limited.* Washington, DC. 2001.

————. *FBI Management of Its Automated Information Systems.* Washington, DC. 1983.

————. *FBI Reorganization: Initial Steps Encouraging but Broad Transformation Needed.* Washington, DC. 2002.

————. *FBI Reorganization: Progress Made in Efforts to Transform but Major Challenges Continue.* Washington, DC. 2003.

————. *FBI Taking Actions to Comply Fully with the Privacy Act.* Washington, DC. 1977.

————. *FBI Transformation: Human Capital Strategies May Assist the FBI in Its Commitments to Address Its Top Priorities.* Washington, DC. 2004.

————. *The FBI's System for Managing Investigative Resources and Measuring Results—Improvements Are Being Made.* Washington, DC. 1978.

————. *FBI-DEA Task Forces: An Unsuccessful Attempt at Joint Operations.* Washington, DC. 1982.

————. *Federal Bureau of Investigation's Conduct of Domestic Intelligence Operations Under the Attorney General's Guidelines.* Washington, DC. 1977.

————. *International Terrorism: FBI Investigates Domestic Activities to Identify Terrorists.* Washington, DC. 1990.

————. *International Terrorism: Status of GAO's Review of the FBI's International Terrorism Program.* Washington, DC. 1989.

————. *The Multi-State Regional Intelligence Projects—Who Will Oversee These Federally Funded Networks?* Washington, DC. 1980.

————. *National Crime Information Center: Legislation Needed to Deter Misuse of Criminal Justice Information.* Washington, DC. 1993.

————. Statement of Elmer B. Staats, Comptroller General of the United States. Before the Subcommittee on Civil and Constitutional Rights, House Committee on the Judiciary on Domestic Intelligence Operations of the Federal Bureau of Investigation. Washington, DC. February 24, 1976.

————. Statement of Elmer B. Staats, Comptroller General of the United States. Before the Subcommittee on Civil Rights and Constitutional Rights, House Committee on the Judiciary, on Domestic Intelligence Operations of the Federal Bureau of Investigation. Washington, DC. September 24, 1975.

————. Statement of Victor I. Lowe, Director, General Government Division [General Accounting Office]. Before the Subcommittee on Government Information and Individual Rights, House Government Operations Committee, on the Federal Bureau of Investigation's Conduct of Internal Inquiries Concerning Allegations of Improper Conduct by FBI Employees. Washington, DC. July 21, 1977.

————. Summary Statement of Victor L. Lowe, Director, General Government Division. Before the Subcommittee on Civil and Constitutional Rights, House Committee on the Judiciary, on the Federal Bureau of Investigation's Conduct of Domestic Intelligence Operations Under the Attorney General's Guidelines. Washington, DC. November 9, 1977.

————. *Transportation Security Administration: Progress and Challenges Faced in Strengthening Three Key Security Programs.* Washington, DC. 2012.

Gentry, Curt. *J. Edgar Hoover: The Man and the Secrets.* New York. Norton. 1991.

George, Roger Z., and James B Bruce, eds. *Analyzing Intelligence: National Security Practitioners' Perspectives.* Washington, DC. Georgetown University Press. 2014.

Government Accountability Office. *Aviation Security: TSA Has Enhanced Its Explosives Detection Requirements for Checked Baggage but Additional Screening Actions Are Needed.* Washington, DC. 2011.

————. *Bureau of Alcohol, Tobacco, Firearms, and Explosive: Enhancing Data Collection Could Improve Management of Investigations.* Washington, DC. 2014.

————. *Combating Nuclear Smuggling: DHS Has Made Progress Deploying Radiation Detection Equipment at U.S. Ports of Entry but Concerns Remain.* Washington, DC. 2006.

————. *Combating Nuclear Smuggling: DNDO Has Not Yet Collected Most of the National Laboratories' Test Results on Radiation Portal Monitors in Support of DNDOs Testing and Development Program.* Washington, DC. 2007.

————. *Combating Nuclear Smuggling: Inadequate Communication and Oversight Hampered DHS Efforts to Develop an Advanced Radiography System to Detect Nuclear Materials.* Washington, DC. 2010.

————. *Combating Terrorism: Federal Agencies Face Continuing Challenges in Addressing Terrorist Financing and Money Laundering.* Washington, DC. 2004.

————. *Confidential Informants: Updates to Policy and Additional Guidance Would Improve Oversight by DOJ and DHS Agencies.* Washington, DC. 2015.

————. *Critical Infrastructure Protection: Department of Homeland Security Faces Challenges in Fulfilling Cybersecurity Responsibilities.* Washington, DC. 2005.

————. *Critical Infrastructure Protection: DHS List of Priority Assets Needs to Be Validated and Reported to Congress.* Washington, DC. 2013.

————. *Critical Infrastructure Protection: DHS Risk Assessments Inform Owner and Operator Protection Efforts and Departmental Strategic Planning.* Washington, DC. 2017.

————. *Cybersecurity: DHS's National Integration Center Generally Performs Required Functions but Needs to Evaluate Its Activities More Completely.* Washington, DC. 2017.

————. *DHS Intelligence Analysis: Additional Actions Needed to Address Analytic Priorities and Workforce Challenges.* Washington, DC. 2014.

————. *Drug Control: Better Coordination with the Department of Homeland Security and an Updated Accountability Framework Can Further Enhance DEA's Efforts to Meet Post–9/11 Responsibilities.* Washington, DC. 2009.

————. *FBI Transformation: Data Inconclusive on Effects of Shift to Counterterrorism-Related Priorities on Traditional Crime Enforcement.* Washington, DC. 2004.

————. *Federal Bureau of Investigation: Actions Needed to Document Security Decisions and Address Issues with Condition of Headquarters Buildings.* Washington, DC. 2011.

————. *Federal Bureau of Investigation: Weak Controls over Trilogy Project Led to Payment of Questionable Contractor Costs and Missing Assets.* Washington, DC. 2006.

————. *Firearms Trafficking: U.S. Efforts to Combat Arms Trafficking to Mexico Face Planning and Coordination Challenges.* Washington, DC. 2009.

————. *Homeland Security: Federal Efforts Are Helping to Alleviate Some Challenges Encountered by State and Local Information Fusion Centers.* Washington, DC. 2007.

————. *Homeland Security: Federal Efforts Are Helping to Address Some Challenges Faced by State and Local Fusion Centers.* Washington, DC. 2008.

————. *Information Security: FBI Needs to Address Weaknesses in Critical Network.* Washington, DC. 2007.

————. *Information Sharing: DHS Is Assessing Fusion Center Capabilities and Results but Needs to More Accurately Account for Federal Funding Provided to Centers.* Washington, DC. 2014.

————. *Information Sharing: Federal Agencies Are Helping Fusion Centers Build and Sustain Capabilities and Protect Privacy but Could Better Measure Results.* Washington, DC. 2010.

————. *Information Technology: FBI Has Largely Staffed Key Modernization Program but Strategic Approach to Managing Program's Human Capital Is Needed.* Washington, DC. 2006.

————. *Information Technology: FBI Is Building Management Capabilities Essential to Successful System Deployments but Challenges Remain.* Washington, DC.

————. *Information Technology: FBI Is Taking Steps to Develop an Enterprise Architecture but Much Remains to Be Accomplished.* Washington, DC. 2005.

————. *National Protection and Programs Directorate: Factors to Consider When Reorganizing.* Washington, DC. 2015.

————. *Terrorist Financing: U.S. Agencies Should Systematically Assess Terrorists' Use of Alternative Financing Mechanisms.* Washington, DC. 2003.

————. *Vacancies Have Declined but FBI Has Not Assessed the Long-Term Sustainability of Its Strategy for Addressing Vacancies.* Washington, DC. 2012.

Graff, Garrett M. *The Threat Matrix: The FBI at War in the Age of Global Terror.* New York. Little, Brown. 2011.

Gulati, Ranjay, Jan Rivkin, and Ryan Raffaelli. *Does "What We Do" Make Us "Who We Are"? Organizational Design and Identity Change at the Federal Bureau of Investigation.* Cambridge. Harvard Business School. 2016.

Johnson, Loch. *America's Secret Power: The CIA in a Democratic Society.* New York. Oxford University Press. 1991.

Krouse, William J. *The Bureau of Alcohol, Tobacco, Firearms, and Explosives (ATF): Budget and Operations.* Washington, DC. Congressional Research Service. 2008.

Haddal, Chad C. *Border Security: Key Agencies and Their Missions.* Washington, DC. Congressional Research Service. 2010.

Hamilton, Lee, and Thomas Kean. *Without Precedent: The Inside Story of the 9/11 Commission.* New York. Vintage. 2007.

Harris, Shane. *The Watchers: The Rise of America's Surveillance State.* New York. Penguin. 2010.

Heffter, Clyde R. *A Fresh Look at Collection Requirements.* Langley. Central Intelligence Agency. 1995.

Helms, Richard. *A Look over My Shoulder: A Life in the Central Intelligence Agency.* New York. Random. 2003.

Herbig, Katherine L. *Changes in Espionage by Americans: 1947–2007.* Washington, DC. Department of Defense, Defense Personnel Security Research Center. 2008.

Inspectors General of the Department of Defense, Department of Justice, Central Intelligence Agency, National Security Agency, and Office of the Director of National Intelligence. *Report on the President's Surveillance Program.* Vol. 1. Washington, DC. 2009.

Inspectors General of the Intelligence Community, Central Intelligence Agency, Department of Justice, and Department of Homeland Security. *Unclassified Summary of Information Handling and Sharing Prior to the April 15, 2013, Boston Marathon Bombings.* Washington, DC. 2014.

Inspectors General of the Intelligence Community, Department of Homeland Security, and Department of Justice. *Review of Domestic Sharing of Counterterrorism Information.* Washington, DC. 2017.

Intelligence and National Security Alliance. *Protecting the Homeland: Intelligence Integration 15 Years After 9/11.* Washington, DC. 2016.

Kaiser, Frederick. *Law Enforcement Reorganization at the Federal Level.* Washington, DC. Congressional Research Service. 1979.

Kris, David S. *Modernizing the Foreign Intelligence Surveillance Act.* Washington, DC. Brookings Institution. 2007.

Krouse, William J. *Terrorist Watch List Screening and Background Checks for Firearms.* Washington, DC. Congressional Research Service. 2013.

Kubic, Thomas T., Deputy Assistant Director, Federal Bureau of Investigation. Before the House Committee on the Judiciary, Subcommittee on Crime. Washington, DC. June 12, 2001.

LaFraniere, Sharon. "FBI Reassigns 300 Counterspies to Crime-Fighting." *Washington Post.* January 9, 1992.

Lake, Jennifer E. *Department of Homeland Security: Consolidation of Border and Transportation Security Agencies.* Washington, DC. Congressional Research Service. 2003.

———. *Homeland Security Department: FY2011 Appropriations.* Washington, DC. Congressional Research Service. 2011.

Lavin, Marvin M. *Intelligence Constraints of the 1970s and Domestic Terrorism.* Vol. 2, *Survey of Legal, Legislative, and Administrative Constraints.* Santa Monica. Rand. 1982.

Liu, Edward C. *Reauthorization of the FISA Amendment Act.* Washington, DC. Congressional Research Service. 2013.

Lowenthal, Mark M. *Intelligence: From Secrets to Policy.* 2nd ed. Washington, DC. Congressional Quarterly. 2003.

Masse, Todd, and William Krouse. *The FBI: Past, Present, and Future.* Washington, DC. Congressional Research Service. 2003.

Masse, Todd, Siobhan O'Neil, and John Rollins. *Fusion Centers: Issues and Options for Congress.* Washington, DC. Congressional Research Service. 2007.

Mayer, Matt. A. *Consolidate Domestic Intelligence Entities Under the FBI.* Washington, DC. American Enterprise Institute. 2016.

McGroddy, James, and Herbert S. Lin. *A Review of the FBI's Trilogy Information Technology Modernization Program.* Washington, DC. National Research Council of the National Academies. 2004.

National Academy of Public Administration. *Transforming the FBI: Integrating Management Functions Under a Chief Management Officer.* Washington, DC. 2006.

———. *Transforming the FBI: Progress and Challenges.* Washington, DC. 2005.

———. *Transforming the FBI: Roadmap to an Effective Human Capital Program.* Washington, DC. 2005.

National Commission on Terrorist Attacks upon the United States. *The 9/11 Commission Report.* New York. Norton. 2004.

National Security Agency. *American Cryptology During the Cold War.* Book 3, *Retrenchment and Reform, 1972–1980.* Washington, DC. 1998.

New York Civil Liberties Union v. United States Department of Justice. June 24, 2008.

9/11 Review Commission. *The FBI: Protecting the Homeland in the 21st Century.* Washington, DC. 2015.

Office of the Director of National Intelligence. *Domestic Approach to National Intelligence.* Washington, DC. 2016.

———. *Statistical Transparency Report Regarding Use of National Security Authorities for Calendar Year 2016.* Washington, DC. 2017.

Office of the Inspector General. *Audit of the Bureau of Alcohol, Tobacco, Firearms, and Explosives' Use of Income-Generating, Undercover Operations.* Washington, DC. Department of Justice. 2013.

———. *Audit of the Department of Justice's Use and Support of Unmanned Aircraft Systems.* Washington, DC. Department of Justice. 2015.

———. *Audit of the Federal Bureau of Investigation's and the National Security Division's Efforts to Coordinate and Address Terrorist Financing.* Washington, DC. Department of Justice. 2013.

———. *Audit of the Federal Bureau of Investigation's Cyber Threat Prioritization.* Washington, DC. Department of Justice. 2016.

———. *Audit of the Federal Bureau of Investigation's Implementation of Its Next Generation Cyber Initiative.* Washington, DC. Department of Justice. 2015.

———. *Audit of the Federal Bureau of Investigation's Philadelphia Regional Computer Forensic Laboratory, Radnor, Pennsylvania.* Washington, DC. Department of Justice. 2015.

———. *Audit of the Status of the Federal Bureau of Investigation's Sentinel Program.* Washington, DC. Department of Justice. 2014.

———. *Coordination Between FBI and ICE on Investigations of Terrorist Financing.* Washington, DC. Department of Homeland Security. 2007.

———. *Explosives Investigation Coordination Between the Federal Bureau of Investigation and the Bureau of Alcohol, Tobacco, Firearms, and Explosives.* Washington, DC. Department of Justice. 2009.

———. *The External Effects of the Federal Bureau of Investigation's Reprioritization Efforts* (redacted for public release). Washington, DC. Department of Justice. 2005.

———. *The FBI Laboratory: An Investigation into Laboratory Practices and Alleged Misconduct in Explosives-Related and Other Cases.* Washington, DC. Department of Justice. 1997.

———. *Federal Bureau of Investigation Casework and Human Resource Allocation.* Washington, DC. Department of Justice. 2003.

———. *The Federal Bureau of Investigation's Ability to Address the National Security Cyber Intrusion Threat.* Washington, DC. Department of Justice. 2012.

———. *The Federal Bureau of Investigation's Aviation Operations.* Washington, DC. Department of Justice. 2012.

———. *The Federal Bureau of Investigation's Compliance with the Attorney General's Investigative Guidelines.* Washington, DC. Department of Justice. 2005.

———. *The Federal Bureau of Investigation's Efforts to Hire, Train, and Retain Intelligence Analysts.* Washington, DC. Department of Justice. 2005.

———. *The Federal Bureau of Investigation's Efforts to Improve the Sharing of Intelligence and Other Information.* Washington, DC. Department of Justice. 2003.

————. *The Federal Bureau of Investigation's Foreign Language Program—Translation of Counterterrorism and Counterintelligence Foreign Language Material.* Washington, DC. Department of Justice. 2004.

————. *Federal Bureau of Investigation's Foreign Language Translation Program Follow-Up.* Washington, DC. Department of Justice. 2005.

————. *The Federal Bureau of Investigation's Foreign Terrorist Tracking Task Force.* Washington, DC. Department of Justice. 2013.

————. *The Federal Bureau of Investigation's Implementation of Information Technology Recommendations.* Washington, DC. Department of Justice. 2003.

————. *Federal Bureau of Investigation's Management of Information Technology Investments.* Washington, DC. Department of Justice. 2002.

————. *The Federal Bureau of Investigation's Management of the Trilogy Information Technology Modernization Project.* Washington, DC. Department of Justice. 2005.

————. *The Federal Bureau of Investigation's Pre-Acquisition Planning for and Controls over the Sentinel Case Management System.* Washington, DC. Department of Justice. 2006.

————. *The Federal Bureau of Investigation's Terrorist Threat and Suspicious Incident Tracking System.* Washington, DC. Department of Justice. 2008.

————. *The Federal Bureau of Investigation's Terrorist Watchlist Nomination Practices.* Washington, DC. Department of Justice. 2009.

————. *The Federal Bureau of Investigation's Weapons of Mass Destruction Coordinator Program.* Washington, DC. Department of Justice. 2009.

————. *Follow-Up Audit of the Federal Bureau of Investigation's Efforts to Hire, Train, Retain Intelligence Analysts.* Washington, DC. Department of Justice. 2007.

————. *Follow-Up Audit of the Terrorist Screening Center.* Washington, DC. Department of Justice. 2007.

————. *Implementation of the Communications Assistance for Law Enforcement Act by the Federal Bureau of Investigation.* Washington, DC. Department of Justice. 2008.

————. *Interim Report on the Department of Justice's Use and Support of Unmanned Aircraft Systems.* Washington, DC. Department of Justice. 2013.

————. *Interim Report on the Federal Bureau of Investigation's Implementation of the Sentinel Project.* Washington, DC. Department of Justice. 2012.

————. *The Internal Effects of the Federal Bureau of Investigation's Reprioritization.* Washington, DC. Department of Justice. 2014.

————. *Investigation of Allegations of Cheating on the FBI's Domestic Investigations and Operations Guide (DIOG) Exam.* Washington, DC. Department of Justice. 2010.

————. *A Review of Allegations of a Double Standard of Discipline at the FBI.* Washington, DC. Department of Justice. 2002.

————. *A Review of ATF's Operation Fast and Furious.* Washington, DC. Department of Justice. 2012.

————. *A Review of ATF's Undercover Storefront Operations.* Washington, DC. Department of Justice. 2016.

————. *A Review of the Department's Anti-Gang Intelligence and Coordination Centers.* Washington, DC. Department of Justice. 2009.

————. *A Review of the Department's Use of the Material Witness Statute with a Focus on Select National Security Matters.* Washington, DC. Department of Justice. 2014.

————. *Review of the Drug Enforcement Administration's El Paso Intelligence Center.* Washington, DC. Department of Justice. 2010.

————. *A Review of the FBI's Handling of Intelligence Information Related to the September 11 Attacks.* Washington, DC. Department of Justice. 2004.

————. *A Review of the FBI's Involvement in and Observations of Detainee Interrogations in Guantanamo Bay, Afghanistan, and Iraq.* Washington, DC. Department of Justice. 2009.

————. *A Review of the Federal Bureau of Investigation's Activities Under Section 702 of the Foreign Intelligence Surveillance Act Amendments Act of 2008.* Washington, DC. Department of Justice. 2016.

————. *A Review of the Federal Bureau of Investigation's Counterterrorism Program: Threat Assessment, Strategic Planning, and Resource Management.* Washington, DC. Department of Justice. 2002.

————. *A Review of the Federal Bureau of Investigation's Use of Exigent Letters and Other Informal Requests for Telephone Letters.* Washington, DC. Department of Justice. 2010.

————. *A Review of the Federal Bureau of Investigation's Use of National Security Letters.* Washington, DC. Department of Justice. 2007.

————. *A Review of Federal Bureau of Investigation's Use of Section 215 Orders for Business Records.* Washington, DC. Department of Justice. 2007.

————. *Review of the Organized Crime Drug Enforcement Task Forces Fusion Center.* Washington, DC. Department of Justice. 2014.

————. *Review of the Terrorist Screening Center.* Washington, DC. Department of Justice. 2005.

Office of Public Affairs. *Community Outreach in Field Offices: Corporate Policy Directive and Policy Implementation Guide.* Washington, DC. Federal Bureau of Investigation. 2013.

Painter, William L. *Department of Homeland Security: FY2013 Appropriations.* Washington, DC. Congressional Research Service. 2013.

Parson, Chelsea, and Arkadi Gerney. *The Bureau and the Bureau: A Review of the Bureau of Alcohol, Tobacco, Firearms, and Explosives and a Proposal to Merge It with the Federal Bureau of Investigation.* Washington, DC. Center for American Progress. 2015.

Partnership for Public Service. *Cyber In-Security II: Closing the Federal Talent Gap.* Washington, DC. April 2015.

Powers, Richard Gid. *Broken: The Troubled Past and Uncertain Future of the FBI.* New York. Free Press. 2004.

Privacy and Civil Liberties Oversight Board. *Report on the Surveillance Program Operated Pursuant to Section 702 of the Foreign Intelligence Surveillance Act.* Washington, DC. 2014.

Rafalko, Frank J. *A Counterintelligence Reader.* Vols. 2–3. Washington, DC. Office of the National Counterintelligence Executive. 2011.

Randol, Mark A. *The Department of Homeland Security Intelligence Enterprise: Operational Overview and Oversight Challenges for Congress.* Washington, DC. Congressional Research Service. 2010.

Reese, Shawn. *Selected Federal Homeland Security Assistance Programs: A Summary.* Washington, DC. Congressional Research Service. 2008.

Relyea, Harold C. *Homeland Security: Department Organization and Management.* Washington, DC. Congressional Research Service. 2002.

Relyea, Harold C., and Henry B. Hogue. *Department of Homeland Security Reorganization: The 2SR Initiative.* Washington, DC. Congressional Research Service. 2005.

Rensselaer. Lee. *Homeland Security Office: Issues and Options.* Washington, DC. Congressional Research Service. 2002.

Reuter, Peter. *Licensing Criminals: Police and Informants.* Santa Monica. Rand. 1982.

Richelson, Jeffrey. *The U.S. Intelligence Community.* 6th ed. Boulder. Westview. 2011.

Riebling, Mark. *Wedge: The Secret War Between the FBI and the CIA.* New York. Knopf. 1994.

Riley, K. Jack, Gregory F. Treverton, Jeremy M. Wilson, and Lois M. Davis. *State and Local Intelligence in the War on Terrorism.* Santa Monica. Rand. 2005.

Rivkin, Jan W., Michael Roberto, and Ranjay Gulati. *Federal Bureau of Investigation 2009.* Cambridge. Harvard Business School. 2010.

Rogers, David E. *Creating the Secret State: The Origins of the Central Intelligence Agency, 1943–1947.* Lawrence. University Press of Kansas. 2000.

Rollins, John. *Fusion Centers: Issues and Options for Congress.* Washington, DC. Congressional Research Service. 2008.

Special Security Center. *Intelligence Community Classification and Control Marking Implementation Manual.* Washington, DC. Office of the Director of National Intelligence. 2009.

Treverton, Gregory. *The Next Steps in Reshaping Intelligence.* Santa Monica. Rand. 2005.

———. *Reshaping National Intelligence for an Age of Information.* New York. Cambridge University Press. 2003.

Tromblay, Darren E. *The Domestic Intelligence Enterprise: History, Development, and Operations.* Boca Raton, FL. CRC/Taylor and Francis. 2015.

———. "The Threat Review and Prioritization Trap: How the FBI's New Threat Review and Prioritization Process Compounds the Bureau's Oldest Problems." *Intelligence and National Security* 31, no. 5 (2016): 762–770.

Tromblay, Darren E., and Robert Spelbrink. *Securing U.S. Innovation: The Challenge of Preserving a Competitive Advantage in the Creation of Knowledge.* Lanham, MD. Rowman and Littlefield. 2016.

Ungar, Sanford J. *The FBI.* New York. Little, Brown. 1976.

US Department of Justice. *FY 2014 Authorization and Budget Request to Congress.* Washington, DC. 2013.

———. *Law Enforcement Intelligence: A Guide for State, Local, and Tribal Law Enforcement Agencies.* Washington, DC. 2004.

US House Committee on Appropriations. *Appropriations, Department of Justice, 1924.* Pt. 2. 1922.

———. *Commerce, Justice, Science, and Related Agencies Appropriations for 2009.* Pt. 1. 2009.

———. *Commerce, Justice, Science, and Related Agencies Appropriations for 2012.* Pt. 7. 2011.

———. *Commerce, Justice, Science, and Related Agencies Appropriations for 2014.* Pt. 2B. 2013.

———. *Commerce, Justice, Science, and Related Agencies Appropriations for Fiscal Year 2015.* 2015.

———. *Commerce, Justice, Science, and Related Agencies Appropriations for 2017.* Pt. 2B. 2016.

———. *Departments of Commerce, Justice, and State, the Judiciary, and Related Agencies Appropriations for 1985.* Pt. 8. 1984.

———. *Departments of Commerce, Justice, and State, the Judiciary, and Related Agencies Appropriations for 1988.* Pt. 4. 1987.

———. *Departments of Commerce, Justice, and State, the Judiciary, and Related Agencies Appropriations for 1990.* Pt. 2. 1989.

———. *Departments of Commerce, Justice, and State, the Judiciary, and Related Agencies Appropriations for 1993.* Pt. 2B. 1992.

———. *Departments of Commerce, Justice, and State, the Judiciary, and Related Agencies Appropriations for 1998.* 1997.

———. *Departments of Commerce, Justice, and State, the Judiciary, and Related Agencies Appropriations for 1999.* Pt. 6. 1998.

———. *Departments of Commerce, Justice, and State, the Judiciary, and Related Agencies Appropriations for 2000.* Pt. 6. 1999.

———. *Departments of Commerce, Justice, and State, the Judiciary, and Related Agencies Appropriations for 2001.* Pt. 2. 2000.

———. *Departments of Commerce, Justice, and State, the Judiciary, and Related Agencies appropriations for 2004.* Pt. 10. 2003.

————. *Departments of Commerce, Justice, and State, the Judiciary, and Related Agencies Appropriations for 2005*. Pt. 10. 2004.

————. *Department of Defense Appropriations*. Before a Subcommittee of the Committee on Appropriations. 1975.

————. *Department of Homeland Security Appropriations for 2005*. Pt. 6. 2004.

————. *Department of Homeland Security Appropriations for 2007*. Pt. 1A. 2006.

————. *Department of Homeland Security Appropriations for 2009*. Pt. 1B. 2008.

————. *Department of Homeland Security Appropriations for 2016*. Pt. 1A. 2015.

————. *Department of Homeland Security Appropriations for 2017*. Pt. 1C. 2016.

————. *Department of Homeland Security Appropriations for 2018*. Pt. 1C. 2017.

————. *Department of Justice Appropriations Bill, 1930*. 1928.

————. *Department of Justice Appropriation Bill for 1938*. 1937.

————. *Department of Justice Appropriation Bill for 1943*. 1942.

————. *Departments of State, Justice, and Commerce, the Judiciary, and Related Agencies Appropriations for 1966*. 1965.

————. *Departments of State, Justice, and Commerce, the Judiciary, and Related Agencies Appropriations for 1976*. Pt. 2. 1975.

————. *Departments of State, Justice, and Commerce, the Judiciary, and Related Agencies Appropriations for 1979*. Pt. 6. 1978.

————. *Departments of State, Justice, and Commerce, the Judiciary, and Related Agencies Appropriations for Fiscal Year 1980*. 1979.

————. *Science, the Departments of State, Justice, and Commerce, and Related Agencies Appropriations for 2007*. Pt. 2. 2006.

US House Committee on Government Operations. *Central Intelligence Agency Exemption in the Privacy Act of 1974*. 1975.

————. *Freedom of Information Reform Act*. 1984.

————. *Notification to Victims of Improper Intelligence Agency Activities*. 1976.

US House Committee on Government Reform. *Everything Secret Degenerates: The FBI's Use of Murderers as Informants*. 2004.

US House Committee on Homeland Security. *Advancing the Homeland Security Information Sharing Environment: A Review of the National Network of Fusion Centers*. 2017.

————. *The Department of Homeland Security: An Assessment of the Department and a Roadmap for Its Future*. 2012.

————. *The DHS Intelligence Enterprise: Past, Present, and Future*. 2011.

————. *A DHS Intelligence Enterprise: Still Just a Vision or Reality?* 2010.

————. *Drugs and Security in a Post–September 11 World: Coordinating the Counternarcotics Mission at the Department of Homeland Security*. 2004.

————. *Examining the Mission, Structure, and Reorganization Effort of the National Protection and Programs Directorate*. 2015.

————. *The Future of Fusion Centers: Potential Promise and Dangers*. 2009.

————. *Is the Office of Intelligence and Analysis Adequately Connected to the Broader Homeland Communities?* 2010.

————. *The National Network of Fusion Centers*. Majority Staff Report. 2013.

————. *A Report Card on Homeland Security Information Sharing*. 2008.

————. *Reviewing the Department of Homeland Security's Intelligence Enterprise*. Majority Staff Report. 2016.

————. *The Road to Boston: Counterterrorism Challenges and Lessons from the Marathon Bombing*. 2014.

————. *State and Local Fusion Centers and the Role of DHS*. 2006.

————. *The Way Forward with Fusion Centers: Challenges and Strategies for Change*. 2007.

————. *Worldwide Threats to the Homeland*. 2014.

US House Committee on Internal Security. *Domestic Intelligence Operations for Internal Security Purposes*. 1974.

US House Committee on the Judiciary. *Department of Homeland Security Transition: Bureau of Immigration and Customs Enforcement.* 2003.

———. *Dismantling of the Bureau of Alcohol, Tobacco, and Firearms.* Before the Subcommittee on Crime of the Committee on the Judiciary. 1981.

———. *Enforcement Efforts of the Bureau of Alcohol, Tobacco, and Firearms.* 1982.

———. *FBI Domestic Security Guidelines.* 1980.

———. *FBI Oversight.* 1980.

———. *FBI Oversight and Authorization, Fiscal Year 1993.* 1992.

———. *FBI Undercover Guidelines.* 1981.

———. *Federal Bureau of Investigation.* 2009, 2014.

———. *Legislative Charter for the FBI.* 1980.

———. *Oversight of the Federal Bureau of Investigation.* 2013.

———. *Section 702 of the Foreign Intelligence Surveillance Act* (2017).

———. *Surveillance.* Pt. 1. 1975.

———. *Undercover Storefront Operations: Continued Oversight of ATF's Reckless Investigative Techniques.* 2014.

———. *Wiretapping and Electronic Surveillance.* 1974.

US House Committee on the Judiciary and the House Select Committee on Homeland Security. *Terrorist Threat Integration Center (TTIC) and Its Relationship with the Departments of Justice and Homeland Security.* 2003.

US House Committee on Oversight and Government Reform. *United States Secret Service: An Agency in Crisis.* 2015.

US House Permanent Select Committee on Intelligence. *H.R. 6588, the National Intelligence Act of 1980.* 1980.

———. *IC21: The Intelligence Community in the 21st Century.* 1996.

———. *U.S. Intelligence Agencies and Activities: Intelligence Costs and Fiscal Procedures.* Pt. 1. 1975.

US House Select Committee on Homeland Security. *How Is America Safer? A Progress Report on the Department of Homeland Security.* 2003.

US Senate Committee on Government Operations. *Federal Drug Enforcement.* Pt. 4. 1976.

———. *Reorganization Plan No. 2 of 1973.* Pt. 1. 1973.

US Senate Committee on Homeland Security and Government Affairs. *Department of Homeland Security Status Report: Assessing Challenges and Measuring Progress.* S. Doc. 110-588. 2007.

———. *Department of Homeland Security's Budget Submission for Fiscal Year 2006.* S. Doc. 109-8. 2005.

———. *Federal Support for and Involvement in State and Local Fusion Centers.* Majority and Minority Staff Report. 2012.

———. *Focus on Fusion Centers: A Progress Report.* S. Doc 110-694. 2008.

———. *The Homeland Security Department's Budget Submission for Fiscal Year 2012.* S. Doc. 112-196. 2011.

———. *Nuclear Terrorism: Strengthening Our Domestic Defenses.* S. Doc. 111-1096. Pts. 1–2. 2010.

———. *The Progress of the DHS Chief Intelligence Officer.* 2006.

———. *Ten Years After 9/11: 2011.* 2012.

———. *U.S. Department of Homeland Security: Second Stage Review.* S. Doc. 109-359. 2005.

US Senate Committee on the Judiciary. *The "Carnivore" Controversy: Electronic Surveillance and Privacy in the Digital Age.* Serial no. 106-105. 2000.

———. *Cyber Security: Responding to the Threat of Cyber Crime and Terrorism.* Before the Subcommittee on Crime and Terrorism of the Committee on the Judiciary. S. Doc. 112-167. 2011.

———. *DEA Oversight and Authorization.* S. Doc. 98-91. 1983.

———. *DEA Oversight and Budget Authorization.* 1982.

————. *DEA Oversight and Budget Authorization.* S. Doc 98-794. 1984.

————. *Domestic Security (Levi) Guidelines.* 1982.

————. *Electronic Surveillance within the United States for Foreign Intelligence Purposes.* 1976.

————. *FBI Charter Act of 1979.* S. 1612. Serial no. 96-53. 1979.

————. *FBI Oversight.* 1977.

————. *FBI Oversight Hearing.* 1982.

————. *FBI Oversight: Terrorism and Other Topics.* S. Doc. 108-804. 2004.

————. *FBI Statutory Charter.* S. Doc. 521-60. Pts. 1–2. 1978.

————. *FBI Statutory Charter—Appendix.* S. Doc 521-38. Pt. 3. 1978.

————. *Federal Bureau of Investigation.* 2007.

————. *Federal Bureau of Investigation Oversight.* S. Doc. 109-763. 2005.

————. *The Federal Bureau of Investigation's Strategic Plan and Progress on Reform.* S. Doc. 110-793. 2007.

————. *The Future of Drones in America's Law Enforcement and Privacy Considerations.* 2013.

————. *Impact of Attorney General's Guidelines for Domestic Security Investigations (the Levi Guidelines).* S. Rep. 98-134. 1983.

————. *Improving Our Ability to Fight Cybercrime: Oversight of the National Infrastructure Protection Center.* S. Doc. 107-366. 2001.

————. *The Nationwide Drive Against Law Enforcement Intelligence Operations.* Pt. 2. 1975.

————. *Oversight of the FBI.* S. Doc. 107-447. 2001.

————. *Oversight of the Federal Bureau of Investigation.* S. Doc. 110-881. 2007.

————. *Oversight of the Federal Bureau of Investigation.* S. Doc. 110-910. 2008.

————. *Oversight of the Federal Bureau of Investigation.* 2011.

————. *Reforming the FBI in the 21st Century.* S. Hrg. 107-961. 2002.

————. *Surveillance Technology: Policy and Implications—An Analysis and Compendium of Materials.* 1976.

————. *Undercover Operations Act.* S. Hrg. 98-1288. 1985.

————. *Warrantless Wiretapping and Electronic Surveillance, 1974.* 1974.

US Senate Select Committee on Intelligence, House Permanent Select Committee on Intelligence. *Joint Inquiry into Intelligence Community Activities Before and After the Terrorist Attacks of September 11, 2001.* S. Rep. 107-351. H.R. Rep. 107-792. 2002.

————. *National Intelligence Reorganization and Reform Act of 1978.* 1978.

————. *S.2525 National Intelligence Reorganization and Reform Act.* 1978.

US Senate Select Committee to Study Government Operations. *Federal Bureau of Investigation: Hearings on S. Res. 21.* 1975.

————. *Final Report of the Select Committee to Study Governmental Operations with Respect to Intelligence Activities.* S. Doc. 95-755. Book 2. 1976.

————. *Final Report of the Select Committee to Study Governmental Operations with Respect to Intelligence Activities: Senate Resolution 21.* Vols. 5–6. 1976.

————. *Foreign and Military Intelligence: Final Report of the Select Committee to Study Governmental Operations with Respect to Intelligence Activities.* S. Doc. 94-755. Book 1. 1976.

————. *Intelligence Activities and the Rights of Americans. Final Report of the Select Committee to Study Governmental Operations with Respect to Intelligence Activities.* S. Doc. 94-755. Book 2. 1976.

————. *Supplementary Detailed Staff Reports on Intelligence Activities and the Rights of Americans.* S. Rep 94-755. Book 3. 1976.

————. *Supplementary Reports on Intelligence Activities.* S. Doc. 94-755. 1976.

Vina, Stephen R. *Homeland Security: Scope of the Secretary's Reorganization Authority.* Washington, DC. Congressional Research Service. 2005.

Warner, Michael, and J. Kenneth McDonald. *U.S. Intelligence Community Reform Studies Since 1947.* Washington, DC. Central Intelligence Agency. 2005.

Weiner, Tim. *Enemies: A History of the FBI.* New York. Random. 2012.

Wildhorn, Sorrell, Brian Michael Jenkins, and Marvin M. Lavin. *Intelligence Constraints of the 1970s and Domestic Terrorism.* Vol. 1, *Effects on the Incident Investigation and Prosecution of Terrorist Activity.* Santa Monica. Rand, 1982.

William H. Webster Commission. *Final Report on the Federal Bureau of Investigation, Counterterrorism Intelligence, and the Events at Fort Hood, Texas, on November 5, 2009.* Washington, DC. 2010.

Zegart, Amy. *Spying Blind: The CIA, the FBI, and the Origins of 9/11.* Princeton. Princeton University Press. 2007.

Index

Interagency influences, 17–19
Interagency Threat Assessment and Coordination Group (ITACG), 180–182
Internal Revenue Service (IRS), 17
Investigative Services Division (ISD), 13–14
Iran, 62, 161
Iraq, 64
IRS. *See* Internal Revenue Service
IRTPA. *See* Intelligence Reform and Terrorism Prevention Act
ISD. *See* Investigative Services Division
Israel, 136–137
ITACG. *See* Interagency Threat Assessment and Coordination Group

Johnson, Jeh, 30, 128
Joint Regional Intelligence Groups (JRIGs), 70
Joint Terrorism Task Forces (JTTFs), 126–127, 129–130, 150, 182–184
JRIGs. *See* Joint Regional Intelligence Groups
JTTFs. *See* Joint Terrorism Task Forces

Katzenbach, Nicholas deBelleville, 12
Kelley, Clarence, 15
Knowledge assessment, 204

LAPD. *See* Los Angeles Police Department
Law enforcement: CJIS for, 16–17; collaboration for, 117; crime and, 92, 158–160; economics of, 20, 159–160; FBI and, 187; IMINT for, 100; intelligence and, 36–37; OLEC for, 182; policy for, 17–18; for security, 2–3; technology for, 15, 40, 110–111, 126; threat analysis for, 125–126; US intelligence and, 19
Law Enforcement Assistance Administration (LEAA), 20
Law Enforcement Online (LEO), 197
Law Enforcement Support Center (LESC), 200–201
LEAA. *See* Law Enforcement Assistance Administration
Leadership: bureaucracy and, 35–39, 202–203; in CIA, 86; for counterintelligence, 47–48; economics of, 128–129; 9/11 Review Commission on, 67–68; of OI&A, 126–127; in US intelligence, 175–179
Leahy, Patrick, 31
Legislation: Foreign Intelligence Surveillance Amendment Act (2008), 156; Homeland Security Act (2002), 117; IRTPA, 54, 173, 175–176; National Security Act (1947), 143; for 9/11 Review Commission, 199; for PRISM, 156; for security, 26–27; USA PATRIOT Act, 197

Leiter, Michael, 174–175
LEO. *See* Law Enforcement Online
LESC. *See* Law Enforcement Support Center
Levi, Edward, 12
Libya, 64
Lieberman, Joseph, 25–27
The Looming Tower (Wright), 82
Los Angeles Police Department (LAPD), 161–162

MASINT. *See* Measures and signatures intelligence
Master Threat Issue List, 43
McCabe, Andrew, 52
McCone, John, 146
McKinsey and Company, 88–89
Measures and signatures intelligence (MASINT), 100, 103–106
Mergers, of government, 148–152
al-Mihdar, Khalid, 50
Military Intelligence Division of the War Department (US), 11
MINARET, 154–156
Mueller, Robert, III, 12, 213–214, 217; legacy of, 30–32, 47–51, 58, 60, 69, 71–72, 79, 85, 87–93, 187, 198, 209–210; reputation of, 35–39, 51–53, 66–67, 83–84, 150–151, 160–161, 212

NAO. *See* National Applications Office
NAPA. *See* National Academy of Public Administration
Napolitano, Janet, 29–30
Narcotics, 11, 18–19, 92, 155
NASA. *See* National Aeronautics and Space Administration
National Academy of Public Administration (NAPA), 54, 68, 89
National Aeronautics and Space Administration (NASA), 132
National Applications Office (NAO), 135–137
National Capital Planning Commission, 2–3
National Counterproliferation Center (NCPC), 173
National Counterterrorism Center (NCTC), 7, 173–175, 175*fig*, 179–180
National Crime Information Center, 217
National Cyber Investigative Joint Task Force (NCIJTF), 59, 188–189, 218
National Cybersecurity and Communications Integration Center (NCCIC), 101–102, 218
National Gang Intelligence Center (NGIC), 186–188
National Geospatial Intelligence Agency (NGA), 137–138

About the Book

Initiated in the aftermath of the September 11 terrorist attacks, have the reforms of the US intelligence enterprise served their purpose? What have been the results of the creation of the Department of Homeland Security, the Office of the Director of National Intelligence, and a reorganized FBI? Have they helped to reduce blind spots and redundancies in resources and responsibilities . . . and to prevent misuses of intelligence and law enforcement? How did a disaster like the Snowden scandal happen?

Darren Tromblay answers these questions in his thorough, often provocative, assessment of post–9/11 US domestic intelligence activities in the pursuit of national security.

Darren E. Tromblay has served as an intelligence analyst with the US government since 2005. He holds graduate degrees from George Washington University and the National Defense Intelligence College and has published widely on domestic security issues.